W9-CBK-982

Striking Back

Striking Back

A Jewish Commando's War Against the Nazis

Peter Masters

PRESIDIO

Library of Congress Cataloging-in-Publication Data

Masters, Peter, 1922–
    Striking back : a Jewish commando's war against the Nazis / Peter Masters.
        p.   cm.
    ISBN 0-89141-629-3 (hardcover)
    1. Masters, Peter, 1922–   . 2. Great Britain. Army—Parachute troops—Biography. 3. World War, 1939–1945—Participation, Jewish. 4. Refugees, Jewish—Great Britain—Biography. 5. Jews—Austria—Vienna—Biography. 6. Holocaust, Jewish (1939–1945)—Austria—personal narratives. 7. Austria—Ethnic relations. I Title.
D810.J4M3847   1997   97-24416
940.54'4941—dc21   CIP
                                                       r97

Photos courtesy of the author, the Imperial War Museum, Edwina Hilton, Col. Bruce Beattie, Freddy Hepworth, Ron Gilbert, Ian Harris, and Eva de Becker.

Printed in the United States of America

This book is dedicated to the nineteen 3 Troopers killed in action.
Also, to all and sundries who saved my life, one time or other.
And to Alice, who made it worth living.

Contents

Foreword

Of all the hundreds of veterans I've interviewed and the many more whose unpublished or oral history memoirs I've read, Peter Masters stands out as one of the best storytellers. He has a good sense of pace and timing, and of telling detail. I was with him among a group of D day veterans as he told his personal D day story—he had every man in the room leaning forward, wanting to know what happened next.

And of these hundreds of veterans I've interviewed, Peter Masters has one of the best stories to tell. The Jewish kid from Vienna, a pacifist, becomes a member of the elite British commandos, and contributes more than his fair share in combat to help destroy the Wehrmacht, and with it Hitler's Germany.

Combat is the most extreme experience a person can go through. Those of us who have never been in combat can only try to imagine it and can never fully comprehend it. Peter Masters takes us as close to combat as is possible to do in words. This is a classic account of what is was like to be front line infantry in World War II.

STEPHEN E. AMBROSE

Preface

I went back to North Wales not long ago, to Aberdovey, where I first became a Commando soldier. The hills and mountains where we panted up and down, day and night, look friendlier now that there is no fear of RTU: return to unit, in case we couldn't hack it. The little mansion that had been the Skipper's billet is now the Plas Penhelig Hotel, a lovely place with excellent cuisine. I sat on the stone wall of the terrace surrounded by the flowers, just as I had done years ago when I had to think up my new name in a couple of minutes. I reflected that I had been born there, or at any rate reborn. Nary a soul remembers us nor how we disturbed their sleep with things that go bump in the night. There is no trace of us ever having been in Aberdovey, except one.

On the little church is a stone slab facing the sea. It looks like a World War I memorial, old and weatherbeaten. But it says World War II and lists a few names of villagers killed while serving in the Welsh Fusiliers, or other units. The name engraved at the bottom of that stone reads "Commando Max Laddy, 10 CU". It would no doubt astonish the parishioners to learn that it was our Max Lewinsky, the nephew of the famous Austrian actor, and a ballet dancer himself. Max had fished a grenade splinter out of my rear end with his scissors while I was unconscious. He was killed on D day. I imagine that his Aberdovey wife had his name added to the local lads on that stone, headed by the sentence: "LEST WE FORGET."

Acknowledgments

When I contributed to Professor Stephen Ambrose's book *D-Day*, I told him that I had been working on a book about 3 Troop, No. 10 Commando. I felt that our story should be told, the story of an argumentative bunch of mostly young Jewish refugees who volunteered for special and hazardous duty. The antithesis of "lambs to the slaughter," we fought and many of us died. Most were wounded, some several times, many so severely that they were forced to leave the army.

The well-known historian encouraged me and made helpful suggestions. What I had begun as tape recordings while walking my dog now plunged me into the unexplored jungle of the word processor. I would still be hopelessly lost in it if it were not for my "gurus": Renee Schick, Cathy Gant, and my intrepid tennis partner and friend Fred Howell, who stayed with me when more fainthearted, normal people would have abandoned me.

Then there came Ian Dear, the British author, and editor of numerous important books on World War II. Having been a Royal Marine officer himself between 1953 and 1957 and having written *Ten Commando* about our parent unit, he was uniquely familiar with my scenario and its dramatis personae. Happily, I was able to assist him a little with research for some of his books because of the lucky happenstance of my living in the Washington, D.C., area. Thus I had access to the U.S. National Archives, where I spent interesting days in his behalf. He patiently and generously undertook to edit my effort, insisting on my being sequential and accurate. I learned from him that just having been there does not guarantee that one's perceptions are factual. He also wisely crossed out some of my favorite sentences in which I showed off what I fancied to be my literary erudition. In other words, he tried to keep me honest and straightforward.

Acknowledgments

And of course I am very grateful to my 3 Troop comrades in arms, some of whom were particularly helpful: Manfred Gans, Harry Nomburg, Ian Harris, Peter Terry, Henry Geiser, George Kendall, Tony Firth, Stephan Ross, Gerald Nichols, John Envers, George Saunders, Colin Anson, George Lane, Michael Merton, Paul Streeten, Hupf Fraser, Ronnie Gilbert, Richard Tennant, and Leslie Trevor. Harry Andrews's friend Herbert Aronson told me about Harry's fight with the flywheel. Tom Bell of 6 Commando told me about one of their No. 1 Troop's darkest hours, which he experienced with less luck than I had.

The Skipper's wife, Edwina Hilton, Ronnie Gilbert, MBE, Freddy Hepworth, Ian Harris, MM, and Bruce Beattie kindly allowed me the use of some of their photos.

My wife, Alice, undeterred by having listened to my stories throughout our long and happy marriage, helped me with angelic patience in the proofreading. In the process, she made many suggestions in her unique, down-to-earth, logical way, thus constructively defoliating overly flowery lines that contain mixed metaphors, such as this one.

Introduction: The Yellow Star

Hardly a 3 Trooper had been forced to wear a yellow star in his native country. Most were lucky enough to leave their homelands before the Nazis required Jewish citizens to wear the star, under penalty of death, a return to medieval racism. The star had the mock-Hebrew lettered word *Jude* (Jew) inscribed in it. In the Middle Ages, the symbol was a yellow pointed hat. It signaled that the wearer had no civil rights. Eventually, it marked a person who had not even the right to live.

Knobby Kendall (George Knobloch), a tall, bald lawyer, an older and serious minded member of 3 Troop, told me that "someone ought to write about the role of light forces in modern warfare."

"Knobby," I assured him, "I'm writing about the young men of 3 Troop—who they were, what they did, what became of them—but von Clausewitz I'm not!"

"Just go ahead and write, and some of it is bound to come through."

So I went ahead. But the story I want to tell is of these young men: of us. Shocked by history, desperate, and in danger, we were threatened first by Hitler—that vast, unswerving scourge, that creator of hell on earth. Then, by our own choice, we fought for the opportunity to counter seemingly insurmountable odds. Those who died preferred their fate to being gassed and cremated by the Nazi brute. Those of us who survived feel that the remainder of our lives is a bonus to be cherished.

The discussion had come up in Normandy: what did "the sweet life" mean to us? During a fierce bombardment, pressed against the gravelly side of my narrow hole in the ground, I reflected:

What "the Sweet Life" Means to Me

When thunder meant not storm, but guns,
life then was precious to the ones
who gasped for it on many a beach;
Life, then, was sweet for all and each.
This is the reason, then, I give:
The sweet life is the life I live!

Prologue: Into the Wild Blue Yonder

The Whitley Armstrong twin-engine bomber revved up its motors, increasing the vibration in its fuselage. There were ten of us in the plane, with a Royal Air Force (RAF) instructor, Sgt. Roy Bladen, in charge. Harry Andrews sat nearest to the aperture—a tapering hole in the middle of the floor—through which we were about to make our first parachute jump. Harry was really Hans Arnstein from Germany, and I, Peter Arany from Austria, was now called Peter Masters. I had never flown before this beautiful, sunny October day in 1942.

"Hey, Harry, how high are we?"

"We're still on the tarmac," he shouted back. "Haven't even moved yet!"

Suddenly, the plane throbbed and started to roll forward. Twenty seconds later I felt it lifting off. I contained myself for what I thought was a respectable amount of time. "Harry, how high now?"

He made himself look down, past his feet, past the dark rim of the hole, into the abyss of a verdant landscape below. Perhaps it was just the reflection of the fields that made Harry's slim face look green beneath the lock of black hair protruding from his beige parachute helmet.

"Must be about three hundred feet—we just flew over a church steeple—and don't ask me again."

Sergeant Bladen stood in the dispatcher's position, near the aperture. He had taken us through a week of simulated parachute jumps, torturing us with all kinds of unpleasant gadgetry in the hangar. The usual three months of fitness training had been waived for us, on the assumption that we were already thoroughly trained Commandos. We had done well enough, though our welterweight prizefighter, Richard Abramowitz—now known as Dicky Arlen—had almost killed himself jumping from a platform sixty feet above the ground before being fitted with the fall-breaking harness.

1

What Bladen didn't understand about this "shower" (his RAF jargon for an unruly bunch of men) was who we were. All of us had ordinary English names—Andrews, Arlen, Kershaw, Masters—yet there was hardly one among us who spoke English without an accent. The Poles who came through his unit always wore a shoulder flash that read *Poland,* as did the French, the Dutch, and the Czechs. But this peculiar mob was wearing English regimental badges, the Queen's Own, the Buffs, the Hampshires. Where had the British Army found these odds and sods?

Bladen, however, hadn't become a parachute instructor without also becoming a psychologist. We had told him, as we had been ordered to tell anyone who asked who we were, a lot of cock-and-bull stories. So he had decided to satisfy his curiosity by going to work on Wasserman, now called Watson. A wiry, little balding man, Watson was older than most of us and perhaps more upset than we were by the prospect of his first jump. He also had a more pronounced foreign accent than the rest of us did.

"OK, Watson, you're number one. Before you jump, answer me one question. And remember, I'm your parachute instructor, who looks after your safety like a father, so tell me the truth. Are you men Danes? Swiss?"

With an effort, Watson pulled himself together. He knew the rules about security.

"You vill laugh, Sergeant," he said. "Ve are Brittisch."

The red light came on, and Sergeant Bladen saw the possibility of defeat, for the green light signaling the men to go would follow in twenty seconds.

"Action stations, number one!" he yelled, and made a last desperate attempt: "Go on, Watson, you can tell *me!*"

"I vill tell you downstairs, Sarge," Watson yelled back, and jumped.

The rest of us sat on the hard metal floor of the plane, awaiting our turn to leap out into the wide sky, toward the landscape far below. As my turn came closer, I tried to remember what the sergeant had taught us. "A good exit is most important—feet and knees together, semirelaxed so you can see the tips of your toes below your knees. Grab the outside of your trousers with your hands and keep your elbows pressed into your sides. And do a nice roll—feet, hip, and opposite shoulder—when you land."

And I remembered what von Kagerer-Stein, now called Didi Fuller, had told us. He was one of us, but he had jumped before, at least eight times. Which entitled him to wear blue and white embroidered parachute wings on his battle-dress sleeve, and to tell us what it was like. "There's not much to it. No rip cord, and a static line opens your chute whether you like it or not. One thing is very important though. When you jump, don't look down. It'll only scare you. Look up. And when you do, what do you see? Blue. Now, that's a good color—blue. It's what you're supposed to see."

"Any more?"

"Yes, indeed. Keep looking up, for soon blue will no longer be the right color to see. What you want to see now is the color of your parachute when it opens. White, or khaki, or a camouflage-patterned khaki, green, and brown. All of them are real good colors. If you still see blue, it means that when you do look down, you'll see a little white rectangle with a red cross painted on top of it, moving across all that green to a place *right under you*. What you're seeing is an ambulance rushing to where you are going to land, to pick up what's left of you."

Suddenly, it was my turn, for there was Sergeant Bladen's voice: "Action stations, go!" And I was out there in the sun. My chute opened and it was beautiful—khaki and beautiful. The scenery below was beautiful, life was beautiful. That wise RAF sergeant had taught me all the right stuff.

1 Vienna, City of My Dreams

I was walking past Hammerling Park in Vienna's 8th District when I bumped into Janak. It was a lovely day in 1938. Spring was almost here. I was sixteen years old, and Janak, a lanky, gray-eyed lad, had been in my class in elementary school on the Albert Platz. We had not seen each other since, so we talked about what we had been up to. I was surprised to see that Janak was wearing a badge on his lapel: the three silver arrows of the Social Democratic Party. That was clearly an act of bravado, for all opposition parties had been repressed by the nationalistic Austrian government of Chancellor Kurt von Schuschnigg.

We chatted for a while, moving aside to make room for a short man in washed-out blue coveralls who was carrying a long metal pipe; he was presumably a plumber or construction worker. Then a tall, red-haired boy, who looked about eighteen years old, approached wearing the brown-shirted uniform of the Hitler Youth. The Austrian government had only recently been pressured by Hitler into legalizing the Nazi Party, which previously was outlawed because of its hate policies and terror tactics.

Janak winked at me and spat contemptuously on the sidewalk, almost at the feet of the approaching boy. That surprised me, for the Nazi was a lot bigger than either of us. Janak's action proved that he was not only a Social Democrat, but also a militant one. So there I was, a Jewish boy standing next to Hammerling Park with my dangerously provocative friend, knowing that our country was in jeopardy from Nazi Germany, our powerful neighbor. Under the circumstances it would have been wise to avoid any confrontation.

The tall uniformed boy pulled a lanyard out of his pocket and blew three shrill blasts into the whistle attached to it. Suddenly, the park was teeming with onrushing brown uniforms. Janak dashed off hastily to the right and I to the left.

"See you later," he yelled.

Luckily, I knew the neighborhood well between my high school and my home. With a mob in hot pursuit bent on beating me up, I faked one direction and ran in the other at the next corner. That enabled me to dart into a cleaning shop owned by the mother of a Jewish boy I knew slightly. When I told her I was being chased by a Nazi gang, she sounded upset.

"You can run out the back, but you can't hide here. I don't want any trouble."

I was out of there before she finished her sentence. I dove into the entranceway of a block of apartment houses on the next street. I knew that the building had three other exits, so even if someone had seen me go in, they could not tell where I would come out. When I did emerge, I relaxed. But I walked speedily toward home, just one block to go, just past the stage door of the Stadt Theater.

From that doorway my red-haired Nazi adversary jumped and hit me over the head. He must have known where I lived and taken a shortcut for the ambush. I had no doubt that he would blow the whistle again.

But who was coming down my street but the man with the metal pipe. He stopped next to us, entangled like predator and prey. Then the muscular little man put the pipe down gently on the pavement and whacked my tormentor in the face with a combination of right-left uppercuts.

"Next time, pick on somebody your own size," he growled as my enemy slunk away, howling.

I got home all right, but the incident was an evil portent.

On 15 January, Hitler summoned Schuschnigg to Berchtesgaden to discuss a treaty pertaining to the borders between the two countries. It turned out to be a bullying session designed to intimidate and to wring concessions from the vulnerable Austrian head of state. Hitler underscored his threatening posture in a radio speech on 20 January. Schuschnigg responded on 9 March, calling for a plebiscite to allow the Austrian people to assert their wish to remain independent from the German Reich. There is little doubt that the populace would have supported him by more than 60 percent at that time. Hitler therefore could not afford to let the voting take place, and he issued an ultimatum on 11 March. In a final speech, Schuschnigg—to our utter shock—resigned. "I yield to brute force," he said. "God save Austria." On the next day the German Army marched into Austria. Hitler triumphantly entered the provincial town of Linz near the village of his birth. Dejectedly, we were glued to the radio.

"Sepp Wolkersdorfer has been in jail for as long as anyone can remember, but now he is mayor of Linz," stated the announcer. Cheering Nazi crowds lined the streets to greet the German Army as it came across the border. Waves of *Luftwaffe* bombers flew low circles over Vienna, low enough so that everybody could clearly see the Nazi insignia on what seemed to be an endless procession. A Nazi attorney named Seyss-Inquart was installed as chancellor without an election. Then Hitler ordered his own plebiscite.

I accompanied our cook, Paula, to the neighborhood polling place, set up in an empty shop on the corner of our street. A male official with a swastika armband checked Paula's name in the register and handed her a ballot. It was a small rectangular piece of white paper on which just one question was printed: "Do you wish Austria to be incorporated into the German Reich?" Below it there were two circles, one marked *yes* and one marked *no*. I noticed the heavy-handedness: the first circle was as big as a large silver coin; the second circle was the size of a shirt button, the word *no* so tiny that it was barely visible.

"Over there is our secret voting booth," said the man with the swastika, pointing to an enclosure with a drawstring curtain, "but since you are probably going to vote yes, Fräulein, you can do it right here."

"I think I'd like to go to the booth," said Paula.

"Indeed? Now, what was your name again . . . let me see." And he marked an *X* next to it on the register. She walked over to the booth, holding her head high, and pulled the curtain shut behind her. She did not know that she was risking her freedom, or perhaps even her life. Others did: thus 99.8 percent voted yes for the incorporation, the *Anschluss*—a number so high that it clearly proved the clumsy lie it represented. Austria thus ceased to exist.

School started again on 21 March, but there were only speeches, no lessons. The Jewish pupils were segregated and told: "You are merely tolerated guests in this country."

All over Vienna, and indeed all over Austria, Jewish businesses, the ones belonging to the families of these "guests," were defaced with graffiti: "Don't buy from Jews." Nazi commissars were installed in them, and a short time later the businesses were stolen altogether, or "requisitioned."

Arbitrary arrests became a daily routine, many times in the streets; other people were forced to scrub the sidewalks and house walls to remove the political slogans left behind by Schuschnigg supporters. Usually this had to be done by well-dressed Jewish victims with tooth-brushes, as jeering onlookers surrounded them. Jewish citizens were picked up by police or Nazi bands with swastika armbands during house or apartment searches for weapons or anti-Nazi political books or material. These were, of course, looting binges.

My family was affected immediately. My divorced father felt most threatened, being an adult Jewish male. As soon as the Nazis took over, he tried to ski into Switzerland, but he encountered heavy armed patrol activity on the border. He abandoned that attempt and took a train instead. He noticed that a class of small schoolchildren was not being checked by the border guards, who seemed to know them. He mingled with the children, pretending to be a teacher. He waved to the guards and was out of Austria—free!

He managed to hitchhike to Bern, carefully avoiding the Swiss police, for it was already rumored that they mercilessly returned refugees to the nearest Nazi border point—to an almost certain death. He sought help from his cousin who was first tenor of the Bern Opera. A maid at his cousin's house informed my father that *Herr Kammersänger* was on tour and that she could not let him in. Could he come by again in a day or two? At that moment two men in raincoats identified themselves as plainclothes police and ar-rested him.

As the detectives marched him off, they happened to bump into his relative, the opera singer, back from his trip abroad. "Let go of this man!" he exclaimed. Recognizing him as a celebrity, they complied. "I shall be personally responsible for him, and he will be a guest in my house." There my father stayed for several months, until he moved on to Belgium en route to Britain.

My eighteen-year old sister, Eva, had also wanted to leave Austria right away, to join her girlfriend Renee, who was leaving for Italy the day after the *Anschluss*. (Who knew which direction was safe?) My mother would not hear of it. "We go together, or we don't go. My work, our home, our friends and relatives are here. What would we do elsewhere? If things get really bad, we can leave later."

Many Austrian Jews believed in this foolish sentiment, almost always with deadly consequences. In downtown Vienna my mother had been working with her youngest sister, Ida, who was somewhat eccentric. She was an early motorist as well as an early independent businesswoman who owned the Modellhaus Ydelle, a millinery salon one block from Vienna's St. Stephen's Cathedral. Every year my Aunt Ida went to Paris to look at the new fashion collections. She couldn't afford to buy many of the hats, but she sat up in her hotel room all night and drew from memory what she had seen. When she got back to Vienna, she modified what she had sketched into original Viennese creations.

When my parents were divorced, Aunt Ida generously took my mother on as a partner. Noting that many British customers enamored with Vienna came to the shop each year, my mother suggested that Ida should visit London as well as Paris. Ida didn't think much of the idea, for she considered British fashion inferior to French fashion. But she agreed reluctantly to the experiment, which she described as "a mere hop across the Channel—probably a waste of time."

In London in the spring of 1937, she met people in the fashion business, and impressed them with her Continental charm. A man offered her a job to manage the millinery department of an Oxford Street department store. She turned him down, explaining that she was perfectly happy in her own successful business. Smitten or clairvoyant, the London tycoon said that he would keep the offer open for a year. That year would have been up in April 1938.

After the *Anschluss,* on the ides of March of that year, my aunt's business was immediately confiscated by the Nazis. She wired her acceptance to the London tycoon and left for England on 29 April. The department store was a professional step down for her, but she was quite a curiosity in London—an early arrival from the Nazis' first expansionist invasion. At work and at parties, she was asked how she liked life in a new country, and whether she was happy in London. At that, Ida would burst into tears. How could she be happy when her loved ones were in jeopardy? Naively, they wondered why she could not simply bring all her family out. Ida explained the problems of the immigration laws, but she pointed out that a British subject could invite her relatives, or employ them as domestics, or gardeners, or anything.

Aunt Ida's tactics worked: she managed to get fourteen people out of Austria: my mother, my sister, eleven others, and me. She saved our lives. From then on I forgave my Aunt Ida all her eccentricities.

Before my family and I left Vienna, I had been worried because the Hitler Youth boy knew where I lived. After the Nazis had taken over, there were absolutely no restraints on what the boy could do to me and my family. When our doorbell rang, a chill ran down our spines. Were they coming for us? Were the threatening phone calls from him? From someone put up to calling by him? From an envious neighbor? One night there was a call every hour on the hour ordering us to report instantly to the police or to the SS to perform unspecified tasks. We felt compelled to telephone the police to check the authenticity of the orders.

"We don't know a thing about it, but if they want you Jews, you must do as you are told."

"You still haven't gone?" said the next call, on the hour, like clockwork. "The Gestapo will pick you up in the morning." Our cook, Paula, looked out our third floor window at dawn while we hurried to prepare some provisions to go hiking in the Vienna Woods. We intended to check carefully whether it was safe to return in the evening, or to try to find a route of escape. Paula rushed in, pale and breathless: "They're coming! A Gestapo car just pulled up in front of the house."

"Throw the rucksack into a closet and sit down," I ordered. "Pretend to read a book or something, so they don't say we were trying to escape." I did what I had suggested, and my mother and sister followed suit. Trembling, we sat and waited for the doorbell to ring. We waited, and waited, and waited. . . . No doorbell, no knock; nobody came for us. After some minutes, which seemed like hours, I pulled myself together, crept to the window, and peeped over the sill. An olive green convertible was parked in front of the house. Nobody was in it, but a framed picture of Schuschnigg, the glass smashed, lay on the backseat. The letters *GStP* were clearly visible on the car door. It could hardly have been a coincidence. It was someone who knew that the Gestapo had business in our apartment house and thought it worthwhile to stay up all night making phone calls to terrify us, or to make us report to some Nazi authority, where our fate would be uncertain at best. Similarly victimized people were known to commit suicide. We moved to my grandfather's house after that. I didn't like having to sleep in his double bed with him, but at least no old adversaries knew where I lived.

Daily rumors were circulating on the safest routes out of Austria at about the time that we finally had assembled all our papers, visas, and affidavits. Fly to Zurich was the word on 20 August. Flying had seemed a luxury to us until then; none of us had ever flown. And because the Nazis would allow one to take only ten deutsche marks out of the country, the expense didn't matter. But it was not to be. On that day the rumor mill said that a refugee-filled plane en route to Zurich had been ordered to turn around and land in Germany, where all Jewish passengers were immediately sent to a concentration camp.

What route now? We chose the night train to Munich, through the middle of Nazi Germany, through Stuttgart and Karlsruhe to cross the French frontier from Kehl to Strassbourg. We left on 21 August.

The lone Frenchman who shared our compartment proved to be a great asset. At the border three Nazi officials scanned all the passengers. They thought we were one French family as they checked our luggage. The last one checked the passports. "Hey, this isn't one family at all, but one French gentleman and a bunch of Jews. Let's look them over again," he exclaimed.

"Oh, to hell with it," grumbled his boss, and they left.

As we crossed into France, my mother poured each of us a glass of Cognac. Our French "father" got one, too. Then she poured one sacrificial glass, filled to the brim, and threw it out the window of the train as we sped toward Paris. We arrived there four hours late, for others had been less cursorily inspected at the border than we had been.

Freedom! Out of the clutches of the Nazis, I might yet live to fight them.

2 But Who Are You Really?

I sympathized with Roy Bladen, our RAF parachute instructor, for wanting to know more about our strange group. I would have told him gladly, if I'd been allowed to, that officially we were part of No. 3 Troop of 10 Inter-Allied Commando, which was otherwise composed of French, Norwegian, Belgian, Dutch, Polish, and Yugoslav personnel. Number 3 Troop consisted entirely of what were called friendly enemy aliens: mostly German, Austrian, and Hungarian subjects, with a few other nationalities mixed in. There was one common denominator: all of us were refugees from the Nazis and spoke fluent German. Most of us were Jews.

To protect our true identities, we had been ordered by the War Office to change our names. We had been told to invent a plausible reason for our foreign accents and to destroy all documents and personal belongings that might compromise our new identities. We were then given Commando training, which qualified us to wear the elite green beret, and were taught everything there was to know about the German Army—its organization, weapons, paperwork, tactics, and methodology.

Most of us had grown up in Central or Eastern European towns, the children of a whole class range of parents, though it is true that the upper and middle class "non-Aryans" had had a better chance of escaping the Nazi terror. The poor were often less mobile and less informed in the early stages of the Nazi takeover as to what was going on and what options were available for escape. This handicap amounted to a death sentence for the majority of these innocents.

The upper class frequently had sent their sons abroad to be educated, so that many of these men were safe. The middle class tried to pack up their families and emigrate when the situation in their hometowns became too threatening, but because the Nazis in many places gradually tightened their noose, families delayed until it became difficult or impossible to leave. The numbers who could have saved themselves were fewer because some were lulled into a false security by having been respected citizens in their communities, and by the human tendency to leave "together, or not at all."

In easygoing Austria, people felt that they could always leave later, although the first impact of violence had caused some to stampede across the nearest frontiers. But the foolish sentiment that "this cannot happen here" already had to be modified to "this cannot last for long here." It was hoped that the great Western powers would intervene. But they didn't. Some didn't even open their doors to the persecuted. Those that did accepted only small numbers, thus condemning millions of Jewish men and women to death—and with them, unbelievably, more than a million children.

There had always been anti-Semitism in Germany and Austria, at times not much more than an ethnic remark. Young Nazis were considered fanatics, the unstable lunatic fringe. Don't martyr them, and they will go away. Ignore them or, as the Austrian idiom has it, "Don't even ignore them."

But the situation worsened rapidly. In the first few days after the *Anschluss,* fights broke out. There had always been political skirmishes between opposing parties, but it quickly became apparent that the police, which used to protect the victimized, now supported the perpetrators as long as they wore a Nazi badge or an armband, and their prey was a Jew.

Jews' bank accounts were blocked. My grandfather, who had just been awarded an honor scroll by his guild of gold- and silversmiths for his long and distinguished artistry, worked at home in semi-retirement. That did not deter the Nazis from placing a commissar in his apartment. It turned out to be the owner of a small jewelry shop in the suburbs, who seemed embarrassed by his new status.

My grandfather, who was in his seventies, called a family meeting after the traditional Friday night family dinner. He couldn't grasp the situation. Having been a quiet, highly respected, law-abiding citizen all his life, he found it impossible to understand that the law no longer protected him. On the contrary, the law had now become his enemy, for the Nuremberg Laws took away the Jews' civil rights, and the law-enforcement officers now sided with the crooks. Eventually, it was not only the civil rights they took away, but the right to live.

"The commissar is a nice enough man," my grandfather said, "but I have a real problem: what shall I call him? *Herr Kommissar* sounds too formal, *Herr Mautner* too casual . . ."

He rejected all suggestions by family members for one reason or another. The dilemma was left unsolved until the following Friday's family dinner, when he solved it once and for all. "He likes to hike, just like me," my grandfather announced, almost happily. "We went for a long hike in the Vienna Woods last Sunday. He has trouble keeping up with me, of course, less experienced as he is. But it suddenly came to me that I shall call him *lieber freund* (dear friend).

My grandfather was finally persuaded by my mother, family, and friends to emigrate. He went to Belgium, because his name was well known among the pearl, diamond, and precious-stone dealers in Antwerp. He even came to London to visit my mother and her three sisters, all of whom had been brought out by my Aunt Ida. They tried to convince him to stay in England. He refused, feeling that he would be a burden to his children because he didn't speak English and therefore could not work. He returned to Antwerp, where he was respected, and he did speak French.

Friends offered to hide him on a remote farm when the German Blitzkrieg overran Belgium and Holland. But before considering their possibly lifesaving offer, which certainly risked their lives, my grandfather had two questions: would he be able to have a bath every day? And would he be able to go for a daily walk?

That would be out of the question, he was told. He was to be hidden in an attic or a cellar, and the only water he would have would be a bucket put once a day outside his hiding place. Once in a while at night, he might come out for a brief stretch, when the coast was clear.

As far as my grandfather was concerned, these restrictions eliminated the option of hiding.

But he was tired of running. He did make one last effort to get away, on foot—as was his way—to France. The crowded highways, choked with families running for their lives, were dive-bombed and machine gunned by the *Luftwaffe*. Reports reached us in England that he had been seen, with a bandaged head wound, trudging back to Antwerp, having abandoned all hope.

One final act remained. He had carved a space out of his doorjamb, and there he hid some of the remnants of his merchandise: a few diamonds, rubies, emeralds, pearls, and some gold dust. He hoped that his children might somehow retrieve their inheritance. Then he packed his hiking rucksack and waited for the Nazis. He did not have to wait long. An extraordinarily gifted and remarkably fit man of seventy-four, who had designed and made tiaras for the Hapsburgs, was considered redundant, or even a threat to the Nazi master race. They deported him to a concentration camp, where he was murdered.

After the war my mother went to look for the cache of valuables, in the apartment in the Plantin en Moretus Lei 210, having been informed of its existence and whereabouts by a trusted messenger. She found the niche in the doorjamb with some difficulty, for it was well hidden, but it was empty.

My grandfather, Arnold Metzger, could have been saved simply by staying in England as a welcome burden to his daughters. He never sufficiently faced the reality of man's inhumanity to man to realize that he was walking to his own death. This has weighed heavily on all the surviving family. Was it just stupidity, or the naiveté of an honest man, stubborn in his faith, confident that his own integrity would assure him the hard-earned respect he deserved?

Respect had been a recurring theme in his life. When he had been in business, he had had a unique insurance policy with Lloyd's of London. All his valuable shipments, of diamonds, pearls, precious stones, and his beautifully designed and crafted jewelry, whether they were coming or going, were fully covered, without documentation, merely on his say-so. And in all the years in which he had plied his trade, he had never filed a single claim. Not that he had never suffered any loss, but he deemed it more important to maintain his standing, his respect, than be reimbursed for what he considered a minor material setback. He was clearly out of step with his abysmal times.

What is even more appalling is that he experienced only the beginnings of what became a worse nightmare. Many of the more than

6 million Jews killed during the Holocaust went through painful, tortuous tightenings of the noose that he never witnessed. One by one, every necessity of life was taken away, forbidden, outlawed: work, public transportation, medical care, communication, human contacts, lodging, and food. One victim was set against the other, as the price of illusory momentary survival. On reflection, Arnold Metzger's end seems simple.

In Germany and Austria, the future members of 3 Troop—teenagers mostly—had always been exposed to a certain amount of anti-Semitism, even before the advent of the Nazi regime. Anti-Semitism had been a political hobbyhorse, semisupported by the church, reinforced by a depressed economy. Notwithstanding the fact that Jews were a mainstay of the cultural life of these countries—perhaps because of that—an unwashed envy from below and a condescending disparaging disqualification from above combined to promote a Jewish "angst," which caused some to flee the stigma of their religion, not from conviction but "for the sake of the children."

Some of our young men of 3 Troop, thereafter, were not told by their parents that they were Jewish, until the implementation of the 1935 Nuremberg Laws (in which the Nazis decreed severe restrictions on anyone who did not have three Aryan grandparents) necessitated such candor. Other families were practicing Jews but were still assimilated as patriotic Germans or Austrians. Yet others were Zionists, hoping for a Jewish state. And still others were nonpracticing Jews, who remained Jews only because they felt it would be disloyal and cowardly to abandon their religion.

Few of us had attended Jewish schools until forced to do so. We went to schools whose members mixed freely. We studied together, played sports together, grew up together. But even before the Nazis, the conservative anti-Socialist, anti-Nazi government of Austria reorganized all high school classes into pure Catholic ones and all others lumped together—Protestants, Atheists, Agnostics, Jews, and even Greek Orthodox. Members of my high school soccer team, newly divided by this reorganization, protested bitterly. It was to no avail, of course, for the racist heart knows neither charity nor reason, and it does not appreciate the loss of an irreplaceable center forward.

Soon the repaired and patched soccer teams were mutilated once again. Under the Nazis the new classes were Aryan and non-Aryan, whatever their professed religion. They hadn't heard about not changing a winning team, either.

But in Germany, by consensus and acclaim, Steve Ross (Stephan Rosskamm) continued to play for his old integrated soccer eleven for a surprisingly long time. And the principal of Tony Firth's (Hans Georg Fürth) high school interceded with his mother not to send his star hockey goalkeeper out of Germany just yet, at least not until the hockey championship was over. With the atmosphere becoming more threatening, Frau Fürth sent him to England anyway, the survival of her son taking precedence, in her mind, over that of his hitherto unbeaten team. Without Tony to guard the goal, the team was eliminated in the next round.

Until the end of 1938, the Nazi persecution of Jews across the country had been so gradual as to seem almost gentle from some of the future victims' point of view. But when a frustrated Polish-Jewish youngster shot a minor German embassy official in Paris (because the ambassador—the highest accessible representative of the Reich—happened to be out), Hitler used the occasion to unleash a vicious, murderous, "spontaneous" outburst against all Jews in every township or hamlet. What followed was *Kristallnacht*—the night of broken glass—when on 9 November 1938 synagogues were torched and store windows were smashed, Jews were beaten and some were killed.

Stephan Rosskamm, in spite of his star status, was arrested with his father at this time. The Rosskamms were the only Jewish family in Stephan's hometown of Schwarza near Meiningen in the German province of Thuringia. The local Nazi authorities were apologetic, for Rosskamm Senior was the respected owner of a department store and a close friend of the mayor. The full impact of what lay ahead was as yet totally unknown to both perpetrators and victims. "You know how it is, Herr Rosskamm, the higher-ups and the Gestapo have issued orders. We have to arrest all male Jews of the town, and that means both of you, but we shall release you and your son soon."

The Rosskamms were held in the county seat prison in Suhl. It was winter, and the nights in jail were bitterly cold. "Remind me to sell better blankets to the prison director, Stephan," said father to son. "These are clearly not our quality merchandise."

When it turned out that other men and youths from surrounding areas had been sent to the concentration camp in Buchenwald, the threat of what the future might hold began to sink in with a chill that could not be overcome even by Herr Rosskamm's top-quality blankets. Stephan, who was sixteen when he and his father were released, took a train to Berlin to check the possibilities of getting out of Germany—across any border. There he found panic and turmoil; suddenly a foreboding of the dire, deadly future had become apparent across the entire land. So many Jewish women everywhere had their husbands taken from them that they felt compelled, at long last, to try to flee abroad. If they could not, or would not, leave without their husbands, they wanted at least to get their children out. No longer was it a case of "together, or not at all."

Young Rosskamm was shocked when he encountered these terrified women in the capital, many of them young with small children. The Jewish agencies that had been handling the previous comparatively slow trickle of emigrants were overwhelmed by the sudden onslaught of would-be clients. Stephan told me the following story.

"There was such disorder that I felt someone had to do something. No! I felt that if I didn't do something, nobody would; a mass of frightened mothers clutching their children would stand in confused lines day and night, not daring to leave to eat or sleep or go to the bathroom for fear of losing their place in the queue to get out of the country. As often as not, even when they arrived at the head of the queue to plead their case, they were told, 'Come back tomorrow . . .'" And Stephan added: "I became a man—I had to. I organized a number system for those queuing, and I instilled some kind of order. It worked."

When the process was running smoothly, Stephan added his name to the list of one of the transports that was being organized. It went by train through Cologne across the Dutch frontier, then to the Hook of Holland, and by ship to England, where a boys' camp called Dovercourt had been hastily set up in the cabins of a working-class holiday resort.

Watson, the target of Roy Bladen's effort to solve the riddle of 3 Troop's identity, remembered nothing as amusing as the suggested upgrading of prison blankets. Instead, he remembered wearing a uniform of flimsy pajamas, with broad vertical black and gray stripes, which hung loosely from his emaciated shoulders. He remembered the day a fellow inmate somehow managed to escape from the Dachau concentration camp: he stood next to his brother in the chill rain, standing at attention from six in the evening until the following noon, when simply shifting one's weight from one foot to the other meant risking one's life. So everyone stood perfectly still until the ill-fated man was caught and brought back. The guards hung a drum around his neck and paraded him up and down. He had to beat the drum while they beat him to death to the accompaniment of its hollow sound. Then the weakened, ill-fed inmates were allowed to slink off and go on living, at least for a while. The worst of it was that they had to admit to themselves that they were glad the man had been caught so that their ordeal was ended. Watson's twenty-two-year-old brother died of pneumonia brought on by hypothermia, a lack of food, and forced labor. It was recorded as "a natural death" in the camp's record books.

The Watson brothers' crime was that they had attempted to flee to Holland after *Kristallnacht*. While Watson was in Dachau, his wife succeeded in buying tickets to China for them and their two children (China was one of the very few countries that generously allowed Jewish refugees to enter), and he managed to finagle his release from Dachau on the understanding that they would leave immediately. Just then an uncle in the United States came through with an affidavit for his nephew, which brought about Watson's actual release.

Instead of China, Watson chose to go to England, planning to have his wife and children join him as soon as he was established there. He quickly found a job for himself and his wife, and sent for her, but then war broke out and his hopes for the future turned to dust: it was too late for his family to escape. They were murdered. Watson stayed in England and eventually found his way into 3 Troop.

Many of our British hosts were intrigued with the fact that we spoke English, at least after a fashion, and that many of us were well educated. (The scholastic standards in our countries of origin were rather advanced, and "general knowledge" had always been a Central European goal, almost an end in itself.) That made us, at the outset, exotic conversation pieces, like coffee table books. Well-meaning people invited friends for a viewing of their refugees—not necessarily live-in refugees, but ones they were helping, sponsoring, or employing.

Those "exhibits" were the lucky ones. The unlucky ones were still lining up in consulates across the Channel, trying to learn to become electricians and shirtmakers, or to train for other nonlanguage-dependent occupations. Many were taking Spanish or English conversation classes. Above all they were writing letters to friends who had made it "out," letters to long-forgotten relatives who had in turn forgotten their increasingly desperate kinfolk. Some, who had unusual surnames, scanned the telephone directories of foreign cities for addresses of people with identical names. Were they not perhaps related? Fearful of the censor, all these letters contained veiled cries for help, stressing, as much as they dared, the extreme urgency of their request for shelter, for a safe place for themselves or at least for their children. The most important goal was to find someone to take them in, as domestics, as gardeners . . . as anything.

A few of No. 3 Troop had come to Britain in a gentler fashion and missed the phase of being impoverished refugees. Freddy Gray (Manfred Gans) had been sent to school in England by his parents. Leslie Scott (Uli Steiner), the scion of an affluent German-Jewish family, came to London from school in Switzerland. The father of Kurt Meyer (Peter Moody) was a psychiatrist whose skills were exportable. The father of Peter Wells (Auerhahn) was in the import-export business and could shift his base of operation fairly easily, without his son suffering from the dismal poverty that was in store for many of the rest of us.

Peter Terry was another lucky one. Born Peter Tischler on 21 June 1924, he was the youngest member of No. 3 Troop. His father was a well-known Viennese dentist and his mother came from a Jewish-Viennese patrician family. Her father had been awarded the title "Hofrat" (court counselor) by the Hapsburgs, an honor given for distinguished government service. Peter's father had headed an Aus-

trian Army field hospital on the Russian front in World War I, and
two of his mother's brothers had been killed in that war.
Peter's early childhood was spent in the Central European comfort of the well-to-do. The Tischler family lived in a villa in the elegant Viennese district of Grinzing. From there, at the age of twelve,
he was sent to an English boarding school called Frensham, presumably prompted by his parents' Anglophilia. Peter remembers:

> In early March 1938, when I was not yet fourteen, I re-
> turned to Vienna for the Easter holidays just in time to hear
> the Austrian chancellor, Kurt von Schuschnigg, announce
> the German invasion over the radio. "I yield to brute
> force . . . ," he said, his voice cracking with emotion. That
> night we received a telephone call from the Duke of Wind-
> sor, who had been one of my father's patients, asking if he
> could be of help. At the time the Duke was staying in the
> south of France (he had abdicated the British throne two
> years earlier), and he urged my father to leave the coun-
> try immediately. But my father declined.

Two days later, standing on the balcony of the Tischlers' new in-
town flat in the Ringstrasse, Peter watched the German Army enter
the city. He did not return to school in England, as his parents felt
the family should stay together in the hope that the Nazi excesses
would pass. Among his father's other patients was an attorney who
had occasionally been a guest in their house. His name was Seyss-
Inquart. For years he had hidden his then illegal membership in the
Nazi Party, but now he became the new chancellor.* In gratitude for
dental services rendered, he provided Peter's father with a document
stating that he was not to be molested and that the brass plaque reading "Dr. Tischler" outside his practice was not to be defaced with anti-
Jewish slogans.

---

*A popular underground verse of that time went: *"Seyss-Inquarten, Seyss in Quin-
ten, sind beschissen vorn und hinten"* (Seyss in quarts, Seyss in quints, we are shat
upon back and front). Seyss-Inquart subsequently became the Nazi governor of
occupied Holland and was later executed by the Dutch.

Armed with this piece of paper, the doctor took Peter one Sunday morning in May to Vienna's Prater district to walk among that
park's shady avenue of old trees. Suddenly they found themselves surrounded by brown-shirted Nazi thugs who had seen that they were
not displaying the little aluminum swastika badge worn by virtually
all non-Jewish Viennese.

Their leader glanced arrogantly at his father's precious document
and decided that it did not apply to Peter. Therefore Peter would
have to accompany him into custody. Naturally, Tischler senior went
along. During the next few hours, together with thousands of other
Jews who had been rounded up all over Vienna, they were subjected
to numerous indignities, from being forced to scrub anti-Nazi slogans off the streets to standing among a mob screaming anti-Jewish
insults at them, all with the regular police standing by. The rabid
brownshirts arrested a few "good" Austrians, including one policeman, because they dared to protest this madness. Hours later the ar-
restees were made to stand facing the Danube Canal and told that
anyone turning around would be shot. Some minutes later, Peter,
noting the total silence, did turn around and found that the brownshirts had disappeared. Their place had been taken by taxicabs
whose drivers saw a chance of making money from all these people
hoping to get away as quickly as possible.

That night Peter heard his father say, "Now we leave." The problem was, where to? The necessary visas to enter foreign countries
were by now almost impossible to obtain. Their only hope was to try
to contact the Duke of Windsor to see if his offer of help still stood;
this they did. However, the next day Dr. Tischler was arrested and
taken to Vienna's Hôtel Métropole, which was now the Gestapo headquarters. During days of interrogation, it transpired that one of the
Tischler's former servants had told the Gestapo that the servant had
been dismissed years ago because he had been a member of the illegal Nazi Party. Peter recalls:

> Then a miracle happened. The same Gestapo interrogator
> who had started each session with the sentence 'Are you the Jew
> Tischler?' entered my father's cell and addressed him as "Herr
> Doktor." He took my father out to the street where a car flying

the Union Jack from its fenders was waiting to take him to the safety of the British Embassy. Thanks to the Duke, this car remained at our disposal for the rest of our stay in Vienna, until we were able to complete the numerous formalities to leave the country. The British flag ensured that we could move about the city unhindered by the roving band of uniformed Nazis and their opportunistic camp followers.

The Duke had sponsored us by providing an affidavit required by the British immigration authorities, and thus we arrived in London as honored guests. The Duke's secretary, Sir Geoffrey Thomas, awaited us at Victoria Station and took us to temporary quarters in someone's empty house in the fashionable London district of St. John's Wood.

I returned to Frensham, finished school, and went to Cambridge. A year later, two days after my eighteenth birthday, I walked into the Bloomsbury office of one Major Davidson, a tall, impressive man with curly gray, almost collar-length, hair. I told him I wished to join the Pioneer Corps, the only part of the British Army that a friendly enemy alien was allowed to join at that time. I felt I had to "do my bit" to get back at the Nazis and to repay my British hosts for giving us asylum.

A week after my arrival at a Pioneer company in Warwickshire, I began my efforts to transfer to a fighting unit. These finally resulted in my being sent, together with others, to be interviewed by the man who was to become our Skipper.

What Peter Terry did not know is that I, then sixteen years old, had walked along the Alserstrasse in Vienna and had come upon a luxurious car, parked at the sidewalk, flying the Union Jack from its fender. In it was what I took to be a British family with a young boy. For a moment I considered approaching the protected foreigners, begging them for help for myself and my family, but my shyness had made me hesitate. I had enviously watched the car take off and disappear in traffic.

Happily, the Aranys—my mother, my sister, and I—did get out. It was wonderful to have escaped, even though we were almost destitute and the world news grew more depressing every day.

One night a man wearing a leather coat and boots strutted past the drab rooming house in London where I lived with my mother and sister. To my horror I heard him whistle the Horst Wessel song—the party hymn of the Nazis. It sent a chill down my spine, as if he had followed me all the way from Vienna. It took me days to recover from that British Fascist passerby.

I recall going sightseeing at that time, in this great new city, to the Tower of London with my sister, Eva. When we were done, we discovered to our shock that we had only enough money between us for one sandwich or the fare home. We were both so hungry that we opted for the food. Marginally reinvigorated, we set out for home on foot. The hike to that rooming house in Warrington Crescent, Maida Vale in West London, took several hours.

To my European eyes, the red brick walls of this four-story house looked shabbily unfinished. At home there would have been a veneer of stucco to cover the bricks, usually richly decorated with scrollwork and multilayered ledges. Without it these dwellings looked naked and impoverished. But in back there was a huge lush green lawn shared by our street and the one behind us. Neatly uniformed English schoolchildren romped there, turning cartwheels and playing tag. We had had nothing like it even in Vienna, but I never dared to venture out there. Who knew whether it was verboten? The inhibitions of living under the Nazis still hung heavily over me. How was I ever going to get the chance to fight them, let alone to vanquish them?

In daily living, every conceivable utility was activated by a separate coin meter. One dusky evening I was at home alone when a click in the corner accompanied the lights going out, and I didn't have a single sixpence to feed the wretched machine. While I waited as patiently as a sixteen year old could manage for some family member to come home, the doorbell sounded. It rang four times, which meant that it was for us. I opened the front door, and a tall, elegant man stood before me in British city garb—striped pants, dark jacket, Homburg hat, briefcase, umbrella, and the obligatory rolled-up *Times* under his arm. He asked for me! He introduced himself as the Honourable Ralph Roper-Curzon, representing the Boy Scouts of Great Britain. He said he had been sent to welcome me, a Scout for eight years, to the United Kingdom. A great moment in a boy's life. He obviously expected to be asked in. My teenage mentality pitted manners versus embarrassment. It was clearly my move, and for a moment of panic I was tempted to bang the door shut and hide. Instead, I stammered: "Before I ask you to come in, sir, do you happen to have sixpence on you to turn on the lights?"

3 Friendly Enemy Aliens—Behind Barbed Wire

When we were allowed to enter the United Kingdom as refugees from Nazism, we looked upon ourselves as guests, on whose courteous gratitude and political nonparticipation our hosts could rely. Yet some of us could not keep ourselves from warning our benefactors of the gathering storm. Having just come from under the ostentatious display of a boastful power, and encountering the general indifference of what seemed to us an idyllic, free country, we considered it our duty to sound an urgent alarm. We had seen the Nazis' formidable tanks and planes but nothing even faintly resembling such power in England. Once in a while we saw old-fashioned military double-decker aircraft, yellow-painted Tiger Moths, sputtering on training missions, but we never saw any armor on the ground. Convinced that Hitler was bent on world domination, we tried desperately to communicate our fears in conversations, so much so that some of our comments reached the press.

The British press reacted with shocked outrage—not about the message but about us messengers. Its right-wing columnists, particularly, complained. "These émigrés are jeopardizing our relations with our good friends the Germans," wrote one of them before the outbreak of war. After it, the same man, Ward Price of the *Daily Mail,* wrote: "How do we know these people are not spies? Anybody can say that he is a refugee."

At first the British lived up to their reputation for tolerance. Enemy aliens were rounded up, but it wasn't until the German invasion of France and the Low Countries, and the invasion panic that followed it, that wide-scale internment occurred. It was then that many of us friendly enemy aliens went through a third metamorphosis, that of an internee. For me, the first had been from a sheltered life of the more or less assimilated Central European middle class high school student to the harassed object of hatred, contempt, ridicule, and ostracism in my own country. The second was the transformation into a penniless refugee, because the Nazis permitted us to take only the ludicrously small sum of ten deutsche marks each out of the country. The fresh air of freedom was worth far more, of course, but still the meager finances cramped the style of most of us. How can you try to get a date when you can't even buy one cinema ticket? We were trying to grow up and prove ourselves.

The third metamorphosis—being locked up behind barbed wire—was hard to accept with equanimity. Although we sympathized with our British hosts' concern about the threat of a fifth column of infiltrated spies posing as refugees, we also knew that we were the real thing: refugees. We had no trouble at all telling friend from foe, and we would have been happy to help our jailers identify any suspect elements among us, had there been any. We who had hoped to fight the common enemy were held prisoners by our own side, probably for the duration of the war—our war! What we wanted was to help.

In October 1938, shortly after I arrived in England, my rescuer, Aunt Ida, found me a job on a farm in Berkshire, in Hurley on Thames between Henley and Maidenhead. I wasn't paid at Wilfred Long's Frogmill Farm, but I got board and lodging and thus was able to avoid being a burden for my mother. I got tougher from the hard work, which would stand me in good stead in the war that was surely coming, the one in which I hoped to fight. Advancing stealthily in my silent Wellingtons when I made the rounds shutting up the chicken houses in the lush English meadows at night, I pretended to be stalking imaginary foes.

One summer evening all hands on Frogmill Farm were busy tending the hay. In England one proverbially makes hay while the sun shines, but in haying season the sun shines so rarely that the work tends to extend into dusk and beyond. I was feeding the elevator, a conveyor belt of spikes hauling pitchfork loads of hay up unto the rick. As I worked opposite "the old man" himself, Wilfred Long, his critical eye corroborated his firm belief in my incompetence. His tongue, sharper than the prongs of my clumsy pitchfork, berated me in a constant stream of explicit invective, which was redundant after his initial pronouncement: "You are a no-good city kid."

While I was trying hard to prove otherwise, I risked a moment's pause. (According to Mr. Long, no row of elevator spikes was allowed to pass empty—"damn waste of petrol.")

Taking my life and my handkerchief into my hand, I stopped just long enough to wipe the blinding sweat out of my eyes. I saw . . . ah! What did I see?

A man was walking down the lane toward us, silhouetted against the sun. It looks like my father—ridiculous—couldn't be. He was in Belgium without papers. Typical of my father's enterprise, he had carved a likeness of George Bernard Shaw and mailed it to him, asking for help to get into Britain. The famous man replied, on a picture postcard of his bearded photo portrait. "Thank you for the very spirited bust. I have no influence at the Home Office, but I have forwarded your letter thither. It is an excellent letter. I cannot improve on it. G. Bernard Shaw."

The stranger continued down Black Boy Lane and looked across at us in the distance. Then he opened the wrought iron hoop that held the gate shut and strode across the golden stubble field. He was indeed my father. With the macho flamboyance of an ex-officer of the Austro-Hungarian Imperial Army, he threw off his jacket and rolled up his sleeves: "I help!"

Mr. Long paled, flushed, and paled again, reflecting under his breath, "Now there are two of you, when one of you had been one too many."

My father had stowed away on a Polish steamer, hidden under a pile of coal. After dark he had sneaked ashore and hitchhiked to the Long farm. The Longs had no choice but to invite him to dinner, since there was no other place to go, especially without money. The large family sat around the kitchen table. My father was very hungry—so much so, that it embarrassed me, his teenage son, who had been trying to prove himself, or at least to be inconspicuous. But worse was still to come. Suddenly, my father nudged me. "I think I must make speech," he whispered very audibly.

"No!" I almost shouted.

Too late. He had leaped to his feet. "Ladies and gentlemen, first of all I want to thank you for your hostility."

I gasped: "Wrong word!"

"Why? Host—hostility!" He made a flowery speech in broken English. After dinner he left to give himself up to the police. A few weeks later he was released, for the time being. Even without papers he was another friendly enemy alien.

On 3 September 1939 the war started. Britain and France had issued an ultimatum to Hitler to desist from invading Poland, but Hitler, confident of his superior strength and preparedness, ignored it and pressed relentlessly on. Early in May 1940, Holland and Belgium surrendered. I wrote in my diary: "The Nazis are making too much progress for my taste." I had already adopted British understatement, for the truth was that I was very depressed.

On 24 May a police detective drove up the winding lane to Frogmill Farm. The area had been declared a "defence zone" by the War Office, and enemy aliens (even friendly ones such as I) had to leave at once. Coincidentally, I received a scholarship to an art school in London. I had applied in case I might not succeed in the field of agriculture. So I moved in with my mother, who was doing so well that she now lived in a garden flat in Hampstead in northwest London. It was an exciting new experience to cycle to school near Victoria Station every day.

On the first day, my schedule read, "Life Class/second floor." I assumed that that meant drawing still life compositions—a bowl of fruit, a vase of flowers. Imagine my surprise when I discovered a young blond woman in the room, draped over a chaise lounge entirely naked. My reaction was one of total shock, and I backed out hurriedly into the corridor and went to the men's room to comb my hair. After a while I gathered myself together and tiptoed back into class, sat down, and made a small, modest drawing of the lovely lady. Ah, art indeed!

On 14 June the Germans entered Paris. Three days later my budding art career was cut short: the school closed "because of the imminent danger of invasion." I carried my portfolio, such as it was, home on my bicycle. I couldn't carry my art materials as well, so I decided to pick them up later. Alas, it was not to be. The next day the arrests of friendly aliens began, prompted by the decline of the Allied fortunes of war. The knock at our Hampstead door came early in the morning.

"No time to wash and shave . . . sorry," said the officer.

I had the impression that the policemen on the aliens' beat had to bring in a certain quota each day, and that the quantity was much more important than the character, or even the identity of their targets. We later heard that one Black Maria (the police van of London's Finest) had pulled up in front of some university digs. "Are you Hans Schmidt?" the young man who answered the door was asked by the officer.

"No," replied the student truthfully. "I'm Tom Jones, his roommate."

"You come along then, you'll do. You can explain to the sergeant at the station who you are, and who you are not."

This explanation and its subsequent corroboration would mean at least two weeks in a camp. The police did not seem to understand what it was all about. Although my arrest was expected, I knew I was not singled out but was one of many that day.

Feeling dejected, I found myself on the second floor of the Hampstead police station with a roomful of German and Austrian refugees of all ages. One little old man in a long brown overcoat was looking anxiously out of the window because his wife had promised to bring him a sandwich, as his departure from home had been so hasty. At last he spotted her, rushing around the corner below with a brown paper bag. He managed a forlorn wave of the hand, to catch her eye.

"Get away from there," yelled an officer. "I saw you making signs to someone. You try that once more and you'll be in a cell."

Shortly afterward a more kindly sergeant asked whether anyone wanted to be escorted to the bathroom. Most of us raised our hands, but the little man was late. He was still intimidated and rather crestfallen from his rebuke, but after the excitement of the altercation he felt the need of the bathroom more keenly than anybody. So he tried to catch up with the group as we left by the far door, to be marched downstairs.

"You again," screeched his antagonist from before. "Up to the same old tricks, trying to sneak out." He yanked the old man out of the line.

Internment was toughest on the older men, but we all felt that it was haphazard and often disorganized. The problems confronting the Home Secretary were whom to intern, where to intern them, and what manpower to use to implement this difficult program. He answered the first question by having most males from sixteen year olds on up arrested. Some women were included but in much smaller numbers, though with no greater reason for suspicion. Unfortunately, the first category included me and many of the would-be volunteers to fight Hitler. What frustration! In the camps the guards were soldiers. Some grasped their assignment and some did not. Some were simply superannuated, tired, third class; they fell asleep on duty. We would toss pebbles up at them in their watchtowers to wake them when their orderly sergeant approached, for we felt sorry for them and didn't want them to get into trouble. We were on the same side, after all.

The camp commandant's attitude could make all the difference in the world to his charges. The commandant of Lingfield in Surrey, where I was interned, ran three different kitchens in his camp: regular, vegetarian, and kosher. Nowhere did any army regulations prescribe this kind of humanitarian effort. When I arrived, I found to my surprise that my father had preceded me there by a few days. I had not been in daily contact with him, and therefore did not know that he had been reinterned.

"Which meals did you sign up for?" he asked with apparent concern.

"Regular," I replied.

"Wrong," he said.

"Which should I have signed up for? Kosher?"

"Wrong again."

"Vegetarian?"

"Wrong, wrong, wrong. All three, of course." He added anxiously, "And you'd better not mind starting entrees again after dessert.

Some of the meal serving times overlap, and you'll have to run from one dining hut to the other, but it'll be the only way a growing lad like you can get enough to eat in this place."

The choices of camps varied. Some were examples of the British genius for improvisation. Based on the appreciation that racecourses are generally well fenced so that no one can gain admission without a ticket, plus the fact that horse racing had been suspended as an inessential luxury for the duration of the war, several of these establishments were converted into internment camps. Familiar to any race goer, the racecourses were now surrounded by an extra barbed wire fence. Numbers of watchtowers were equidistantly spaced around the huge enclosures, and gates were constructed. The inmates poured into Ascot, Lingfield, and Kempton Park.

Some camps were in boarding houses on the Isle of Man, where tourism was dormant because of the location in the Irish Sea, under threat of German U-boats. Another was located in a workers' housing development near Liverpool.

"And where are you sleeping?" asked my father at Lingfield racecourse.

"In the stables, on a straw palliasse," I replied.

"No good," he said.

"I know, but where should I be sleeping?"

"Members' enclosure, grandstand—leave it to me." He buttonholed an officer and told him he wanted to keep an eye on his son, "a young lad among all these men, you understand, sir."

"Is there any room for an extra bunk?"

"Yes, sir!" said my father, and he pushed all the other bunks tightly together to make space for me. I moved to the glassed-in luxury penthouse forthwith.

In Lingfield we were guarded by the Queen's Own Royal West Kent Regiment, in which I was to become a sergeant—much, much later. On the second day in camp, I had a run-in with a corporal of my future regiment. I had volunteered to peel potatoes, and while I was so occupied the rest of my newly arrived group was given the opportunity to take toothbrushes and razors out of their luggage, which was still locked up in a shed. Not being there, I missed that access. Returning from the cookhouse, I appealed to our guards to let me get at my little suitcase. They said no. In my naiveté I said that I had missed something important for purely altruistic reasons and that surely I had the right to my toiletries, the same as everybody else. "The 'right'?" screamed the corporal. He drew his Smith & Wesson revolver and pointed it at my head. "Let me tell you something about rights. I have the right to shoot you. You have no rights at all." I had tried the wings of freedom, even as an internee, and crashed.

In the paddock at Lingfield I met Harry Nomburg. It was during a handball game—the European version of that sport, more popular in Germany than in Austria. Harry came from Coburg, one of two sons of Georg and Lotte Nomburg. That town boasted of an early eruption of Nazism, and when the Nomburg business was torched by brown-shirted hooligans, the family moved to Berlin. They felt safe there as Herr Nomburg ran his overcoat business downtown, convinced that the urban sophistication of the capital also meant a more urbane conduct by its citizens and officials.

But as the Nazi noose slowly tightened, the Nomburgs became convinced that they had to get the boys out, the younger to Palestine and Harry on a children's transport to England. Unfortunately, Georg and Lotte lingered far too long themselves. Foolishly, they had believed that Hitler was really after the Communists, perhaps particularly Jewish Communists. They could not accept that law-abiding citizens such as themselves could be considered "enemies of the state"—their state, their Germany. They were deported to Lodz ghetto in Silesia, where most inmates either starved to death or were later deported to death camps. Harry never heard from them again.

As Harry and I stood next to each other in that paddock in Lingfield, we never envisioned that we were destined to land together as British Commandos on the same Normandy beach.

Meanwhile, 2,000 internees were shipped to Canada and 2,000 more to Australia. Because the destinations of transports leaving the camps were never announced, my father and I tried hard to join a departing classmate of mine. We failed. He was deported to Australia on the bad ship *Dunera*. Their guards were an unfortunate choice. They came from a unit that had just returned from Dunkirk, where they had heard of the Nazis' treatment of camp inmates and prisoners. The guards thought they were dealing with the perpetrators of these atrocities. Their apparent ambition was not to be outdone in brutality; their colonel was subsequently cashiered, and compensation claims were litigated for years.

Five who later joined No. 3 Troop—Hans Georg Fürth (Firth), Vogel (Villiers), Goldschmied (Dwelly), Gerald Nell (Nichols), and Carlebach (Carson)—all sailed on the *Dunera*.

Fürth immediately put up his hand when a call went out for experienced butchers. He wasn't a butcher at all, but he saw it as the opportunity it was, to escape the misery of the hold and to be close to the best coinage available—food. He was not disappointed. He slept in his own hammock for the rest of the trip and, unlike his shipmates, he was never hungry.

Nell also pulled off a major coup, with an idea that came to him before he was interned. His Aryan father had died when Gerald was fifteen years old, but his mother was Jewish. The teenager had wanted to get out of Germany and persuaded her to let him go to England, which was then still possible with his German passport. In London Gerald took the first job he could find. When the war seemed imminent, he was worried about his mother left behind in Germany, so he went to the German embassy and told them: "I am of military age. Would you be so good as to contact me right away if you are about to call up young men?"

One day they phoned and Gerald thanked them sincerely. Armed with that first-rate intelligence of mobilization, he then called his mother in Berlin. "Mother, please drop everything you're doing and come out at once."

She wisely followed his advice, but almost lingered in Holland too long. Luckily, she did manage to get aboard the last ship out and to join her anxious son in the United Kingdom. He went into internment and to Australia with a load off his mind.

Life in most internment camps was not too bad, if one had no family responsibilities, no relatives depending on one as a breadwinner. In some camps soccer uniforms and equipment were issued almost before food. An entire soccer league was established in one of the bigger camps, at Huyton near Liverpool, bearing witness to the popularity of that game in Germany, Austria, and Hungary, and to the sportsmanship of the British, to whom life without soccer must have appeared as cruel and unusual punishment.

There was some good player material among the internees, lads who had played for well-known German teams such as Eintracht-Frankfurt. Being Jewish had not disqualified them in the early days of the Nazi regime, when their exceptional talent had exempted them briefly from persecution. But that had not lasted long. And now, in more friendly confinement, the British commandants likewise could not suppress their own sporting instincts. One of them traded a famous gourmet hotel chef for a center forward from another camp, and a violinist for a goalkeeper. But culture also had its day. A stiff price was extracted when one commandant determined to reunite the popular piano duo of Ravich and Landauer, who had been interned initially in two different camps.

There were some odd characters among the inmates. Apart from a random cross section of humanity between the ages of sixteen and seventy, there was a little man in a blue serge suit who wore a rainbow of British World War I medal ribbons. He had lived in Britain most of his life, having come from Germany as a boy before the institution of immigration visas. He would proudly show off photos of his sons in the British Navy and RAF. Now he found himself behind barbed wire, bewildered because of one awful omission. He had never bothered to apply for naturalization. He had felt so much at home that it had never occurred to him.

After an extended period of incarceration, forms were distributed to give the internees an opportunity to apply for their release. Here was a chance for advocacy: to stress past anti-Nazi activity or essential war-effort work in which internees had been engaged. There was also a space to list character references, British citizens who had known the applicant for more than six years. Having arrived in the United Kingdom only a couple of years previously meant automatic disqualification for a majority. Not having known a single British subject, intimately or otherwise, for six years, I felt doomed to dwell in confinement for the duration of hostilities. It looked as though my life would be put on hold for years, and with it my ambition to fight Hitler. It was depressing, frustrating, and hard to bear.

One young man thought he had a better prospect: under "references" he wrote "His Majesty King George VI." This earned him a quick appearance before the commandant.

"I trust this is not facetious."

"I would not toy with my liberty, sir."

"Well, would you mind . . . amplifying this . . . a little? How does His Majesty know you?" asked the perplexed commandant.

"Actually, I do mind, sir. But if you must know, and I suppose you must, he is my first cousin." And truly, he was a German Saxe-Coburg or Hohenzollern prince, studying in London, incognito. It took him another two weeks to regain his liberty.

My own pessimism proved to be unwarranted. I had underrated the determination and power of my mother. She had decided to undergo surgery, in the hope of getting me out on compassionate grounds. I think that she had a hysterectomy, but in those days that was considered unmentionable. All she told me afterward was that she had postponed her operation several times, and that she recognized this as the opportune moment, as it might get me released. She enlisted the sponsor whom my Aunt Ida had found to help her enter the country.

In the meantime, my father and I had been separated. He wound up in Huyton near Liverpool, and I on the Isle of Man. He continued his efforts to get us reunited, and actually succeeded in having me sent on a mailboat, under escort of a British soldier with a rifle and bayonet, to join him in Huyton.

A telegram arrived there on 11 August 1940 from Marjorie Raphael, the Chief Girl Guide of Great Britain. "Please release Peter Arany at once," it said, "as his mother has to have major surgery. Peter has been a Boy Scout for ten years and is most reliable."

The poor commandant had no idea what to do about this unprecedented request. He sought guidance from the War Office, which was somewhat preoccupied with the German air raids that had recently begun. The verdict was that it would be better to let me go than to risk the wrath of thousands of uniformed little girls—a second front within the British Isles, so to speak. But the official forgot (or could it have been a fiendish plot?) to give me back my identity papers. Instead, I had to report to the Hampstead police, of evil memory.

"Where is your Alien Registration card?" was the sergeant's first question upon my arrival in the very building from which I had begun my prison career.

"It's in Huyton, near Liverpool, as far as I know."

So they issued me a new one ("We can't let you walk around without identification; they should never have let you go without it."), and to my delight they stamped it "Exempt from Internment."

It was a short-lived joy.

"Just a moment," said the police sergeant as I was almost out the door. He called me back to his desk, poised his pen, and inserted the ugly word *Temporarily* in oversized all-too-legible blue script.

But then they forgot me! There I was, roaming London among the ever-intensifying air raids, five or six a day, with Nazi Dornier and Junkers-88 bombers throbbing overhead throughout each night, and bombs whistling agonizingly amid the crackle of the antiaircraft guns. By day there were higher flying formations similarly engaged, plus occasional sneak attacks.

It was the late afternoon of 26 October. I had gone to the Piccadilly Circus branch of Boot's the Chemist in the heart of London to buy my sister a birthday present. I purchased a bottle of Paris Soir eau de cologne, and as I came to the exit door, an elderly couple arrived at the same time. Politely, I stepped aside and said, "After you."

Then there was a tremendous explosion. No air raid warning had sounded. The man and woman jumped right back into Boot's, possibly aided by the blast from outside, and joined me in trying to find a relatively safe place under the counter to get away from all the glass fixtures. When no further explosion came, I stood up and found myself facing a sales clerk, a slight man with steel-rimmed glasses, who said: "Are you being helped, sir?" It was a fine display of British nonchalance.

"Just waiting for it to calm down a bit, thank you," I replied, and waved my paper bag with the little blue bottle at him, by way of an alibi. He almost made me feel ashamed for having ducked for cover. When I stepped outside, I found everyone in Piccadilly Circus gravitating toward the far side of the street, where a cloud of smoke and dust revealed the explosion site. I walked toward it and turned onto a side street behind the Regent Palace Hotel, where I came upon the first of several bizarre sights. A middle-aged man was rushing away from the scene, walking rapidly past me. He wore a gray jacket, a porkpie hat, and short underpants. Before I had a chance to reflect upon this unconventional spectacle (Where had he been? Where was he going? Had his trousers been blown off?), the next weird spectacle came into view, a horse and cart, like the ones that commonly carried vegetables, being led by the driver. Man, horse, and wagon were one monochromatic gray, from top to toe, from hat to horseshoe, covered in debris dust.

This was immediately followed by yet another and more harrowing sight. Rescuers were carrying out several small children, covered with that same debris dust, all gray except for some splashes of red. I could not tell whether these children were alive or dead. They did not move, and their dreadful gray overlay contributed to their inanimate appearance. They were being carried from a pile of rubble one and a half stories high, where a three-story house had stood on Brewer Street.

The final appalling scene was on the level where the third floor had been. A tiny fragment of its floor—the hearth—about one foot in depth and three feet wide, remained attached to the adjacent house. On it stood a blond woman in a black dress, screaming and wringing her hands.

I could only speculate what it must have been like in that room when, without warning, the world around her disintegrated. Had she been there with her children, those wounded or dead gray bundles I had seen? Or had she been in an office, with her coworkers suddenly disappearing along with the furniture, the ceiling, the roof, three out of four walls, and almost all of the floor?

The drama ended right there, at least for the spectators, for firemen and air raid wardens arrived and shooed us away. They needed access for their equipment, to try to get her down before she fell off her narrow perch. As the police joined the emergency crews in clearing the crowd from Brewer Street, I walked back to Piccadilly. For a few blocks I could tell which of the pedestrians I encountered had witnessed the same scenes, at least the children and the blonde, for the horror still showed in their eyes.

• • •

When the internment powers continued to ignore me, temporarily, I took a job in a Polish publishing house behind the British Museum. Recommended by a family friend, I became a humble office boy. Shortly after my mother's release from the hospital, there was an item on the news that His Majesty's Armed Forces had lowered the age for joining up from twenty to eighteen, my age exactly. I volunteered immediately for the Auxiliary Military Pioneer Corps, my only option, on 3 September 1940, precisely one year after the war began. I was told I would be called up within a week or two. Actually, it took eight weeks.

Meanwhile, the air raids grew in quantity and intensity. My mother was recuperating quite satisfactorily and had ventured out of the house for the first time. She and I were at home on 26 September when there was knock at the door. When I opened it, I faced a man who looked like the stereotypical detective, raincoat and all.

"Peter Arany? I'm from Scotland Yard." He flashed credentials.

Here we go again, I thought. "Won't you come in and have a seat? Can I offer you a drink?"

"No, I'm on duty. And how is your mother?"

"Quite well, thank you . . . I mean still a bit weak, of course." We were in the living room. My mother sat on the lounge chair in the corner.

"Ah, ma'am, now I can ask you myself. Have you gone back to work?"

"Oh, no, I'm not up to that yet," said my mother, perhaps a little too quickly.

"Are you quite sure of that?" asked the detective. It was obvious that he thought she was.

I hurried to intercede and said to my mother: "I have an idea. You keep a diary, don't you? Why don't you fish it out and read this gentleman what you've been doing since you've gotten home?"

The detective liked the idea, and my mother went to get her little red pocket diary. She skimmed over her very limited activities. Then she came to the date two days ago.

"Oh, the day before yesterday I went to my fashion business for the first time, just to visit, mind you, and to see how they were doing without me. I was only there for an hour or so."

An air raid began at that moment. There had been an air raid warning signal all along, which was not unusual. People went about their business and sought cover only when "it sounded near." This was in keeping with any number of "Business as Usual" signs on many shops, even partially bombed out ones.

But this particular air raid was not just near, it was practically on top of us. The long, haunting, menacing whistle of the bombs went on and on, finally ending in an ear-shattering explosion. My mother, Scotland Yard, and I met under the dining table, hoping that its top and legs would hold if the ceiling came down on us. It was as if we had rehearsed a synchronized dive.

The windows and even the walls were visibly shaking, and acrid yellow dust emanated from some cracks. But the ceiling held, and we came out from under the table. The excitement of the close call, compounded by the policemen's presence and its implications, proved too much for my mother. She collapsed into her chair and began to shake and scream.

When our visitor heard and saw her seizure, he said to me, "Better get her a brandy, and I think I'll have one myself, now."

He became more talkative. "We knew, of course, that you had been to your workplace, Mrs. Arany. Monday, 23 September, at ten-twenty-seven it was. But I accept your explanation, for I can see that you are not well enough to get along without your son. I believe you're nice folks, and I hope that you'll feel better soon. Perhaps it would help you if I tell you some good news. We hear a lot of things at the Yard that we're not supposed to talk about, but I know you'll appreciate this, and keep it to yourselves: the war will be over by Christmas!"

As he was taking his leave, I said: "By the way, I joined the Army last week."

"Great." he replied. "Why didn't you tell me?"

"You didn't ask me about myself."

"Well, we can't intern one of His Majesty's soldiers, can we? Besides, your mother will need you until you get called up. It's been a pleasure meeting you."

4 Pining in the Pioneer Corps

The fourth metamorphosis for us young refugees was the Pioneer Corps. Some of us had joined this British Army unit as the only option open to us to take part in the war effort. Others joined so that they could escape internment. Yet others had enlisted in the units of their choice, only to be dumped into the Pioneer Corps when their enemy alien status came to the attention of the authorities.

Our occupation was manual labor: loading and unloading railroad cars, building roads, testing Bailey bridges. It was a dreary existence—dull, unchallenging work. We tried to get put on task work, where we had a given amount of work to accomplish and were then free to do what we wanted. For most of us, this was to pursue the opposite sex. The only trouble was that the Army did not feel constrained to adhere to fair labor practices. If unloading three carloads of coal dust each was the required amount for one week, and we managed to clean ourselves up and cycle seven miles to our dates by half past three in the afternoon, it would be four carloads the following week, as they upped the ante. It would then become a matter of pride for us horny young blades to work even faster and get to town by quarter to three.

My own as yet undeveloped sex life was seriously retarded by Lance Corporal Kury. He was not even a bona fide refugee. He told us some story about having been born on a ship in German territorial waters, "and that's why they stuck me into this 'ere outfit." He had the best-polished pair of boots in the company. No doubt it was they and his gleaming brass regimental cap badge and greatcoat buttons that had elevated him to the lofty lance corporal level.

When we yearned to go out, Kury was polishing something; there he would sit, a slim, pink-faced figure with a ridiculous mustache, his boots and buttons next to him on his cot as he polished away as if it were fun. He was determined that we should do the same. As neither example nor inspiration converted any of us, he bullied us instead. "No going out," he would announce, "until yer can shave in the reflection of yer boots."

It was infuriating and frustrating, an early encounter with the harsh realization that military discipline cannot be circumvented effectively by the novice.

Kury was by no means the only reason why some of us wanted to get out of the Pioneer Corps. The war was going on before our very eyes. How were we supposed to satisfy our immense motivation to fight the Nazis by unloading freight cars?

As time passed, some of us were promoted to noncommissioned officer (NCO) rank. Whereas the majority of senior NCOs initially had been British, more and more of us became sergeants and even occasionally a quartermaster—a warrant officer grade no less. Great excitement greeted the arrival of our first refugee second lieutenant. But it was not much comfort to us run-of-the-mill, rank-and-file youngsters, who had no qualifications other than our enthusiasm to fight the Germans.

In desperation, we wrote letters to Members of Parliament, to the press, to anybody who might support us in our endeavor. I wrote to a columnist called Cassandra, who promised to help members of the Armed Forces. After a long waiting period, I received a reply: "No hope . . . a matter of policy . . . contact the War Office." Sure.

Meanwhile, there had been shifts within the Pioneer Corps; at least I had escaped Kury's grasp when several others and I were transferred to Long Marsden, seven miles from Stratford-upon-Avon. Luckily, my friend Marischka, son of the famous Viennese matinee idol Hubert Marischka, was also posted there. He was my mentor in all things pertaining to sex.

Zwetschi was his nickname. Totally unpronounceable by the British and Germans alike, it was a strictly Austrian diminutive of the strictly Austrian word for "plum." It referred to his size and color at birth, but he had changed, naturally, now that he was in his late twenties. In fact, he was the most handsome, charming, charismatic, irresponsible corrupter of morals to be found anywhere. Even in Vienna, mothers would lock up their daughters at the mere mention of Zwetschi's name—usually to no avail, for he was also inventive and ingenious and considered obstacles to sex merely challenges. I had just turned twenty, and Zwetschi was shocked and amazed at virginity in one so ancient.

By and by, we received requests for volunteers—opportunities to transfer to more active units. I had decided a while ago to volunteer first and not concern myself with the details until I was accepted. Thus I began by putting my name down for serving as a listening post in the North African desert, intercepting and interpreting messages between units of Field Marshal Rommel's Afrika Korps. I did not even get an interview. The same thing happened when an obscure parachuting request came down. It was puzzling and frustrating. Much later it was rumored that some bureaucrat, somewhere, had screened out all applicants who had been interned, a totally irrelevant discrimination at this stage.

Yet several men disappeared, one by one. Marischka was sent to Scotland to become a sergeant-ski-instructor, a great loss to me. Others left for destinations unannounced, and apparently unknown even to them.

Then one day there was a tiny typewritten sliver of paper on the company bulletin board: "Anyone wishing to volunteer for special and hazardous duty should come to the office at 1430 tomorrow."

A few young enthusiasts and I lined up outside the company office at the appointed hour. When it was my turn, I was led into a small, bleak room in another Nissen hut. It had been scantily set up for the occasion. A rough gray Army blanket was thrown over a trestle table, behind which sat a slightly built officer. He had a clean-shaven, slim face and was dressed in a raincoat with no rank insignia on the epaulets. He wore dark sunglasses and the peaked cap of an obscure infantry regiment. I memorized the design, three swords in an escutcheon, and learned later that it belonged to the Essex Yeomanry.

"Why do you wish to do special and hazardous work?" he asked in a quiet, voice.

I told him about living under the Nazis from 12 March to 21 August 1938, surely sufficient motivation by itself. "I think part of this war belongs to me, sir."

"Can you shoot? Can you handle a boat? Do you know anything about wireless?"

"I have fired a pellet gun with reasonable accuracy. While I worked on a farm in Berkshire, we used to shoot to break matchsticks stuck in the ground at twenty yards. I have rowed a lot and paddled canoes and my father's foldboat. I don't know anything about sailing, nor do I have any expertise in radios, sir, but I am a quick learner."

Hardly anything else was said. I found that the suspense was parching my throat. My future was in the hands of this man I had only just met.

"In a week or two you will be sent to London for a few days, for more intensive interviews and security clearance. Good luck."

Hurrah! I was on my way at last.

A young man called Mayer with ash blond hair replied, when asked for his reason for wanting to live dangerously: "I have always been interested in cloak-and-dagger operations, sir."

The officer didn't bat an eyelash under the sunglasses. "Thank you very much. We won't be calling you, I'm afraid."

There was also a squat, little fellow-Austrian refugee named Richard Abramowitz in this group of volunteers. Although he was young, he had already acquired the physical characteristics of a prize-fighter: a bull neck, the typical mauled ears, and eyes peering out from little slits that had obviously often been swollen closed. When asked the wireless question, he said: "The only thing I know about it, sir, is how to turn it on and how to turn it off."

But he gave such a dramatic account of his escape from Austria that his motivation for wanting to fight was beyond any shadow of a doubt. He had been with a group of Jews dumped between the German and Belgian border by the Nazis, with the appreciation that the Belgians would not let any of them enter and that the Nazi border guards would shoot the unfortunate group if they attempted to reenter the German Reich. In fact, given the opportunity, they would shoot them even in no-man's-land, whether they tried to return or get away. It had been a harrowing experience before he finally was lucky enough to slip away, under fire, and cross the frontier.

Of course, none of us had the slightest idea of what we were volunteering for. On 17 March 1943, I speculated in my little red leather-bound pocket diary: "Commandos? Don't think so. Other possibilities: Reconnaissance Corps? The latest: agents in Norway, lying low in preparation of an Allied invasion there."

Now that I knew (or hoped) that I would become a member of some special and hazardous outfit, I figured that this novel scenario would more likely than not entail a high standard of physical fitness. I decided therefore to make a concentrated effort to get myself in shape. Happily, an obvious course to achieve my goal was close at hand. The corporal in charge of the hut in which I lived in Long Marsden was one Victor Lenel, from Mannheim, Germany. A man dedicated to exercise to the point of fanaticism, he would get up at the crack of dawn, winter and summer, rain, snow, or shine, and, dressed only in his Army-issue blue gym shorts, he would jog into the Cotswolds landscape. That was in addition to a hard day's manual labor in which he fully participated; despite his elevated rank, Victor was no shirker when it came to work. He shoveled coal and lugged railway sleepers (as we called railroad cross ties) just like the rest of us.

Twice a week Victor took a group of like-minded individuals on cross-country runs. No matter how exhausting the day's exertions in the depot had been, the men chased up and down the countryside until after sundown. Most of us believed they were mad. When I explained that I wanted to join him and why I was embarking on this masochistic enterprise, he welcomed me into his club of runners. "My crazy young brother Ernst has joined some suicide outfit also," he told me. "I think you'll enjoy the running. It's lots of fun."

I had my doubts. The first time I participated, I was panting up a steep mountain when I heard someone remark: "Look at that gorgeous sunset!" I was completely taken aback, for I was too preoccupied with my legs and breathing and the all-too-steep incline of the wooded hillside to be aware of any kind of sun in the sky, let alone its aesthetic qualities.

At the end of the ordeal, those still capable of so doing sprinted the last hundred yards or so, flat out to the camp gate. My ill-considered novice attempt to join them failed dismally. It deteriorated into a limp, and it required grim determination on my part to not sit down, or even lie down in the road. With a last supreme effort of willpower, I made it, but the trouble was that I now could not walk! Shamefacedly dragging myself into our company lines, I wondered how on earth I was going to play soccer for my unit two days hence, as I was the outside right on 77 Company's team.

Luckily, that same Dicky Abramowitz who did not know anything about radios came to my rescue. He had only recently arrived and had been assigned to my hut. He had boxed in the European Youth Finals in Brussels, he told me, but he had decided to quit the gentlemanly art of prizefighting.

"I'm a poet, really," he said, "and I know if I went on, I'd start to look like a boxer."

Alas, too late. But he remembered all about the massage that was required to keep a battered body with sore muscles in fighting condition, so he promised to get me on my feet for the soccer match. He spread a coarse Army blanket on my cot, poised a can of talcum powder, and lunged into his task with gusto.

"This may hurt a little," he said with a fine sense for understatement. This was not a gentle massage. He kneaded and squeezed, knuckled and jabbed, until I gasped and howled. He had insisted on performing this torture just before the game: "It works better that way. Now get up and play!"

Disbelieving, I got to my feet and gingerly tried a couple of steps. Amazingly, my legs felt as good as new, so I played a pretty good game. Two hours after it was over, I wanted to thank Abramowitz once again. But I could not walk another inch. Excruciating pain accompanied every attempt.

For three weeks Dicky massaged me on Tuesdays and Thursdays for the Lenel group, and on Saturdays for soccer.

It is true that I owed Abramowitz a lot. But who would have thought that he would cash that debt by stealing my name? Yet that is precisely what he did, quite soon after the last massage.

5 Stealing My Good Name

It was like going on leave. Six of us were traveling to London on the 1230 train from Stratford-upon-Avon on Friday, 2 April 1943. But this was no leave. No sooner had we arrived at a monstrous red brick building near Baker Street than we were plunged into its basement to be interviewed.

We had been told that we were going for intensive clearance procedures at the Grand Central Hotel on Marylebone High Street. If ever it had been "grand," it must have been a long time ago, before it had been transformed into an all-purpose Army transit facility. So many different activities took place simultaneously that none of us knew what others were doing there.

But to us it was the gateway to a new life—if only we passed the interrogations. Our anxiety was great, because failure was unthinkable. The technique was interesting. There were three typical Army desks in the room, one in front and two behind. At the front desk sat an Army captain with an enormous cavalry mustache, so big that it could be seen from behind. The left rear desk was occupied by a lance corporal clerk and the right one by an ordinary-looking little man wearing horn-rimmed glasses and a blue suit. Into this assembly we were called one at a time and seated facing the mustachioed man.

"What does your father do?" he asked for openers, and then, "What is your political orientation?"

The second question presented a problem, because the "what-does-he-want-to-hear" factor was uppermost in my mind, and he knew it. But I, for one, was also still programmed by a card handed me upon my arrival in England five years earlier. Written by the Refugee Committee, it began: "You are guests of Great Britain . . ." and was full of good advice such as not to damage the property and furniture of others. It also included this gem: "Do not speak loudly in the street, especially not in the evening."

With this in mind, I actually answered the captain softly: "As a guest of Great Britain, it is not for me to participate in political activities."

"Oh, quite so," he replied. "And what newspaper do you read?"

"The *Times*, the *Telegraph*, the *Observer*, whatever."

"And what does your father do?"

"As I just said, sir, he was a jeweler, and he was recently demobbed from the Pioneer Corps because of his age."

"Ah, yes, so you did. And now to another question: what did you say your politics are?"

After a while one felt foolish pointing out that the last question asked had just been answered. Perhaps the man would believe that I had no political convictions at all, and perhaps he would hold that against me. After all, I didn't harbor any subversive views, so why not tell him?

More questions followed, some seemingly trivial and irrelevant. Every now and then, the sole civilian in the room would get up and come out from behind the third desk to hand the captain a paper, and the questioning would take a new turn. A rumor began that the little man in blue was "one of the Big Three of MI-5," British Military Intelligence.

One of our group emerged into the tan-tiled basement corridor where the rest of us were waiting our turn and said: "Phew, that was tough."

"What was?" I asked.

"They wanted to know which of my qualities I was proudest of."

"And how in hell did you answer that one?"

"I said, my good looks!"

At least I had been forewarned. If I were asked that, I decided I'd cite my ability to remain cheerful in adversity, but they never did ask me.

The weekend was upon us, and the interviews at the Grand Central Hotel were not yet complete. On Saturday, orders were posted on the bulletin board. There was to be an obligatory Sunday church parade. Perhaps the marching order was alphabetical by regiments present and accounted for in the hotel.

In any case, the parade proceeded to the church, having marched crisply through downtown London. A small detachment of us, mainly Jewish Auxiliary Military Pioneer Corps men, proudly led the way, followed by Coldstream Guards, Grenadier Guards, and Irish Guards. It felt good to us unarmed labor-unit foreigners to lead that illustrious parade.

It was also good to be in London once more, to smell the aroma of city life again, to be young and, at long last, to have hope for a meaningful future and the chance to fight the Nazis.

At the end of the interviews, we were told that all of us were going to be sent back to our Pioneer Corps units. Those, including me, who had passed the security checks were told that we would soon receive further instructions.

Having to return to the drudgery of the Long Marsden depot did not bother those who had been accepted. The weeks spent waiting were made lighter and infinitely more bearable by the certain knowledge that these were the last coal cars we had to unload, the last railroad cross ties we had to carry on our shoulders, and the last frames we had to lift onto the huge test bridge.

Then, on 14 April, those who had passed the security checks were given travel warrants to the Pioneer Corps base in Bradford, Yorkshire, where most of us had begun our soldiering two years earlier. Then, we were struggling with such problems as keeping in step on the parade ground. This time we felt like old soldiers, familiar with the way the game had to be played, impatient to start our new life. Eight of us were to board a train for an unknown destination three days later. A British Pioneer Corps sergeant, truly an old soldier, persuaded the powers-that-be to send him with us to be in charge of our little group, perhaps hoping he would have a bit of fun and escape his dreary routine for a day.

We had come from different companies and locations. Sachs, Abramowitz, and I were the only ones from 77 Company. On the way, Abramowitz told us about his biggest fight, the European Youth Welterweight finals in Brussels.

"It was bloody bad luck," he said. "I broke my thumb in the first round. Even so, I would have won, for I'm not a quitter. I went right on fighting. But in the eighth the ref noticed it and made me forfeit." His little eyes were glinting as he waved his fists and ducked and weaved, reliving his moment in the limelight.

We transferred to the little steam train that chugs along the coast of North Wales, curious about what fate awaited us. The train stopped at a small station called Dovey Junction.

Suddenly, a dozen men in green berets burst into our compartment. They wore No. 10 Commando shoulder flashes over the round Combined Operations badge. Some had parachute wing insignia on their sleeves and white turtleneck sweaters under their battle-dress blouses. To our surprise, several turned out to be friends who had vanished earlier from the Pioneer Corps.

"Don't ever use the words Pioneer Corps again—it compromises our security. We served together in the Old Hampshires, remember that! Great outfit, the Old Hampshires."

I found myself face-to-face with some of my special pals: Uli Steiner, Stephan Rosskamm, and André Kirschner, all Jewish refugees from 77 Company. I and, in the case of the last two, the company soccer team had sorely missed them in the last few months.

Uli, an intelligent, well-educated individual, introduced himself as Leslie Scott. Rosskamm had become Steve Ross, and the Hungarian Kirschner was now Andrew Kershaw. They had boarded our train as a sort of welcoming committee, and they rode along with us to our destination, Aberdovey, the next stop. There were many questions to be asked by them and by us, for they wanted to know what had happened "back there."

We were even more curious about what was in store for us. "Have you been in action yet?" "Has anybody else managed to escape the Pioneer Corps? Where and when did they go?" "What's it like here?" "Is our old CO in Long Marsden still such a contrary cuss, and has anybody succeeded yet in assassinating his bloody dog?"

That miserable cur used to pounce out from under the table where the major dispensed his brand of military justice, and it would snap at our ankles when we were in enough trouble already and were having to stand rigidly at attention.

All of us new arrivals were caught in a whirlwind of excitement. We heard, in an onslaught of overlapping sentences, that training was bloody murder. "They run us within an inch of our lives. There's no falling out unless you faint. There's no punishment for any infraction, but if you can't hack it, or if you don't fit in for any reason whatsoever, you get an RTU. That means return to unit. It's the worst thing that can happen to you. But the beginning is the toughest."

Hardly anyone of us noticed the afternoon sun on the pretty dunes along the bay between Aberdovey and Aberystwyth, nor the hills on the other side of the railway where soon we were to run our guts out. None of us had ever heard of Aberdovey, nor of Merionethshire. Perhaps some of us had not even heard of North Wales. The lovely song "The Bells of Aberdovey" had not yet reached any of our ears. But that little Welsh seaside resort was to become our first home, our stomping ground, in the Commandos.

When we got off the train, we encountered Troop Sergeant-Major O'Neill, formerly Oskar Hentschel. He was a gaunt, medium-sized, leathery-looking man who yelled and snarled in true sergeant-major fashion, particularly when he noticed the British sergeant who had accompanied us.

"Who are *you?*" he bellowed.

The elderly sergeant identified himself.

"You're under arrest. We didn't ask for any escort."

Troop Sergeant-Major O'Neill then placed the interloper into a waiting truck, under guard. Next he ordered us to remove our forage caps so that no one could see our Pioneer Corps badges.

"Get rid of these. Don't throw them in the garbage, where somebody might find them. Bury them." Then he packed us off into the back of the same truck in which the nervous sergeant was awaiting the outcome of what he had hoped would be a fun trip.

Richard Trojan, who served under the name of Dick Tennant, was at the wheel. This tall, slender Austrian had wavy blond hair, a small mustache, and spectacles. He was a hell-bent driver, so the short distance to our headquarters house up on a hill proved to be a hair-raising experience. Upon arrival we stood around on the flagstone terrace outside, while two 3 Troop sergeants marched the prisoner into the office of the commanding officer. The luckless man's cap had been taken from him, as well as his belt and bayonet.

"Left, right—left, right—halt!" shouted O'Neill. He saluted. "Sir! This noncommissioned officer" (he gave his name, rank, and serial number) "arrived with the other men from Bradford. I believe that he poses a very serious security risk. I respectfully suggest that we kill him, sir!"

"Do you have a method in mind, Sergeant-Major?" asked the slightly built man behind the desk without showing any emotion.

"He could easily have fallen out of the truck, sir."

"He could, at that, Sergeant-Major."

The sergeant was in shock. Who could have anticipated that his little day excursion would have such dire consequences. Who were these madmen?

The soft-spoken, cold-blooded captain let him cringe a little longer before he said: "Sergeant, listen carefully, for your life may well depend on it. You have seen nothing here. You have met nobody. No green berets, no peculiar people. The group of men you accompanied got off the train. You can't remember where, nor do you recall their names. This day never happened. And if, in spite of that, any stories come out of your sergeants' mess, or any of the pubs in or around Bradford or your hometown, I promise you that we are going to get you. Now get the hell out of here before I change my mind. Dismissed. Take him to the station and see that he is on the next train to Bradford."

Meanwhile, the conversation on the terrace had continued unabated. We newcomers were going to be called in alphabetical order to choose ourselves new names and to be issued new Army dog tags and numbers and metal cap badges of the regiments from which we had ostensibly volunteered for the Commandos.

I felt I needed a little quiet concentration to think of a good name, for it would be my turn in a minute. My friends insisted that it was not a big deal. I disagreed, not wanting to be stuck with a poor choice for the future.

"I've got it!" I said finally. "I'll be Peter Arlen."

Having been born Peter Arany twenty years before in Vienna. I thought keeping my initials would be a good idea. It would be easier to get used to. Besides, I had some rather fancy handkerchiefs with "P.A." embroidered in the corner.

Abramowitz was called, the only one ahead of me in the alphabet; he came out a few minutes later.

"Gentlemen, let me introduce myself. My name is Richard Arlen."

I gulped. "You bastard! You stole my name!"

"So I did."

"You heard me say that I'd choose the name Arlen, and just because they called you in first you pinched it!"

"Exactly. Do you want to make something of it?" Dicky Arlen smiled.

I remembered the eight pugilist rounds with the broken thumb. As I have already pointed out, I'm not a hero. I shook my head. But now I hardly had time to think of another name. I consulted my pals.

"How about Garvey?" (To hell with the handkerchiefs; it was the name of a young woman I admired.)

They replied that there was a Garvin in the troop who worked in the office because he had a heart murmur, and the Skipper didn't want to RTU him. It would be too similar a name and have a negative connotation."

I tried another one on them, but they whispered that a troop member with but a slightly different spelling was hovering on the brink of an RTU.

"Next!" came the raspy voice of Troop Sergeant-Major O'Neill. I thought frantically. There had been just one commanding officer, a Major Masters, of one of my old units who had looked like my idea of a real soldier, and he had been a decent sort. He had even swept up for us one evening when we'd been too exhausted to do it ourselves. To that incident and to Arlen's thievery I owe my name. Besides, no other name beginning with an A would come into my head until it was too late, and M, I thought, would commemorate my grandfather, Arnold Metzger.

So I entered the office of the captain commanding No. 3 Troop, 10 Commando. With a little difficulty I recognized the slightly built, unsmiling officer of the dark glasses and the raincoat without rank insignia on the epaulets who had interviewed me in that hut in Long Marsden. Only now the Skipper, Bryan Hilton-Jones, wore his Essex

Yeomanry badge on his green beret. There and then I became No. 6387025 Pvt. Peter Masters, who had volunteered for the Commandos from the Queen's Own Royal West Kent Regiment, who had been born in London, and who was a member of the Church of England. The future looked wonderful. And scary. The fear of not being allowed to fight had now been replaced by the fear of RTU. I knew I would do anything to avoid it. Being superfit was a start. Thank God for the hard work carrying bales of hay at Frogmill Farm; thank God for Corporal Lenel and his crazy cross-country runners.

6 The Toughening Process Begins

I was handed my No. 10 Commando shoulder flashes and the Combined Operations insignia. It showed an RAF eagle perched on a kedge anchor, across which a tommy gun was superimposed, all in bright scarlet red on a navy blue background. For our new cap badges we were arbitrarily divided into four regiments from which we had purportedly volunteered for Commando service: the Queen's Own Royal West Kents (my regiment), the Royal Sussex Regiment, the Buffs (or East Kent Regiment), and the Hampshire Regiment ("the Old Hampshires").

The Queen's Own badge shows a silvered version of the white horse of Kent, over the motto *Invicta*. It seemed a giant step up from the shovel and pickax of the Pioneer Corps. We were told that these metal badges were to be worn over the left eye on our new green berets. Alternatively, we could wear the so-called General Service badge, which showed the royal coat of arms: the lion and the unicorn with the motto *Dieu et mon droit, Honi soit qui mal y pense*.

Our most important instructions came from the Skipper. He told us that we had been chosen for our initiative. Therefore he left it to us to invent a plausible story to account for whatever foreign accent we had. We were issued an Army paybook that bore our new name, our regimental origin and number, our birthplace in Britain, and our religion, the Church of England. This was done not only for our protection but primarily to prevent the enemy from knowing that the British Army had a unit where every man spoke fluent German and was fully trained in knowing all important intricacies about the German Army. We were given the address of a local family where we would live as long as we were in Aberdovey. We would be expected to sign our new name to some papers as per wartime regulations as soon as we arrived at our billets. The Skipper emphasized:

You will then immediately go to your room and scan all your belongings, destroying any evidence of your previous identity. Don't throw it away. Burn it. You will be surprised at how many things you own, letters, books, and so forth, betray your antecedents. You will not fail to destroy them. You will not send or receive mail to or from people with foreign-sounding names. I leave it to your ingenuity to find innocuous methods of communication with your families or next of kin. You will not keep diaries, and you will keep the number of persons who know both your identities to an absolute minimum.

He assured us that we would be furnished all necessary documentation and all the ficticious stories and lies concocted by us would be backed by the authority of the British War Office.

I entered my next of kin in my paybook as Mrs. Clara Masters, mother. I wrote to her under that name, trusting that she would recognize my handwriting.

Leslie Scott had some leave coming, so I asked him to go to see my mother and explain the situation; he had been a frequent guest in our house. He had a good sense of humor, and he came back telling me that he had convinced her what a lovely time we were having and how devoid of danger our future was going to be. I was grateful.

The name of the Welsh family into whose house I would now be moving was written on a slip of paper: Dr. and Mrs. Wright, Cartref (the Welsh name of their two-story house), Aberdovey. I asked directions and lugged my kitbag to the northern end of the village. Theirs was the last house. Beyond it lay only the Chattelard School for Girls, a boarding school that had been evacuated to the safety of North Wales.

I began my new life by burning letters and documents and tearing out title pages from my books. I practiced signing my new name until I could do it in so natural and unaffected a manner that future signatures would not present a problem. When the subject of my family arose, I told the Wrights, and everybody else who asked, that my father had traveled on business extensively in Europe. When he had been posted to Vienna for a prolonged period, he took my mother and me along. When he had been transferred temporarily to an unhealthy tropical climate, my mother joined him, but I was left in Vienna, in the care of a nanny, since I was then a mere babe in arms. Unaccountably, his supposedly brief tour of duty was extended time and again. Because he was in poor health, my mother stayed to look after him, hoping to return any day. They were naturally concerned about me, but they knew I was in good hands with the trusted nanny. Meanwhile, I had started to talk—in German, of course. My parents saw me periodically, on all-too-short visits. At first they were amused by my "linguistic talents" and convinced that I would pick up my native English naturally, when the situation was normalized. Later they grew alarmed, but it was too late: I had to learn English as a second language. They took me back home, posthaste, and avoided all foreign contacts in order to reestablish my own native British persona. This was why I could not remember exact places where we had lived or people I had known. But the damage had been done, and I was afflicted with that "awful, embarrassing" Teutonic accent for the rest of my life.

I had stitched on my Commando shoulder flashes and polished my prancing-horse badge. I affixed it to my green beret and looked in the mirror in my room for a long time and from all angles. Out of the cocoon, a butterfly at last.

Two earlier groups of volunteers had preceded us, having received their initial training at the Commando training center at Achnacarry, Fort William, Scotland. Their tales of that harrowing experience made it sound like Devil's Island but without the creature comforts. Our group of volunteers had not been sent to Achnacarry because, it soon became apparent, the Skipper was perfectly capable of duplicating its worst rigors right here in Aberdovey. Besides, the fewer people who came across us the better. Aberdovey's isolation served that purpose splendidly.

On my first day I had several surprises. There was Cpl. Victor Lenel's crazy brother, the one who had joined the suicide outfit. Ernest Lawrence was his name, and he seemed not only totally rational but a dedicated, serious young man, every bit as fit and tough as his sibling, who had tested our stamina in the cross-country runs in the Cotswolds.

And there was Pvt. Jock MacGregor. To my utter amazement I recognized him as none other than my erstwhile nemesis in the Pioneer Corps, ex-Corporal Kury. He had, of course, been obliged to follow house rules by relinquishing his rank, so we were equals for the time being. I admit that I shuddered when I encountered him in the Commandos. His zealous obstruction of my burgeoning sex life was still too fresh in my mind. I hated Jock MacGregor.

True, there were others to dislike. Sometimes Troop Sergeant-Major O'Neill could irritate all of us. So could Langley (Landau), our efficient administrative sergeant, with his lapses into pomposity. But these were minor antipathies compared with the hatred and fury I reserved for MacGregor. I worked hard to outrank him, and eventually I was promoted to the lofty heights of lance corporal while Jock remained a private. I thought that the slim, tall, provocative, young bullshitter didn't know what he was in for when, much to my pleasure, he was assigned to my detachment when we went into action for the first time on D day. I would, I decided, give him a bit of his own medicine.

But then a funny thing happened: nothing. Having attained the power, the absolute ability to pay him back for all those unconsummated dates, all those undrunk pints of mild and bitter beer, I found that my burning desire for revenge had been totally dissipated. What's more, I actually grew to like him. In times of danger and in depressing circumstances caused by harassing bombardments, casualties, and attrition, Jock never faltered. He remained his usual swashbuckling self, absurdly ignoring the odds. He was a tonic to have around.

Why had he chosen the name MacGregor? He could so easily have been Curry, or Smith. He could have passed in any pub as "one of the boys" because he didn't sound like a foreigner, as did the rest of us. He spoke lousy German. He had been declared an enemy alien because technically he was a German citizen. "I was born on a ship in German territorial waters," he told me once, "son of a British sailor and a German woman." But at another time he said, "I have told so many lies about where I come from that I've forgotten the damn truth. One thing is for sure: I'll never get a passport." Perhaps to put past lies to rest and to acquire a new persona, he had the urge to assume the personality of someone totally different. He was fascinated by the aura of tartan and kilt. The sporran worn with Scots Highland dress, and Scottish dirk, or dagger, drew him like magnets, so he became MacGregor.

We took to the hills almost immediately upon our arrival in Aberdovey. The rolling landscape and the cold bluish sunlight that fell on this war-deserted Welsh seaside resort produced a bleak setting for our self-imposed ordeal. The pale yellow-green slopes were dotted with Commando trainees chasing up and down, odd young men wearing khaki drab and woolen stocking caps of that same colorless hue, or else sporting our flamboyant green berets. We moved silently on rubber-soled boots and then banged away noisily with weapons and explosives of various types.

All movement among the training sites in the dunes and mountainous surroundings was done on the double. The first day, we panted up the steep grades led by some of the old hands. Michael Merton (Blumenfeld) ran ahead of my group, and when he came to a farm fence—the type where three horizontal poles are affixed between vertical posts about five feet high—he headed straight for it. Without breaking his stride he reached up with one hand on the top pole and vaulted over it. I found it a startling accomplishment. How on earth was I going to do that? But remembering the ever-present threat of RTU, I saw no alternative but to have a go at it, and to my amazement I made it over.

Every week we had at least one speed march and one assault march. The first started out in formation, with an officer in the lead. We would be dressed in full field service marching order (FSMO), including weapons and ammunition, as specified in printed daily orders. The leader would break into a run whenever he so decided, and we would have to do the same. Then he changed back to a rapid march step, and so did we. The timing of these changes had little or nothing to do with the gradient of the road, so that often we found ourselves running uphill, and our initial neat formation was soon loosened or abandoned. Keeping up was essential. That applied equally to assault marches, which were similar to speed marches except that they were cross-country.

"There will be no falling out," said the standing order. Fainting constituted an arguable exception. The marches usually lasted an hour or so. On the road, we covered a distance of six to seven miles.

One march took two hours and covered more than eleven miles. Jimmy Monahan, the Irish poet who was our second-in-command, was the leader on that occasion. A quiet, reserved, and elegant man, he didn't say much, but he set a ferocious pace. Toward the end of these marches, it had become fashionable to finish the last hundred yards or so with a spurt of sprinting, for those who could still muster the strength, just as Victor Lenel had done in our Old Hampshire cross-country runs. The leader always held a slightly unfair advantage, because he knew when and where he would declare the run to be over. Therefore, he alone knew exactly when to start sprinting. But some of us learned to judge the leader's intentions with remarkable accuracy. When the end of a run seemed near, several runners would almost draw parallel with him, then watch him with eagle eyes. (It was "not done" to break into the sprint before he did.) Occasionally, the alertness paid off, and a few of us were able to overtake him at the last moment, which seemed to irk him considerably.

Bryan Hilton-Jones was a remarkable athlete. He was demanding of every one of us, but he would never ask us to do anything that he would not first do himself. In fact, we learned to exercise caution even when joking about challenges. For example, someone might say in jest: "Look at that sheer two-story-high wall. Aren't you surprised that the Skipper hasn't made us climb it and then jump down?"

If Hilton-Jones had overheard that remark, he most certainly would have made us do precisely that. The more impossible a challenge seemed, the more he would relish it. First, of course, he would unsmilingly demonstrate how simply and easily the formidable wall could be scaled and how there was nothing to jumping down from its absurd height, if you kept your feet and knees together.

The reason that some of us could occasionally outrun him was simply that there were outstanding runners in our ranks. Freddy Gray (Manfred Gans), Georgie Saunders (Georg Saloschin), Eric Howarth (Erich Nathan), and Ernest Lawrence (Victor Lenel's kid brother), to name a few, could keep up with anybody. The ambition of Peter Moody (Kurt Meyer) was to break the four-minute mile, and we were sure he would. Tall and muscular, he was dedicated to all sports and was a walking encyclopedia on any of them. He could not fathom why his enthusiasm was not shared by everyone. On marches or truck rides, or enplaned to parachute, he would conduct sports quizzes "to pass the time."

Moody's quizzes were a lonely game, for only he knew who had come in second in the 1926 Grand National horse race. But he didn't seem to notice. And the quizzes did help to pass the time, sort of.

There were other challengers to the Skipper's fitness. Maurice Latimer (Moritz Levy), the wiry little Jewish Socialist from the German Sudetenland and another Czech named Taylor, and James Griffith (Kurt Glaser) had all fought in the Spanish civil war in the International Brigade on the Loyalist side. They had all experienced hardship and extreme physical exertion, which held no threat for them now. Neither did it intimidate Geoff Broadman (Gottfried Sruh), an Austrian judo expert, or Bryan Fenton (Feder), a good soccer player. All of them relished the idea of being able to overtake the Skipper on that final spurt at the end of a speed march, if only because he seemed to mind them doing so.

But many of us had no such ambitions, or at least no realistic hope of ever accomplishing such a feat, except in our dreams. We were concerned, rather, with just keeping up, and avoiding the RTU. We munched glucose tablets for quick energy. Whenever I put one in my mouth, Hamilton (Reich) would appear next to me and ask whether he could have one. "How about one for special friends?" he would always ask. Some of us even decided to give up alcohol, not that there were any intemperate drinkers among us. But an occasional Scotch chased by a pint or two of mild or bitter beer was, after all, a military tradition. Word was out how that glassful might cost you your fourth wind during a run, for we were pushed way beyond our second and third winds as a matter of routine. For most of us, the answer was total abstinence. No smoking went without saying.

On one particularly hot day, when a disproportionate number of us did collapse, the usually unemotional Skipper was livid. This manifested itself in a scowl that would have passed for mild displeasure in a more sanguine person. But for Bryan Hilton-Jones it was truly unusual.

"What if this were the real thing? Would you conk out by the roadside? Would you leave others if they could not carry on? From now on, when I say there is no falling out, there is no falling out. If someone faints, you simply bring him along."

The next day's speed march was especially grueling, no doubt by design. Even I, whose stamina was not outstanding, took over a fading friend's rifle. When that was good for only half a mile or so, two of us took him between us, wrapping his arms around our shoulders, holding his wrists firmly in our hands. Breathing hard, we tried to pant encouragement into his ears. "Keep paddling your feet, for Chrissake." We told him it would reduce the friction of letting them drag.

After another mile we were so exhausted that we needed two others to help us. It was a peculiar sight—a team of four, gasping and sweating, our weapons sticking out at odd angles. We made it, but no one sprinted the final hundred yards that day.

One of the fittest athletes in the troop was Freddy Gray (Manfred Gans). He had grown up in the picturesque, thousand-year-old German town of Borken, its old walls and moats only a short run from the Dutch frontier. In fact, his grandfather had moved from Holland to marry his grandmother. Her ancestors had achieved an unusual accomplishment for seventeenth-century Jews. From the year 1610 they had been privileged to live within the walled city, and therefore the Gans clan considered itself proud and patriotic Germans. The tightly knit Jewish community of Borken saw no conflict between their Orthodox Jewish intellectual tradition and their German patriotism. Manfred's father had served in the Army in World War I and lost a leg. He had been active in the politics of the Weimar Republic, the liberal postwar government. Hitler ended all that when Manfred was ten years old. His classmates and former friends no longer talked to him. Many of the now ostracized Jewish families were descendants of Sephardic Jews, driven from Spain centuries earlier by the Inquisition. Was this leading up to a repetition of that dreaded time, or something like the pogroms of Russia and Poland?

Zionism offered an answer to Manfred's older brother, all of fifteen years of age when he went to Palestine in 1935. Manfred was dispatched to England where he threw himself into this new adventure with characteristic enthusiasm, trying to pass his high school certificate in a mere four months, and failing dismally because he didn't yet speak the language well enough.

"I was able to talk to anybody and everybody after a fashion," recalls Freddy. "I was happy. Well, almost. The prospect of never again seeing the beautiful fields, forests, flatlands, mountains, towns, and villages where I grew up filled me with occasional pangs of sadness. Hitler's Reich would last for generations, and I would never be able to return." Worse still, his parents were still there. It was proving impossible for them to get out. The war had started, and he went through the usual 3 Trooper progression: internment, Pioneer Corps, and then Aberdovey.

"I soon felt confident that I could handle any combat with my former high school classmates, now undoubtedly officers in Hitler's Army, Air Force, Navy, or Waffen-SS."

One of the activities of the toughening process that reinforced that confidence was rigorous practice in unarmed combat. Geoff Broadman (Gottfried Sruh) was one instructor, and Ducky Dwelly (Werner Goldschmied) and Bryan Fenton (Feder) were the others. They taught us how to defend ourselves against attacks with bayonets, handguns, and knives, preceded by the following common-sense maxims: if your enemy is armed and you are not, RUN; if you can't run and get away, do what the man says; and if you can't do that, for whatever reason, and you have cause to believe that he will kill or maim you anyway, then, and only then, try what we're teaching you here. You must practice every day to get your actions grooved and your reflexes sharp. You will probably have only one chance.

Our experts roundly ridiculed the romantic notion that one can get so proficient at unarmed combat that any person attacking with a mere gun or knife is a fool. "The armed fighter has a tremendous advantage, always. And don't you forget it!"

On one occasion I happened to have Leslie Wallen (Weikersheimer) as a partner-opponent. He was one of the strongest men in the troop, yet I had been taught so well that I brought him down quickly. He fell to the ground like a felled oak, and I knelt on his shoulders and bicep muscles to pin him down.

"Very good, Masters," he said with a grin. Then he added, "Do you give up?"

"Are you kidding?" I was sure I had him pinned down.

"I'll say it just once more: do you give up?"

"No!"

Then Leslie Wallen simply got up, and I found myself kneeling way up there, on his shoulders.

"So you don't want to give up," he said as he started to rotate so rapidly that after a few moments the centrifugal force threw me into a corner of the room. I learned another lesson: if I have to tackle an opponent, try to make sure he's my size.

Robbie Villiers (Egon Vogel) was much in demand during unarmed combat sessions. One way of killing an enemy with one's bare hands is the so-called Japanese stranglehold. With one hand under the opponent's chin and the other on top of his head, you twist. In practicing this, one has to be careful, because if executed properly your partner-opponent could end up with a broken neck. But not Villiers. He had a double-jointed neck that you could twist to your heart's content.

Villiers had yet another talent. A master lock picker, he had such sensitive fingers that he could feel the right numbers of the combination of a safe's dials. He had also studied the inner workings of locks so thoroughly that he could open most such devices quickly, sometimes with improvised tools, such as celluloid strips or lengths of wire, if his fingers would not suffice. He taught us to do likewise, but none of us ever came close to his proficiency. If the opportunity to crack safes ever arose, and it did on at least one occasion, we had to resort to our training with high explosives.

In the meantime, Arlen (Abramowitz) had become quite a star. With the same grim determination that had carried him into the eighth round of the European Youth Finals with his broken thumb, he now plunged into each training exercise. When we had a "scheme," as an exercise was called, he would totally disregard the odds and attack vastly superior forces single-handedly. Once he launched himself down a grassy hillside, like a shot from a cannon, into a crowd of twenty "enemies." Before they could believe their eyes, he ripped off six paper armbands for the kill. Then he was easily overpowered, of course, by the other fourteen. Troop Sergeant-Major Oscar O'Neill (Oskar Hentschel), particularly, was impressed. "Good man, Arlen," he said—rare praise indeed.

Some of us felt, perhaps a little enviously, that Arlen was a bit crazy. "He wouldn't try this sort of nonsense if it were the real thing," we grumbled, "or he would be dead pretty damn soon."

As my friend, Arlen, confided in me: "I'm going to get me a Victoria Cross one day, or die in the attempt." Arlen *was* a bit crazy.

7 Learning Our Craft

I was going to write a separate chapter and call it "Sex in Aberdovey." It would easily have been the shortest chapter in this book. For most of us, Aberdovey was synonymous with celibacy. Although Dicky Tennant (Trojan, the mad driver) met and married his lovely Dorothy there, and Max Laddy met his wife there while we were in training, most of us couldn't even find a date. Perhaps our management had chosen the place to keep our minds on our work.

There were probably a few reasonably happy homosexual relationships; no one talked much about it, and there certainly was no perception of uneasiness about their existence, either in training or in combat. Going on patrol provides a good example of what I mean. The percentage of men with whom an experienced and battle-hardened soldier would risk his life is very small indeed. If a cardiac or brain surgeon performs a delicate operation, he makes sure that the operating room team is skilled and reliable, and the surgeon's life is not even at risk. It's the same with anyone going on a reconnaissance patrol into no-man's-land. He makes sure that he has the right team with him. A man's sexual orientation, like the color of his eyes, is irrelevant.

Homosexuals had a special reason to hate the Nazis, for as a group they were among the earliest persecuted inmates of the concentration camps. Whereas Jews were forced to wear the yellow star with the mock-Hebrew lettering JUDE in the center, homosexuals had to wear a pink triangle that assured them the same brutal treatment as the Jews. Racially "pure" Aryans were murdered for their sexual orientation alongside all the other "dangerous enemies" of the state, such as Jews, gypsies, and the mentally retarded.

In spite of the dearth of female companionship in our small Welsh coastal town, Steve Ross could be heard sighing wistfully on our night exercises: "At least all of you will get a few hours' rest, but my land-lady will be waiting for me in her birthday suit as soon as I come in the door." Gerald Nichols (Gerald Nell) could occasionally be seen with a pretty girl, but perhaps he imported them, since he was an unusually enterprising Commando soldier. I got to know Nichols well when he asked the Skipper that I be his second-in-command of our five-man detachment for D day. A slim, willowy young man with blond hair worn straight back, he had a special talent for attracting beautiful women.

To make matters worse, there was the Chattelard School for Girls right next to Dr. Wright's house, where I lived. It was a boarding school for well-to-do young girls. When Switzerland, its previous lo-cation, became almost inaccessible in wartime, the school's man-agement chose a large mansion in this remote Welsh evacuation site. The girls were a comely lot, or perhaps they seemed so attractive be-cause females were so rare in those parts. But, to quote a Viennese saying about young women under the age of consent: "The law has its protective hand over their maidenheads."

Then there was the Webster girl, whose parents had evacuated themselves from one of England's industrial cities to a cottage on a nearby hill. They had planned ahead wisely for her twenty-first birth-day and also evacuated a few cases of impossible-to-buy fine cham-pagne. Now the only missing ingredients for a successful coming-of-age party were some young blades—eligible beaus to dance with and to toast their offspring. Perhaps in desperation, some of us in 3 Troop were invited. Although the auspicious day coincided with a sched-uled night exercise planned for 2300 that very evening, we weren't willing to forgo the party just because we had to be up all night. We did have to leave early to retrieve our weapons, deeming them im-proper dress for the occasion.

I recall being in the lead of the departing guests and our gracious hosts offered to light our way down to the garden gate with some shielded lanterns (because of the wartime blackout).

"Thank you so much, but that will be quite unnecessary," I said, "we are trained to see in the dark!"

What I had overlooked was that the little footpath took a sharp turn at the edge of a rock garden and had a dramatic precipitous

10-foot drop. My feet discovered this fact rather abruptly when suddenly there was no footpath under them. I landed with a crash among the rocks and probably some lovely but invisible rock plants. "Are you all right?" came a solicitous enquiry from above, way above.

"Oh sure!" I said with as much dignity as I could muster, as I limped off to start the night maneuver. Even the most tentative pursuit of sex was fraught with unexpected dangers, obstacles, and frustrations. Imagine my surprise and disbelief when at the end of a strenuous day, having been chased all over the dunes by Troop Sergeant-Major O'Neill, I came upon an extraordinary vision. We were dismissed by the sergeant-major, one at a time, as each of us completed whatever fiendish exertion he had devised for us. As I trudged homeward through the sand, there, at the edge of where a footpath began, was a young blond woman dressed in white.

It was such an unlikely sight—beautiful civilian feminine curves, very young but definitely beyond the Chattelard age group. I could have been forgiven had I thought it a hallucination, or a mirage on a hot day. But I noticed that she was bent over what turned out to be a bicycle and was attempting unsuccessfully to pump air into a flat tire.

"May I be of some assistance?" I asked, instantly forgetting my fatigue.

"Oh, yes, please," she replied gratefully.

"It helps to tighten the valve before you start," I explained, and I began to pump, dashingly.

Suddenly there was a jarring interruption. "Hey, Masters! You can't do that all by yourself. Let me help, too."

It was Oakfield, a lanky, dark-haired member of the fourth and most recent group of volunteers. (I don't recall his real name; he was RTUd soon afterward because he couldn't keep up.) I stepped aside obligingly.

"Be my guest."

Freed from this chore, I was able to take aside my white apparition, find out her name, and ask her to the troop's farewell party in the British Legion Hall the following evening; we were all shortly moving to Eastbourne in preparation for the invasion of Europe.

Oakfield had almost finished pumping, so I had to hurry.

"You will do me the honor, won't you?"

Her name was Jean and she said she would be delighted and was ever so grateful for my assistance. Jean, a nursemaid for the baby of a family who lived near Dr. Wright's house (that explained the white uniform), was punctual to a fault. Yet the joy of seeing her again was marred by a little disappointment. Gone was the simplicity of the virginal starched white uniform. She had exchanged it for pale pink, mauve, and green finery. Even so, the evening was going very well for me until the dangerously good-looking George Saunders interrupted us just before the last waltz.

"Masters, be a sport. I'm on sentry duty next door at the armory. Been standing out there by my lonesome for bloody hours on end. You've got to let me have one dance, just one!" Jean was the only one with whom he wanted to dance, understandably.

I was a sport, especially because I was certain that even daredevil George wouldn't risk absconding from his post for longer than just a few minutes. (Deserting one's post was a court-martial offense punishable in times of war, at least theoretically, by firing squad.) So there could be no question as to who was going to walk Jean—*my* Jean—home.

Foreplay began as we left the dance hall and turned the corner along the seawall. But where do you go in Aberdovey, which consists entirely of one main street on which the dance attendees were now ambling home by the light of the April moon? The dunes were damp and gritty, and to have brought a ground cloth to a dance in fine weather would have been indelicate.

Surprisingly, Jean, who had just finished telling me that she had never been kissed before, whispered a suggestion in my ear: "I know a place . . . just follow me." She took one of my eager and impatient hands in hers and led the way up some steep steps to a gazebo perched on the hillside. It was a beautiful, warm night, and I poured out all my pent-up emotions, strengthened no doubt by our fitness training, thrice before the cock crowed.

Our fitness did not prevent us from suffering a number of injuries in training. When men are being prepared for high-risk warfare, it follows that the honing of their skills and attitude is accompanied by a series of dangers. Our top leadership was well aware of that; therefore a casualty rate of some 70 percent was permitted without inquiry. We had nowhere near that number, although live ammunition was always used in our exercises, live grenades were thrown, and live demolitions exploded in the maneuver area.

We did have several people who had to retire from active service because of training injuries. It should be repeated that the Skipper always did everything difficult or dangerous first, before asking us to do likewise.

Our learning process was mental as well as physical. Pushing our bodies well beyond what many of us had thought possible took not only bodily effort but the right attitude, which was infused by a variety of means.

For example, we played our own version of football, a strange mixture of rugby, soccer, American football, and freestyle wrestling. Almost any kind of tackling, kicking, hitting, and hair-pulling was allowed. At times the ball could be seen lying forgotten in some corner of the field. On the principle "anything goes," no referee was needed.

We had daily lectures on military skills such as signaling, tactics, the handling and interrogation of prisoners, and weaponry. Some of us European middle-class youngsters had grown up with the notion that we were not mechanically minded. I had been brought up to believe that I could not operate a machine more complex than a pair of scissors. Suddenly, I found myself, while blindfolded, stripping and reassembling Bren guns, tommy guns, and Colt .45 pistols. I shall never forget a little black crowfoot-shaped part in an aperture of the Colt, into which a steel locking pin had to be fitted in no more than two minutes. It was hard enough to do when you could see. Blindfolded it was murder.

We needed to learn all about explosives, and we experimented with different kinds—lifting, shattering, and concussion. We assembled fuses with primers and detonators. We watched things blow up and make impressive craters. There was a fun drill with so-called pole-and-scissor charges. The pole charge was a hunk of explosive, usually attached to a piece of two-by-four about three feet long, with a detonator, primer, and fuse attached. Having selected a target, usually a wall or door of a house that we intended to enter forcibly, our team of three would approach the entry point using the best concealment available. We moved up swiftly, leaned the pole charge against the wall, lit the short fuse, and walked away toward cover. We were taught always to walk, not run; if you run you are more likely to trip and fall. Then came the flash and bang, and before the smoke cleared we would rush forward and hurl ourselves through the hole blown into the wall.

The scissor charge consisted of two pieces of wood, nailed or tied together as an X, with chunks of explosive attached to the two upper ends or all four ends. This caused an increased crosscutting effect and usually made a better hole through which to crawl.

Neither of these charges, efficient as they were, always produced the desired effect. Sometimes we rushed into the cloud of smoke after the explosion and banged our heads against the wall. Inexplicably, the amount of explosive that we always used occasionally produced a hole barely big enough to peek through. "It's not an exact science," the experts told us. Still, we all enjoyed it. The danger was just enough to titillate without being too threatening.

Our enthusiasm wasn't shared by the gray-haired lady who lived next door to the bombed house where we practiced. Barbara Frietchie-like, as in Whittier's poem, she looked out of her upstairs window. But what she said was not: "Shoot, if you must, this old gray head," but rather:

"This noise will simply have to stop."

"There's a war on, madam," replied one of the more restrained troop members, trying to drown out the vulgar remarks of the uninhibited. "I shall call Mr. Churchill, and we'll see about that," said she, then she banged the window shut.

We reached the point where we could easily understand why humans can become fascinated by explosives. It is a syndrome probably linked to a toddler building elaborate structures and then gleefully knocking them down. Grown men similarly seem to enjoy blowing things up. It makes a big bang and it's spectacular. Hence our love of fireworks, I suppose.

We were taught to set and disarm booby traps. We had an assortment of these devilish devices, and the attitude that they were intriguing toys came to us quite naturally. Pull-switches, pressure-switches, book-switches, and more. We would set up a roomful of tricks so that if you opened the door, sat down, or picked up a weapon or any article whatsoever, there would be a small pop explosion. (You would have blown yourself up if it had been a real explosive charge instead of just a little percussion cap.) We learned to be careful when touching anything at all: we felt for virtually invisible trip wires, and we edged our fingertips under any article we needed to lift, gingerly from both sides until they met in the middle. We relished putting pressure-switches under bicycle saddles (some of the men rode bicycles) and release-switches under the wheels. Pop! went their bikes as soon as they moved them and pop! again as soon as they sat on them. It was fun and games, but it made us familiar with and confident in handling risks we were bound to encounter.

More than anything else, we learned about the German Army—its weapons, vehicles, organization, documents, methods, and mentality. We learned its tactics, its language, its slang, its drills, and its commands until we knew more about the German Army than about our own, certainly more than most German soldiers knew. The fact that every one of us spoke fluent German was, of course, a tremendous advantage. Some had even served briefly in the German or Austrian Army when it had been customary to serve a voluntary year between high school and college, before the Nazis' anti-Jewish laws had made that impossible.

We also specialized in reconnaissance patrols. The Skipper was a perfectionist, and many things he taught us had applications far beyond their immediate purpose. For instance, out on patrol we turned around periodically, which made it easier to find our way back. "Don't forget," the Skipper would say, "it looks totally different viewed from the other direction."

He also stressed the importance of a quick takeoff. "That's why pilots run to their planes. It takes longer to get to them than it does to get up in them."

An important aspect of our training was to become thoroughly familiar with night operations. Early on we had learned such little tricks as closing one eye and then the other when coming out of a lighted place, to accustom ourselves to the darkness as quickly as possible. We had frequent night exercises, night patrols, night firing, and night house clearing.

Later, the Skipper simply had us turn night into day. For one entire month we had our first formation of the day at 2000 instead of the usual morning assembly; lunch break came at midnight and pay call came once every other week at 0300. At 0500 we were generally off duty. The only real trouble with this timetable was its incompatibility with that of our landladies. We got home at dawn, went to sleep, and got up at noon. No dates, no pubs, no movies. And boiled beef (even though it was a luxury in wartime) and cabbage made for an unappetizing breakfast. Surprisingly, we got used to this schedule. More importantly, we truly became confident in the dark. "The dark is your friend," said the Skipper. "In daylight the enemy can see you better, so they can shoot you more easily. If you keep still at night and blend with the background, you are totally invisible. The defender has an obvious advantage over the attacker, or the reconnoitering intruder. The defender can sit still while the protagonist has to move. Therefore, you have to learn how to move as quietly and as invisibly as humanly possible. Patience is essential."

The Skipper showed us how to move without making a sound by setting our feet down carefully, and rolling our weight slowly from the outside of our rubber-soled boots to the center. We found that we could open a door or mount stairs without the slightest noise just by doing it slowly, maintaining our balance, and keeping in mind how things are constructed. For instance, stairs are less likely to creak near their attachment to the wall than in the middle.

We also learned that when a plane flew overhead, the noise of its engine would hide the sound of any movement we made. We learned how to watch and how to listen, patiently, as if our lives depended on it. We learned how to halt a night patrol at the approach of danger without uttering a word: if the front man perceived danger, he simply stopped and everyone else froze. If we thought we heard or saw something behind us or to one side, we halted the others by squeezing the shoulder of the man in front of us. Everyone stopped instantly and listened like deer perking up their ears and sniffing the wind for minutes on end until the signal to proceed could be given.

This skill we called *zwick-mach,* a German-Jewish word combination meaning "Pinch me." "We're playing *zwick-mach* tonight," meant that a night exercise involving patrol activity had been scheduled. Sometimes the learning process was painful. The night of the Websters's daughter's birthday party we prowled around Aberdovey practicing soundless movement in an inhabited, built-up area. We walked like shadows, freezing and blending into the small town's scenery whenever anyone approached. It became easier toward the small hours of the morning, for the worthy Welsh citizens had all turned in by then. As we descended noiselessly down a last alley, the conclusion of a long and sleepless night, the last man of the last contingent carefully lifted his leg over a garbage can that blocked his path. He knocked off the lid and sent it rolling and rattling down the entire length of the alley. All Aberdovey must have sat up in bed with a start.

The Skipper stepped out of the shadows. "You will now return to the starting point up on the hill above the town and repeat the entire exercise where it began three hours ago. Pick up and replace that lid before you go. Parade tomorrow remains at 0800." (At formation, all equipment had to be polished and shining, all weapons spotless.)

The following night a reconnaissance exercise was scheduled to the nearby town of Towyn, six miles from Aberdovey. The RAF had an airfield there, which we were to infiltrate that night, unseen and unheard, and return with specific information about what we had observed. The RAF was not warned that we were coming, and because there was a war on, we could reasonably expect to be fired upon. To add to the challenge, there was a minefield around the base. The simple answer to these problems was to be careful.

The morning after this exercise had been successfully completed, Tommy Farr (Freytag) appeared at formation sporting a WAAF's Royal Air Force blue hat on his fair hair. He had obviously not been satisfied with just accomplishing his prescribed task of getting into the well-guarded compound and entering the WAAF huts to count their occupants. Now he wanted to show off his captured trophy.

The Skipper took one look at him. "Farr, you will proceed unseen to Towyn RAF base forthwith and replace stolen RAF property precisely where you found it. Then report back to me in exactly two hours. On the double. Dismissed."

A favorite night game of Sergeant-Major O'Neill was deploying a group of us in someone's front garden, having made the point that the darkest place was not necessarily the best in which to hide. Rather it was the one that most closely matched the tones of our clothing in the prevailing light.

As soon as we were hidden, he would ring the front doorbell of the house. "Have you seen any of my chaps, by any chance?" he would ask. Invariably the answer was no. "Please look around. I don't want to intrude on your property, but I could swear I saw them turn in your front gate."

The person who had answered the door would glance around, shake his head, and say that he couldn't see anybody.

"All right, men, get up!" O'Neill would order, and twelve or more men would rise from every fold in the lawn, and one or two from the very steps where O'Neill stood. How the householder jumped when Commandos popped up practically underfoot! That was good fun, and it helped build our confidence for when we would have to rely on being unseen and unheard in enemy territory.

Periodically, Hilton-Jones took us rock climbing. We traveled to Bangor and then to Bethesda, a tiny village in Snowdonia (the vicinity of Mount Snowden). Most of our activity took place in a picturesque valley where brown and gray rocks surrounded a boulder-strewn green hollow. The Skipper told us that he had been climbing there since he was four years old. He knew not only every nook and cranny but every hand- and toehold. The climbs are among the most challenging there are, although the mountains in Snowdonia are much lower than the European Alps. Thus you can find a climb such as the Devil's Kitchen described in guidebooks as "very severe, extremely so,"* which meant, as far as we could figure out, that not only were there hardly any holds, but rocks would fall on you while you were trying to hold on for dear life. Paradoxically, if you managed

---

*Guidebooks have a phraseology all their own—for example, "A nice feeling of exposure can easily be attained on this climb."

to scale a forbidding sheer wall of stone, you could often walk down the other side on a grassy slope.

Surrounded by slate quarries, the little village of Bethesda was an austere, simple place with a certain gaunt charm. The small stone houses offered little in the way of creature comforts. There was cold water only, which had to be drawn from a pump in the kitchen.

After our chilly morning toilet, the Skipper lined us up at the foot of the Ydwal Slabs, a long and high but so-called "easy" sloping wall, furrowed vertically by three cracks, named "Faith," "Hope," and "Charity." He divided us into teams of three to a rope, and off we went in different directions and varying degrees of fright.

It was lonely in those hills—we rarely met other climbers—so it came as a surprise to me one day when I found a shaggy woolen hat on the rocks, a balaclava with a little pom-pom on top. It was brand new and almost the same color as our Army-issue so-called cap-comforters. I continued to wear it after that, when dress orders of the day did not call for green berets, although I felt compelled to remove the cute little pom-pom, as it seemed militarily inappropriate.

Before we began serious climbing, the Skipper had taken us "bouldering," first using one of the many boulders littering the landscape to demonstrate how it was done. These great chunks of rock were plenty high enough to break our neck on but nowhere near as high as the "real" climbs on Crib Goch, Adam and Eve, Tryfaen, Glyderfach, Glyderfawr, or the Devil's Kitchen.

The first time I saw three men bouldering, the middle one was Steve Hudson (Hirsch). As I watched in awe of what awaited me, Steve slipped and fell clean off the rock. The man above him had him belayed on the rope, of course, and it held. However, because he was not directly above Hudson but fifteen feet to his right and ten feet up, what followed looked dramatic and scary. Suspended by his waist, Steve swung horizontally, like a pendulum, into a massive outcropping of the boulder, headfirst. His cap-comforter absorbed some of the blow, and the incident was noted merely as yet another aspect of the toughening process.

After a while the Skipper felt that just climbing up and down the Ydwal Slabs was too easy for us, so he added more sophisticated wrinkles, such as traversing the three cracks, from "Faith" to "Hope" and on to "Charity."

While well up the steeply slanting rock wall, a hundred feet or so, I heard a loud, scraping noise above me. I looked up and saw a shower of falling stones hurtling toward me. I hugged the rock and held on tight, and none of them hit me. But somebody climbing above my team had clearly lost his hold and was likely to come falling by in less than a second. Sure enough, a hand appeared way above, a clutching hand, grabbing for any hold it could and finding only some very tenuous vegetation. The hand was immediately followed by the familiar head of my good friend Steve Ross, looking extremely pale and stressed. Luckily, the weeds to which he was clinging held.

The next day the Skipper thought that some of us were not mustering enough enthusiasm for this favorite sport of his. That morning, he fell us in as usual at the bottom of the Slabs, at attention, then ordered us to stand at ease, and then to "stand easy." This permitted us to react and answer to the surprising words he uttered next: "Is there anyone here who feels that he would rather not climb rocks?" An amazed silence was all he got at first; not even Steve Ross replied. The silence was followed by some tittering in the rear ranks, which irritated the Skipper.

"Come on, seriously, are there those among you who are not getting any true pleasure out of this great activity? If there are, I should like them to take turns climbing with me today. Any volunteers?"

Everybody's hand shot up, even Steve's. But the Skipper chose only his second-in-command, Jimmy Monahan, as well as Andrew Kershaw (André Kirschner, yet another of our Hungarian swimmer-waterpolo players and a good all-around athlete and soccer player), and myself. He led us to a part of the mountains that was unfamiliar to us. There he made another brief speech: "This is a bit more of a challenge than what you've been doing so far. I've been climbing it, or attempting to climb it, since I was a boy. Sometimes I've licked it and sometimes it has licked me. Just follow me and enjoy it." And off he went, disappearing over the ten-foot craggy ledge above us.

Lieutenant Monahan was next, then I, then Andrew. Four on a rope this time was no problem for our intrepid leader. Soon there were plenty of problems for us, however, because there seemed to be fewer hand- and toeholds. Whenever we despaired of finding a place to hold on, a voice would come from above and say: "Just stretch a little farther to your right and you'll find a handhold." And invariably, we did. Although most of the time the Skipper could not see us at all because of overhanging rocks, he knew exactly what difficulties we were facing. There were times where he was more specific: "You've got to stretch farther than you think you can and there at shoulder level is a little recess where you can insert two fingers." And there it was.

Finally, we came into a chimney, so-called because it was shaped like a more or less vertical rock tunnel. This one was not narrow enough to climb by wedging ourselves into it, as the Skipper had taught us. Neither were there any holds that we could discern as all four of us clung to a tiny ledge contemplating the bleak prospect. Three of us were singularly devoid even of theoretical ideas how we might scale the obstacle. It looked insurmountable. Had we taken a vote it would have been 3–1 for turning back.

Kershaw came to the point: "How do you get up this thing?"

"It is rather tricky," admitted the Skipper, "you see, there aren't any holds at all."

We were sure he was right, there.

"How then . . ." continued Kershaw, who was always rather persistent.

"Well," the Skipper said, "the secret to this chimney, which works most of the time, is to step on this sheer vertical rock wall as if there were a foothold where in fact there is none. Then, before your foot has a chance to realize that there's nothing to hold it, you transfer your weight onto the other leg, which in the meantime you have swung forward as far as it will go. It will find a quarter-inch ledge, just big enough to step on. In fact it's big enough to have lunch on. Watch me—here goes."

He did exactly what he had said. He stepped on nothing, and at the critical moment—just before the edge of his boot could slide any substantial distance—he swung his other leg upward past the first one. As soon as it had found the little ledge, he hurled his body after it. All this took place over a substantial, dizzying drop.

It still looked impossible, but now he was out of sight and urging us to follow.

Amazingly, the described method worked for all of us. We all reached the top, thanks to the Skipper "talking us up," a disembodied voice from above that expressed care for our survival. While we were up in the mountains, we also climbed Mount Snowden. Crystal-clear springs spouted down the mountain in rocky beds. We were cautioned not to drink during the climb, because of water discipline, but we found the water delicious and irresistible. As we ascended higher, the brooks and grass were replaced by huge slopes of loose rocks and rock chips. They crested in a gigantic horseshoe-shaped ridge along the top of which we found a footpath.

Suddenly, the weather turned bad, as it does in those mountains. It became dark quickly, and black clouds formed beneath us, with occasional white rags of fog blowing through them. Under such conditions we succumbed to the desire to assume a horizontal position quickly and then to move slowly, if at all, by crawling on our hands and knees. The Skipper would have none of that. He walked along the narrow path with his hands in his pockets, the wind whistling through his trouser legs; contemptuously, he stepped over our prostrate figures and ordered us to get up.

"On your feet! When I was here with 4 Commando we had a meal on this spot!"

"And a pay call too, probably," someone murmured.

To our surprise it was perfectly all right to walk upright. But we did have a keen feeling of danger as we looked at the several-hundred-foot straight drop both right and left. After a short rest at the summit, we ran down the mountain with great exhilaration. On the loose rocks the Skipper taught us the *skrae-run,* which is like skiing without skis. We slid down over the rolling stones, trying to keep our footing or leaning into the slope if that failed. Finally, we galloped over the boulder-strewn, steep-sloping meadows near the base of the mountain.

In Bethesda I was billeted in one of those little stone houses, together with Gary Mason (Weinberg). The second evening there was a dance at the local church and of course we were eager to take part. I had recently received an aftershave lotion from my mother in London. It came in an odd-shaped bottle, was pink and gooey, and had the marvelous attribute of drying in an unbelievably smooth coat on my cheeks. I had never had one as good.

I shared it with Gary for the dance; he was convinced that it had powerful aphrodisiac qualities, which he wanted to try out immediately on the young beauties of downtown Bethesda. Although Bethesda was smaller than Aberdovey, we had passed a number of good-looking females en route to our climbs, so everything boded well for the dance.

Indeed, I met a perfectly gorgeous young lady right away. Agnes had short, silky brown hair and a fresh complexion. Her trim figure had no extraneous bulges; her narrow hips and firm breasts were those of a young athlete. We got along very well at the dance and made a date for the following day after work.

The countryside around Bethesda was romantic and promisingly uninhabited. The same grassy knolls and gorse-patched meadows through which we had panted on our way up and down Snowden provided beautiful vistas and fine concealment. That Army-issue ground cloth, a rubber blanket that folded up neatly and was easily carried, could be brought along without embarrassment, for we had planned a nature walk, fully aware of the possibility of a sudden shower.

Agnes worked as a nurse in the hospital in Bangor. When I had asked her name—my highly original opening line at the dance—she had replied: "It sounds like 'battle' in Latin."

And a battle it turned out to be: a battle of wits, and Agnes won, literally hands down. Bent on seduction, as young soldiers about to go into battle almost always are, I took her for a long walk through much of North Wales. In a display of Commando macho, I carried her light, attractive body when swampy ground even remotely warranted such maneuvers. As I held her, it was an easy and natural move to kiss her, on her cheeks, on her eyes, and on her lovely, unpainted mouth. Ah, that was good kissing in a most attractive setting, and Agnes was charmingly responsive.

But whenever I attempted the slightest follow-up, a gentle touch above or below the belt, she would interrupt smilingly: "I really must tell you what happened at work today . . ."

Then she would recount an astonishingly gory anecdote about a pathetic syphilis patient she had to nurse that very afternoon, sparing me none of the medical details. She would counter my next move with a story of an abortion necessitated by a monstrous malformation caused by venereal disease.

It soon became obvious that these descriptions were part of her carefully planned, ingenious defense strategy. I made a last effort to dissuade her: "Agnes, enough shoptalk!"

But I realized my defeat when she replied: "You talk about rock climbing and I talk about my VD ward."

We walked home hand in hand and kissed twice more: good night and good-bye.

She was as virtuous and chaste as she was beautiful. I had to respect a woman with principles, imagination, and superior tactics. Aphrodisiacs are clearly not altogether reliable.

8 Nearer to the Enemy

On 31 May 1943 the troop left Aberdovey for Eastbourne, a Sussex coastal town in southeast England. The whole of No. 10 Commando, hitherto scattered around the Cambrian coast of North Wales, was to be concentrated there.

After the Commando's arrival in Eastbourne, the commanding officer, Col. Dudley Lister, assembled the entire unit in a local cinema to deliver a melodramatic speech celebrating the occasion.

"We have come two hundred miles nearer to the enemy," he began. Aware that the English Channel was still in between "us" and "them," we were not unduly impressed.

Henceforth we paraded together with the other component of No. 10 on a playing field of a local school. This gave us the opportunity to watch the drills of the other "foreign" troops, which seemed exotic to us compared to what we narrow-mindedly considered our "normal" British way.

But Colonel Lister wanted to weld one homogenous fighting unit out of our fiercely individualistic nationalities. One can sympathize with what must have been his dream of leading his mini–foreign legion into battle. So he attempted more joint exercises: three solid days of road marches in the first week of April, everybody participating. But unfortunately the starting times were so spaced that no troop ever caught sight of their comrades in arms or heard a word of command in a foreign tongue.

The footslogging seemed a bit primitive to us, but we were not to be outdone. To show our disdain for what we considered a heavy-handed test of our fitness, a larger number than usual showed up at the Wintergarden three evenings in succession to dance. We were showing off, of course, after all-day marches of twenty-six, nineteen, and twenty-three miles, respectively, with full equipment, weapons, and ammunition. Actually, the muscles used in dancing are totally different from those used in marching, so the activity proved relaxing.

On one of those nights, 10 Commando's medical officer, Doc Hodges, burst onto the Wintergarden's dance floor. His flamboyant mustache trembling dramatically, he announced: "I need volunteers to help pick up casualties. The French Commandos are fighting some French Canadian outfit stationed nearby. My jeeps and stretchers are outside."

Those of us who were curious or didn't have promising dates answered the call. Apparently, some French Canadian had stabbed a French Commando soldier in a barroom brawl that had escalated from a political argument. Thereupon the French Commandos scheduled an impromptu night exercise, with weapons and ammunition. They positioned their mortars above the French Canadian headquarters and opened fire, or so the story reached us. In the ensuing melee around several taverns of the town, casualties mounted until Doc Hodges and other authorities, and plain common sense, prevailed.

The next day there were several spectacular bandages to be seen in the French troop's ranks. Colonel Lister was livid. He ordered all French Commandos into the same cinema where he had made his "nearer-to-the-enemy" speech, and he berated them in an outburst replete with four-letter words, with all the gusto of the ex-Army heavyweight boxing champion that he was. Because he did not speak French, he had bilingual French officers and warrant officers seated at the end of every row, translating his remarks. Fortunately, most of the remainder of his audience understood no English.

Even more fortunately, the interpreters were astute diplomats. Sidestepping the colonel's earthy barrack-room idioms, they translated: "The commanding officer wishes to congratulate you on your victory over your despicable adversaries. You have fought bravely indeed. He would like to add that if you show the same esprit in the rapidly approaching battle against the *Boche*, Hitler had better beware. Therefore, *Monsieur le Colonel* entreats you to save some of your bravery for our common enemy across the Channel."

The audience loved it and cheered with beaming faces.

"Well, I must say they're taking it very well," commented Lister before he gave the order to fall out.

• • •

Three of us lived in a billet at the end of town with a kindly couple who were both officers in the Salvation Army. The man worked at the post office; we 3 Troopers thought him to be an utter civilian, unfit and totally ignorant of all our many military skills—that is, until he found us practicing the Morse code one day.

"Mind if I show you boys how to do this?" he said and proceeded to dazzle us with his simply unbelievable speed. He seemed twice as large after that, and we took whatever he said more seriously. Thus we were impressed when he sought us out a few days later with an air of mystery.

"Wear your best battle dress when you come home for lunch tomorrow. We're expecting a special guest."

"Who's coming?"

"The general," he said in a voice hushed by respect.

We did what he had asked, and when we came back from the morning's training there he was: the general—the general commanding the Salvation Army, that is.

He was a dapper-looking man with close-cropped gray hair. In an Army uniform he might have passed for a bona fide high-ranking British officer. Lunch went smoothly enough, but it was afterward that matters became a little embarrassing for us Commandos. We had moved to the rarely used parlor with its pair of overstuffed easy chairs in front of the fireplace. The general suggested that we kneel. With varying degrees of enthusiasm, we all knelt on the pink and green flowered carpet. After thanking the Divine Power for bringing him to this house and thanking his hosts for inviting him to "the excellent repast," he continued.

"It is a particular pleasure to share the table with three young men who represent the flower of Britain's manhood. Soon they will set sail for the dark shores of a Godless enemy and do battle with the forces of evil. May the Almighty let them prevail, for their struggle is truly His. And may He bring them back safely to this blessed land to live rich, long lives with their loved ones. So say we in earnest prayer to Jesus Christ, His Son, Amen."

We could not help but appreciate this strange man's serious concern for our well-being. The Jewish religion does not permit genuflecting, but we had no intention of blowing our cover in the circumstances. And there was hardly time for obtaining a rabbinical dispensation.

The next day the Skipper marched us to a playground in a public park where a surface shelter had been erected to provide cover for people caught in the open by hit-and-run raids. There were many such shelters on the streets of Eastbourne, but the Skipper had chosen this one for a particular exercise designed to develop coordination, physical prowess, and plain guts. It was about ten feet high, forty feet long, and eighteen feet wide, built of red brick with a thick gray concrete roof. The shelters were no protection whatever against a direct hit by any sizable bomb, but they were excellent shields against shrapnel fragments and machine-gunning Nazi fighter planes, a frequent startling sight swooping over the town at rooftop height.

Negotiating the overhang of the concrete roof was the day's challenge. The flat slab extended over the vertical walls by about a foot all around.

"We shall climb up onto this roof," said the Skipper, "one at a time, without helping one another. I know there are neither hand- nor footholds. The trick is that you must run straight at the wall, as if it were not there—at it, and up it. Then, just before your feet begin to slide down, you must hurl yourselves outward and upward, get your elbows on top of the roof and pull yourselves up. It's quite simple, really."

As simple as that rock chimney in the mountains of North Wales. Thus spoken, he did precisely what he had described, making it look easy, deceptively so in the opinion of many who slid down with an awful scraping sound, time and again.

Some did manage it on their first try, or their second or third; others looked as if they would never make it, which frustrated the Skipper.

"It's a knack you must acquire, here and *now*."

At last everybody was standing on the roof, some more exhausted than others.

"And now we shall jump down, one at a time, not just sliding off the edge but jumping well out, like this."

It did not look very attractive to all of us standing up there. We had often jumped from greater heights, but here he wanted us to run and take a flying leap. Although the landing place could not be seen, it was clear that it would be a hard, gravel-strewn surface, and we would land with forward and downward momentum from about ten feet up.

After the first three had jumped, the Skipper ordered two of them back up. He criticized them for having jumped without enthusiasm. To remedy their reluctance, he positioned the one who had done it right about four feet out from the shelter, standing at attention. This forced us to leap well out, so that our boots cleared his head.

"And don't you dare duck," he told the rigid sentry. "Nobody's going to touch you. If they do, they'll be taking your place."

Leslie Scott was standing next to me as we awaited our turn in jumping. Vernon Nelson (Zweig), a tall, lanky lad with dark hair and with an elongated handsome head, took his dozen running steps and jumped.

"Well done, Nelson," said the Skipper.

"Poor bugger, Nelson," said Scott.

"Why?" I asked Leslie.

"Do you think the Skipper would lavish such praise on anyone who's going to get up after landing?" replied Leslie.

It was our turn next; first Leslie, then I jumped, clearing the hapless man standing at attention below by no more than an inch. Nelson was still writhing on the ground. During the next month or so, we got used to seeing him limp around with a cast on his leg.

"The toughening process continues," said Leslie.

One morning I was quite late leaving the house to cycle to the parade ground. It was only a ten-minute ride, but it was made more difficult by my being a Bren gunner at the time. Carrying a machine gun, even a light one, on a bicycle is not exactly easy, but because we lived in what was technically a war zone we always took our weapons and ammunition with us to our billets. In fact, it was my secret ambition to shoot down one of those low-flying Messerschmitts with my Bren, and I always kept it leaning by an upstairs window, fully loaded.

Alas, I never got a chance. Only once was I in position at my window when the "cuckoo" warning indicated an impending local attack. (Backward air raid sirens sounded something like the cry of that bird. This was used to distinguish a local-threat air raid from a mere overflight warning.) But the plane, machine-gunning and firing small-caliber shells, was flying so low that I was unable to fire without risking that my bursts would hit people in nearby upstairs windows. For one split second I could see the pilot plainly in his cockpit, then he was gone.

Peter Terry (Tischler) accomplished a totally unprecedented feat that day. He managed to get two battle dresses and one set of khaki fatigues replaced in one fell swoop. Never in the annals of the British Army had anyone succeeded in such a coup. This came about while he was out in his blue P.T. shorts. A 20mm shell from a German fighter hit the closet in his billet and penetrated all three uniforms hanging one behind the other, leaving three holes the size of dinner plates. The normally ultrastingy keeper of our stores didn't even attempt to argue.

But coming back to my hasty ride to our Roborough School parade ground with my Bren—I was confident that I would make it, until I encountered George Saunders panting along the road.

"Hey, Masters!" he yelled, "give me a lift and save my life."

"How the hell do you figure that? Can't you see what I'm carrying?"

"Stop! Stop! I'll sit on the handlebars and hold your Bren. You've got to help me."

Against my better judgement I stopped and he got on. It seemed to work fine at first—downhill—but the extra weight totally exhausted me on the next uphill stretch. Saunders noticed my predicament.

"Let me have a turn pedalling and you hold the gun and sit on the handlebars."

We changed places. This took time, and yet we made it to the parade ground, just as the regimental sergeant-major gave the order to fall in. Everything would have been just fine if it had not been for that extra bit of flamboyant bravado so typical of George Saunders (like the time he left his guard duty post to go to the dance). Instead of pulling up inconspicuously at the side of the parade ground, he couldn't resist riding right smack onto it, drawing spectacular figure eights around and in between the Poles and the

Norwegians forming up. I sat helplessly and all too visibly on my elevated perch. It was such an inevitable invitation to get into deep
trouble that I decided to face the lesser evil and risk breaking my
neck by jumping off with the heavy gun in my arms.

Too late!

"What the devil do you think you're up to? In my office as soon
as you're off this parade, the both of you!" screeched the sergeant-
major, with the expression of a pressure cooker that is about to blow
up. We got off with a tongue lashing, luckily. Men had been RTUd
for less, innocent or not.

With all nationalities of No. 10 Commando together in Eastbourne, it had bothered us that all of them wore uniforms far more
impressive than ours. At first we kept saluting the French noncommissioned officers by mistake, for their uniforms were laden with
gold braid. Almost all ranks wore collar and tie, which in the British
Army is the privilege of officers. Frankly envious, we lobbied for
"equal neckwear" rather than the plain battle dress collar, which had
to have both collar hooks fastened at all times. Eventually, we
achieved partial success. Permission to wear collar and tie was
granted to all ranks of No. 10 Commando, but only at our base. This
really was progress, for when we were away from our base on furlough
we all wore collars and ties anyway, illegally, unless we wore our snazzy
issue white turtlenecks.

Sergeant Bentley, a sharp-featured, spunky man who looked a little like Punch (of the British humor magazine) had been to London for the weekend of 12 and 13 June 1943. About to return to Eastbourne, he happened to bump into Colonel Lister at Victoria
Station. It never occurred to Bentley to avoid encountering our commanding officer, for as a trained Commando soldier he probably
could have boarded the train unseen. To Bentley's surprise the
colonel charged him officially with being improperly dressed, with
the forbidden collar and tie.

Back in Eastbourne, Sergeant Bentley was marched into Colonel
Lister's office by Troop Sgt. Maj. Oscar O'Neill. It turned out to be
one of our troop sergeant major's finest hours. The colonel had pronounced sentence: rank busted to corporal, return to unit.

"I respectfully submit, sir, that this would be double jeopardy," said O'Neill. "Military law, to the best of my knowledge, limits us to just one punishment. May I plead that the colonel chooses the first option only? Sergeant Bentley is one of our ablest noncommissioned officers, and we would miss him when we go into action, sir." Yielding to O'Neill's argument, Colonel Lister imposed one punishment only. He RTUd Bentley. No. 3 Troop never forgave him. Sergeant Bentley was posted "back" to his infantry unit, the Buffs. He had never been there before, of course.

One weekend in Eastbourne, I had a female visitor. I had convinced my Salvation Army hosts that she was my fiancée, and they kindly offered her hospitality in one of the upstairs bedrooms, theirs in fact. They both slept in a Morrison shelter, a sturdy cagelike contraption in the kitchen designed to withstand the weight of the entire house should a bomb cause it to collapse.

Their strict religious morals would not have permitted premarital cohabitation, but I was a Commando soldier about to set sail for the dark shores of a godless enemy, and I had been trained in soundless movement, including the opening and closing of doors. Unfortunately, the upstairs landing was inordinately creaky, and I knew that the kitchen door downstairs was always left open. Luckily, we had also been trained in improvisation and initiative, so I resorted to a different methodology. I opened the door to my room noisily and closed it noisily. Then I went to the bathroom, again making sure that entering and locking the door could be heard downstairs. Then I repeated the same maneuver with my beautiful friend's door and the bathroom door. I followed that procedure several more times— someone might have forgotten something in the bathroom.

Soon, even the most attentive listener could not have known who was where, and I hoped that my downstairs audience would find it indelicate to check up on us—two young lovers now locked naked in each others arms.

But a cuckoo warning sounded—it was unusual for fighter planes to attack at night—and our Salvation Army postman host apparently fearing for our lives charged up the stairs hollering: "Wake up! Wake up! Come downstairs as quickly as you can. Come into our table shelter."

Hastily comprehending that he intended to bust into my lady's chamber first, and that it was up to me to save her honor—and my neck—I jumped out of bed toward the window, pulled down the blackout curtain, and wrapped myself in it. As he opened the door, I yelled, "I have just rushed in here to wake her up. Don't turn on the light whatever you do! I've taken down the blackout to try to get one of the blighters with my Bren."

Later I reflected on the narrow escape, and how I owed it all to the Skipper's training: physical fitness, speed and agility, and quick thinking. I hoped that my ambition to bag a Messerschmitt enhanced my credibility.

In the middle of September, No. 3 Troop was assigned forty miles down the coast at Littlehampton. We were to take over the small-scale sea and airborne reconnaissance role of 4 Troop, 12 Commando, although many of the small-scale operations we were meant to mount did not materialize because of bad weather or other circumstances. The move was approved by one and all, for we were issued sophisticated operational equipment and began to feel that we were really moving nearer to the enemy at last.

We traveled from Eastbourne by train. Our kitbags, supplies, and heavy weapons had been loaded onto trucks, which met us at the railway station upon our arrival. The Skipper had us fall in behind them.

"Attention!" he commanded. "When I give you the order 'dismissed,' you will get your kit bags off the truck and proceed to your individual billets. Form up in front of our St. Leonard's Road headquarters at 0800 hours tomorrow morning. Oh, by the way, is there anyone here who does not volunteer to jump out of an airplane by parachute? If so, raise your hand. Webster and Laddy? I'd like to have a word with you two in the office. Dismissed."

Some said that Max Laddy didn't want to jump because he was a ballet dancer and didn't dare risk injuring his legs. He told me the real reason. "I'll volunteer for whatever comes along, and everybody knows that. The Skipper knows it. Anything except parachuting. I can't stand the thought of it. Call it a phobia, or what you will, I just can't do it, and I told him so, right at the start."

Max was a tall, blondish, square-shouldered, upright man with a lined, weathered face and a straggly mustache. He was a bit older than many of us and was always good-humored and cheerful. He and James Griffith had taken a medical course and acted as our medics, taking care of our injections and giving us first aid. (We were self-sufficient—we had no cooks and hardly any administrative staff, and we lived not in barracks but in private billets.) Laddy also was, with Taylor, one of our most accurate 2-inch-mortar men. He told it like it was, and everybody respected him.

Webster said he had promised his wife he wouldn't parachute. That didn't sound quite as good to us, but both were excused from going with us to the Parachute Training School at Ringway near Manchester. Most of us looked upon this perverse act of plunging into the sky from a plane as a step nearer to our goal of fighting the Nazis, although we were surprised when the Skipper asked us to volunteer yet again.

Several 3 Troopers missed parachuting altogether, not because they were brave enough not to volunteer—it took guts for Webster and Laddy to raise their hands when nobody else did—but because they had been sent to Central Mediterranean Forces (CMF) in North Africa, or to Sicily, Italy, and Yugoslavia, just before 3 Troop went parachuting. There were two lawyers, Sgt. Brian Groves and Knobby Kendall, as well as Wells, Hudson, Ross, Scott, Barnes, Merton, Nelson, Streeten, Miles, Anson, and Franklyn. The last four all participated in the Sicily landings.

Sergeant Broadman, Julian Sayers, and Didi Fuller had already qualified as parachutists. I had envied their sky blue wings with an embroidered white parachute between them when my group of volunteers arrived at Aberdovey. Didi Fuller (von Kagerer-Stein) was an older, tall, homespun Austrian, a good joker and storyteller. He had told us not only all about parachuting but also about a special training course connected with it. It had been rigorous, although they had lived luxuriously in some secret, secluded mansion on an English estate.

"Each morning," he said, "we came bounding down this grand staircase, and the last set of a dozen or so steps we had to jump. At the bottom there was a thin gym mat on which we were expected to land a particular somersault known as a parachute roll—landing on both feet together, then a hip, then the opposite shoulder. But the worst of it was that no sooner would I get up than some character in civilian clothes and a trench coat would pop up from behind a column and say, 'Psst! How would you like to sign up for a civvies operation? We'll drop you someplace disguised as a nun. How about it?'

"I would answer, 'Not today, fellows,' and dash out as fast as I could. I like this uniform. Never fancied being a nun, anyway."

When we got to Ringway, we were divided into so-called syndicates, each consisting of ten men. Mine was Syndicate A, for apple, and Sgt. Roy Bladen of the RAF was in charge. Earlier he had tried his psychological skills on Watson—attempting to find out who we really were—and failed, but they worked this time. He saw to it that the least enthusiastic individual of our stick (as a group of parachutists is called) was selected to jump first. He confided his reasoning to me. "If Walter jumps, how can any of you possibly refuse?"

In early October, on the first day of indoor instruction, the Skipper's release button malfunctioned just as he stepped off a high platform with élan, expecting to swing a couple of times before being released for a parachute landing. There were gym mats on the floor, but they were near the middle of the swing, not right under the launching platform. He dropped straight down from a height of about sixteen feet and was in pain for the next few days. We had all seen him manage jumps from more than twenty feet, but this was a totally unexpected fall.

Corporal Jones (Vladimir Kotka, Russian born) was also hurt, a painful shoulder injury, but he recovered on the last day of our jump training and received permission to try to qualify for his wings along with the rest of us. That meant that in a single day he had to do all eight jumps needed to graduate. A jump at the beginner's stage is supposed to be the equivalent of eight hours of hard physical labor, so poor Jones had his work cut out for him. I recall seeing him, looking increasingly stressed, coming down, having been exempted from gathering his spent chute, running to draw another one, up again, down again. Here comes Jones!

Then the real jumps began. First came the balloon jumps, dubbed "jumping from nothing into sweet fuck-all" because we went up in a flimsy box, a gaping hole in the middle, suspended from a barrage balloon. We had to jump well into the center of the hole, for if we didn't jump far enough, the chute, which was in a pack on our back, would tip us forward and we would hit the opposite side of the box with our forehead, nose, or chin. Fearing such an impact and jumping too far would net a similar fate—hitting the opposite side of the box and "ringing the bell," as it is called in parachutist parlance. Ringway was full of men with sizable plaster bandages on foreheads, noses, and chins—bell ringers all.

The customary procedure was to take everybody up for "air experience" before their first plane jump, and then land them, still enplaned. But in our case that was waived, along with three months of physical conditioning, which the school's management conceded we did not need. Our own bosses were evidently in a hurry to get us through for a planned operational parachute raid. All of us qualified, including Walter, and we proudly stitched the embroidered sky blue wings on our sleeves.

In November 1943 we did one more jump, on Salisbury Plain. It was an experimental jump from a four-engine Halifax bomber, a much faster craft than the old Whitley Armstrong. The relevance of speed is inverted for parachuting purposes. Whereas the Whitley could be slowed to about 90 miles per hour, for gentle exits, the Halifax wouldn't slow much below 220 miles per hour.

That was not the only factor of the experiment. The other was an attempt to jump without containers, with all weapons and equipment strapped to the body. Ordinarily, British procedure was to jump sticks of ten men with two containers on chutes of their own dropping between number 5 and number 6 in each stick. These long, fat, tubular metal boxes were deliberately placed in the middle of the stick, so that all troops would have the quickest possible access to them on the ground. The disadvantage was mainly in having to find them and then dispose of them invisibly in small tactical operations.

On our Halifax jump, these hazards were to be eliminated, or rather traded off for the discomfort of having all the necessary equipment attached to our bodies, plus such extra payloads as might be taken on a Commando raid. I carried a 200-foot hemp rope, used for rappelling down a cliff. With it came a piton, a long steel spike with a steel ring set into it, to which the rope would be fastened. The piton was as big as a small sword.

We were transported to Salisbury Plain on that cold November day in unheated open trucks—not a pleasant trip. When we arrived at the airborne base of our destination, we found that the personnel seemed unprepared for our project. A lone major arranged for us to organize our equipment and to have a meal, which was beginning to assume the aura of a last supper.

Getting dressed was a formidable task; there seemed to be so much to be stashed and not enough places to stash it. In particular, the long steel spike appeared to be getting bigger by the minute. I kept trying to put it in a protected place so I would not impale myself when I landed. I coiled the rope around my chute pack, the obvious and most comfortable place. But that spike! Finally, I remembered that knights of old had to solve a similar problem—not falling on their swords if they fell off their horses in combat. So I girded my piton by my side in the same way they did their swords.

Then the question arose as to whether we wanted to look over the planes before our meal, and we agreed. However, we decided not to undo all that elaborate gear but to go as we were, despite the discomfort that entailed. The gear was held together by an ad hoc issue of grayish green American coveralls with little star-decorated black buttons down the front. These oversized garments were fitted over the entire pack loads, which made us look like the Michelin man, encased in rubber tires.

We walked with some difficulty to the trucks, which took us to the Halifaxes on the runway. We had previously seen silhouette diagrams of that plane, and we were anxious to ask the crew a few questions—first and foremost about the unretractable rear wheel of the landing undercarriage. The front landing gear folded into the wings, but the rear wheel was fixed, sticking out and threatening to snag our parachutes as they opened after leaving the plane.

We met the crew of our plane; I was in Troop Sgt. Maj. Oscar O'Neill's stick of ten men. To our chagrin, O'Neill struck up a "don't I know you from somewhere?" type of conversation with the navigator, followed by an excruciatingly long list of places where their previous meeting might have occured. Some of us wanted to ask what we considered more urgent and relevant questions. At last we managed to get a few words in: "How about that rear wheel?"

Answer: "Don't worry, it'll be fine."

"Have you ever dropped parachutists before from a Halifax?"

"Sure, we dropped some 'slow pairs' last week." ("Slow pairs" meant that as the plane overflew the drop zone, or DZ, only one man jumped; then the plane flew a circular loop, and as it came around to the drop zone again, the second man jumped, completing the "pair.")

"If you've never dropped an entire stick, how long can you keep the plane over the DZ?" I asked.

"What do you mean?" was the alarming reply to what I believed was a self-explanatory question.

"Well, how long can you keep the green-for-go light on once you switch it from the red-running-in light?"

"Oh, I see what you mean. We were going to keep the green on until you're all out."

This was getting downright perturbing.

"That's great. What if by that time we're over Salisbury—the town, not the plain?"

"Ah, I see. You may have a point there . . ."

In between these frustrating attempts at communication, O'Neill was still speculating: "Were you ever stationed in Aldershot, or in Torquay?"

And I continued: "How long do you plan to give us on the red light?"

"About twenty minutes."

"Could you make that twenty seconds? When that running-in light comes on, our first man is poised to push off. Twenty minutes of that would be hard for him to take."

We hoped they saw our point.

To make matters worse, the crew explained that on a Halifax we could not have half the stick forward of the aperture and the other half aft, because the aperture was so placed that only one person could be aft and the other nine would all have to jump from a for-ward position. (An additional problem: splitting the stick allowed for a faster exit than one behind the other in aperture jumping, because the men could swing into the exit hole on an alternating basis, with-out having to wait for their front men to be clear before they could swing in themselves.)

"Well, you fellows want to see the inside of this plane, right?" We clambered on, as best as ten blimpish men could, hoping to get to our lunch soon. And then the plane took off! We were stunned. What was worse, we weren't hooked up yet. Communication was made even more difficult by the noise of the four engines. No stick had ever parachuted from a four-engine aircraft, and here we were, obviously with a novice flight crew too ignorant to let us prepare properly for takeoff.

We tried to protest briefly but then decided we might as well get on with it, even though we were hungry and cold. A more serious problem loomed. The brand-new carabiner snap hooks and pins were so cold and stiff that we could not get our D rings inserted into them to hook ourselves up. (There is no rip cord to be pulled when a stick of parachutists jumps. Each man is hooked up with a so-called static line to the fuselage. It opens his chute automatically.) Our frozen fingers were no help on that icy day. While we were struggling to connect our vital lifelines, the order came from the navigator: "Open the trapdoors. We're running in."

"Just a minute," Troop Sergeant-Major O'Neill said, "we're not hooked up yet."

A couple of minutes later the order was repeated.

"Now just hold on a bloody moment," O'Neill said, as we tried to get the safety pins out and the carabiner opened to receive the D rings. That's when the pilot himself came on the intercom.

"I'm the captain of this ship, and I order you to open the trapdoors."

"And I'm the captain of these men, and I'll be damned if I'll open half a trapdoor before they're all hooked up."

The argument became more strident, but we finally managed to get everybody hooked up, and the trapdoors were opened at last. The red light had come on above the exit hole even as we struggled. Nichols, who would be number one, sat by himself in the aft section of the plane. Kershaw was number two, and I was number three. Griffith was there somewhere, and Harry Drew (Nomburg) was number ten. Griffith had pulled out several lengths of the strop from his chute pack and piled it in a heap beside him.

"What the hell are you doing, James?" I asked.

"I'm trying to reduce the friction of this thing paying out," he answered, "to speed up my free fall so I can pass through the slipstream of the four engines more quickly."

"Do you think it'll work? What if it doesn't?"

James smiled. "We'll soon know."

I was full of admiration, for my own tendency was to follow instructions to the letter and repeat what had worked before, to the point of superstition. At Ringway, on the first plane jump, we had been delayed because the ground wind strength exceeded fifteen knots, which is too much for training jumps. We had had to take off our chutes, and because they had already been adjusted to each man's measurements, Roy Bladen had chalked our names on them before leaning them against the walls of the standby room. He had written my name in letters too large to fit and had run out of space after "MAST." Thereafter, when it had become necessary to mark our names on the parachutes, I wrote "MAST" in exactly the same fashion. Since it had worked the first time, who could say whether I would do as well if I wrote "MASTERS"?

Meanwhile, over Salisbury Plain, it turned out that there had been no need for the crew to panic about opening the trapdoors. We were coasting along for at least the threatened twenty minutes that we had hoped to avoid. It seemed like hours. Gerald Nichols was halfway out of the plane, looking progressively paler. With chattering teeth from the cold wafting up at him, he spread out his arms, when he felt secure enough on a straight stretch, to show us how the aircraft was banking left and right. It was making us ill to watch him.

At long last the green light came on and Nichols jumped. As Andrew Kershaw exited after him, his strop caught my heel and jerked my leg out from under me. The jolt shook me up physically and mentally, for I had heard tales of people being pulled out of a plane helter-skelter, and I knew that a clean exit was essential, especially on a low-level jump from a four-engine aircraft.

Luckily, I was not pulled out, but I worried about holding up the stick. So I hastily stepped into the void, one foot after the other, rather sloppily. Instantly, I was punished for not having my feet and knees together—I started to spin like a top. "If you spin, kick against the direction of the twist." Roy Bladen had taught us. Otherwise, the

lift webs on one's shoulders twist, and then the rigging lines, and finally the unopened canopy itself. The chute can't open, and one has
what the American parachutists call "streamers." The British call it
a "Roman candle." By any name, it results in death.

I kicked against my rotation even before I had an open chute. Yet
I spun so rapidly that the twisted lift webs pressed my head down on
my chest. I kicked some more and strove to push the two lift webs
apart, to free my head. Once I had halted my body rotation, I
strained to hold the lift webs in the proper position and not spin back
the other way. It was a supreme effort, and I sighed with relief when
I became aware that I had succeeded. Then I realized that because
this was to be our lowest jump ever—240 feet—as part of the experiment, I had no time to check my position or determine whether
I was coming in on a forward or backward oscillation. I would be hitting the deck at any second.

I looked down and there was the ground, approaching fast. I was
on a backward swing, almost completely unprepared for hitting the
ground.

Well, here comes one hell of a whack, I remember thinking, but
to my delighted surprise I felt as though I was gently rocking in a
comfortable easy chair. The coiled mountaineering rope had absorbed the shock perfectly, and there I lay, grinning up at the sky,
the piton next to me, not through me.

Not everybody was that lucky. Wallen had fallen into a foxhole and
suffered a bad concussion, and Peter Moody had four thrown lines—
rigging lines that for some reason draped themselves over the
canopy instead of connecting the canopy to the lift webs. One
thrown line results in two half canopies breaking a fall instead of one
full canopy—diagrammatically, an upside-down W instead of an upside-down U (the latter being obviously much more efficient). Four
thrown lines means virtually no effective canopy.

"I jumped last," Moody told us, "and I saw myself passing numbers nine, eight, seven, and six. I was supposed to whip out my switchblade and cut the thrown lines, and I tried that. I got a half-opened
chute when I was ten feet off the ground."

Moody tore a bicep muscle on impact. Because the preparations
for D day had begun, Moody went to see the Skipper and did what

must have been more painful for him than his injury: he said he felt insufficiently recovered and unfit to participate in the D day operation. His standing in the troop was so high that there was not the slightest doubt about his eagerness and enthusiasm to be part of what we had been yearning for.

The Skipper sympathized: "Even when you're unfit, you're about twice as fit as most of the rest of the troop. My advice is go and take part, and don't worry about it." Moody agreed, reluctantly.

On a fine day in early spring in Littlehampton, the highest-ranking Commando officer we had ever seen, Maj. Gen. Sir Robert G. Sturges, K.B.E., C.B., D.S.O., came to brief us for Operation Crossbow, an important series of raids. His visit was appropriately shrouded in secrecy. The small two-story local British Legion Hall had been taken over for the occasion, and guards were posted inconspicuously around it to protect us from accidental or deliberate eavesdroppers, as if Littlehampton were a hotbed of Nazi spies. The real purpose of the general's presence was kept under wraps. Ostensibly, he had come to inspect No. 3 Troop.

The general, a stocky little gray-haired man with his green beret squarely above his serious face, stood on a small wooden crate as an improvised platform while we marched past in formation. After the "eyes right" and the "eyes front," we were halted outside the hall and swiftly sent upstairs.

"Gentlemen," he began, and I felt a chill creeping down my spine. No one had ever addressed us as gentlemen before. I felt that this honor was probably proportionate to the unlikelihood of any of us returning from wherever he was going to send us. He said we would be going farther inland in France than any uniformed British troops had penetrated to date. The operation was to be undertaken by a small group specially equipped with sophisticated weaponry and instruments. The information sought was so important that, should the first group fail, a second one would be dispatched to the objective as soon as practical, and a third, and fourth, and so on—the entire troop if necessary.

"And, gentlemen," he concluded reassuringly, "you will be picked up in the usual manner by the Royal Navy. But should this prove impossible—because you fail to reach the rendezvous on time, or because the Royal Navy is prevented from getting there by weather or enemy activity—the MTB (motor torpedo boat) will return for you the next night. If that doesn't work, I promise you that they will return a fortnight later to the same spot and every fortnight thereafter." The general scanned us, sitting silently on the hard chairs of the Legion Hall, making eye contact with almost all of us. "But," he continued, "if you don't get picked up after the first fortnight, I would start walking if I were you."

"Walking on water," somebody whispered. "I knew we'd be expected to do that sooner or later." "Walk where, sir?" someone else asked out loud.

"Spain, of course. You will receive a specific itinerary," replied General Sturges, "but I must add one other cautionary note. Many operations have been scheduled in the past, and they have not materialized. I know that that is a big blow when you're all keyed up to go, but it can't be helped. The only thing I can do is to wish you good luck."

9 The Pigeons Have Arrived

Operation Crossbow entailed being parachuted into France, near the Pas de Calais, to reconnoiter the V-1 sites there. These were soon to launch the unmanned German doodlebugs, Hitler's revenge weapon targeted at Britain's civilian population, but no one at that time knew exactly what they were.

Our information was considered so important that three different ways were planned to try to get it back to Britain before we returned ourselves: carrier pigeons, strapped across our chests in corrugated cardboard boxes for the jump; an S-phone, a special radio to communicate our descriptions to a plane (a lightweight plywood Mosquito); and a motor torpedo boat carrying an S-phone (in case we made it to the coast but could not be picked up for some reason).

Dry runs on these forms of communications started immediately. We tried to transmit a sample message to a Mosquito by standing in a clearing in a forest and speaking into our S-phone. It didn't seem to work. Although we didn't know it at the time, the plane was supposed to circle around us within the range of the S-phone, but the pilot flew over us instead of around us so that we could transmit only a few words at a time, an unsatisfactory situation. Then the pilot suggested that we should stand in a clearing on top of a hill, which might have increased the range of the S-phone.

"Well," we replied, "sure we can, here in England. But if you expect us to stand on some bare-assed hilltop in enemy-held territory with you drawing attention to us overhead, you must be out of your fucking mind."

It also did not help that they had sent us a Polish pilot who hardly spoke English, and English was what we were speaking, in our usual "accent-free" manner. We cursed the dumb-ass War Office in general, and the dumb-ass RAF in particular.

After token parachute jumps at points inland in Sussex, our training for Crossbow culminated with an exercise in which our teams started out from equidistant places from the coast. The local population and ground forces were not notified of our presence. The Home Guard, for instance, was not alerted so it was up to our skills and caution to move unseen and unheard and not be killed by some conscientious soldier or patriot who had not unreasonably concluded that we must be enemy parachutists or seaborne infiltrators.

The morning that this exercise began, our administrative officer, Lieutenant Langley, emerged from his office at formation time, an unusual occurrence in itself. He strutted toward the Skipper, who was standing in front of the troop, saluted him, and, leaning as close to his ear as he dared, said in the loudest stage whisper I had ever heard: "The pigeons have arrived, sir!"

This became for us, forever afterward, a bon mot, a saying that replaced "the balloon's gone up" and all such similar clichés. We were issued not only the pigeons but still more special equipment, including infrared cameras and the new Patchett machine carbine, a novel-looking gun that none of us cared for much. Its main asset seemed to be that, if we were forced to fire it, the enemy would think that the entire Allied armies were descending upon him because it made such a racket.

We were also given some little bottles we were told contained a liquid that would throw tracker dogs off our trail. This had a surprising consequence. One of our teams had decided to lay up in an unoccupied weekend villa during one day of this final exercise. We were trained in breaking and entering, so the team had no difficulty in getting into the house, which proved to be well stocked with food, wine, and other creature comforts.

Because our total rations consisted of only two twenty-four-hour dehydrated packages for each man, to introduce an element of hardship to the exercise, the food and wine were quickly consumed. Jimmy Monahan, who was in command of this particular team, had some ethical misgivings, but his men persuaded him that these delicacies had been captured by legitimate foraging and thus only added to the realism of the exercise.

The team then retired to the bedrooms for the rest of the day, for what they felt was a well-deserved rest before night fell and they could move on. However, some nearby farm dogs were making a terrible racket, presumably having gotten wind of the unusual goings-on. Although these canines were by no means comparable to trained tracker dogs, our men felt that they might draw someone's attention to their temporary stay in the house. What a wonderful opportunity, someone suggested, to test the antitracking potion.

George Saunders volunteered to distribute the contents of one of the bottles. Using the best available cover, he swiftly darted around the estate walls and fences, sprinkling the liquid liberally hither and yon. Then he and his pals settled down comfortably for a good day's sleep.

Suddenly, they were awakened by the awful howling of numerous dogs. Judging by the sound, they were all around the house. The men looked cautiously out the windows and saw, to their horror, dozens of crazed dogs yelping and jumping around in a frenzy. What was worse, a group of local citizens, attracted by the noise, was making its way toward the house. The team members had to summon all their skills to beat a hasty retreat out a window on the far side of the house. They barely managed to gain the cover of the nearby woods and the dogs did not give chase.

It became obvious that whereas the concoction in the little flasks was indeed efficient in throwing dogs off a trail, the team had misunderstood its method of application. The way it worked—superbly, in fact—was by exciting the animals greatly, in the manner of catnip for cats, in a word, dognip. We subsequently found out that we should have laid a false trail one way and then gone the other. Unfortunately, the War Office had forgotten to include instructions.

That night, when we approached the farm designated as the camouflaged enemy factory that we were to reconnoiter, I was elected, over my unsuccessful protest, to stay at the fringe of the woods to guard the team's packs and mountaineering ropes. The rest of the team could then move freely when infiltrating the objective. I knew that I would have a boring period of waiting, devoid of the excitement and challenge of crawling silently around the buildings in the little valley.

When at long last the men returned, I at least had a chance to exercise my art school training. My friends had made a rather crude drawing of what the buildings looked like, and I translated that into an "artist's impression" of a plan. I drew cows in the fields where they said they had seen some. The result was rather colorful and cartoonlike but a modicum of fun. At least it impressed the Skipper. "Anyone who can come from a reconnaissance patrol and a strenuous exercise in the middle of several nights' exertion and bring back a drawing as explicit and informative as this one is doing all right."

The pigeons proved to be our next problem. In the case of my team, it began when we passed through a little village in the middle of the night. Suddenly, the sirens sounded their undulating cuckoo warning, indicating a local attack. The villagers, to our dismay, responded the way the British often did. They came out of the houses to watch the air raid. Our group of three, Nichols, Mason, and I, flopped down, just in time, by the low garden wall and garden gate of a house on the main street. To our chagrin, a man and a woman came out of the front door, walked to the gate about six feet from us, and leaned on it. They started to discuss the air raid, which they expected to begin at any moment.

I was carrying our carrier pigeon in its corrugated cardboard box strapped to my chest. No sooner had the couple taken up their position than our pigeon decided to go for a walk in its rather confining environment. Its short footsteps resounded like muffled drumbeats from the carton, and in between it tried to show its displeasure at the lack of space by pecking at its walls. "Knock, knock, knock, knock."

"What was that?" asked the man.

"I didn't hear anything," replied the woman.

"Well, I did, and it came from over there."

Although I had my head down, I could feel the man pointing to where my pigeon and I were lying. He continued: "You know, sometimes they pretend to make an air raid, and what they're really doing is dropping spies, parachutists, you never can tell. Those bloody Nazis, they're a crafty bunch."

I didn't like the way this whole thing was going. About this time my pigeon started pecking again.

"I heard it this time," said the woman excitedly. "Shall we call the police or the Home Guard?"

While they were considering that, we decided to get out of there.

The lead man, Nichols, jumped up and took off down the road. Mason and I followed instantly, having been alertly awaiting the signal to move should the situation become critical. We sprinted a quarter of a mile, dived into a field, and converged again a couple of hundred yards farther along. That good couple must have had the shock of their lives.

We spent the night in a copse. Having gathered the information that the exercise demanded, we wrote our findings on the tiny message pad provided and attached it to my pigeon's leg. I for one was glad to be rid of the wretched bird, glad to see it launched into the rosy early morning sky. But the bird didn't seem to be as happy. It flapped its wings a couple of times after takeoff, and then lighted on a nearby tree.

We were appalled. At first we encouraged it with more or less friendly exhortations, but when it turned a deaf ear to all of them, we changed our tune in frustration: "Fly, you bugger! Fuck off home!"

When that, too, was ineffective, we tried throwing sticks and stones at it. When one missile almost hit home, it finally became airborne and headed straight up into the pale sky. It circled above us once and then set a determined course—straight toward France.

"Wrong way," we called after it, "you damned traitor."

Another team told us that their pigeon, unlike ours, was so eager to fly home that it took off almost immediately and with such panache that they never had a chance to fasten the message into the capsule on its leg, and shouts of "Hey, come back" had proved fruitless.

Later, when we had returned to Littlehampton, we confronted the Royal Signal pigeon handlers with our complaints.

"Not all these fine birds behave exactly alike," they replied. "And you must bear in mind that the birds you had were by no means our first-string carrier pigeons. They are far too valuable for a mere exercise. You'll get the A team only for the real thing."

That was comfort indeed. But we couldn't help thinking that *we* didn't have any surrogates for roaming around, liable to be shot by ambitious Home Guard sharpshooters. We were not valuable enough, presumably, to warrant stand-ins.

It had been an exhausting exercise, ending at the Seven Sisters cliff on the Channel coast, between Cuckmore Haven and Birling Gap near Seaford. Seven sheer vertical cliffs 150 to 200 feet high were so snowy white that they seemed to shine in the dark, rivaling the White Cliffs of Dover. Our several teams converged on top of them and used a shielded blue flashlight to signal the motor torpedo boat to pick us up. Then we rappelled down the sheer cliff so as to embark unseen. Such cliffs are likely to be the least defended spots on any coast, because both sides believed that an invasion was unlikely to occur.

But then disaster struck. As Andrew Carson (Carlebach) was being lowered down the cliff, as was the practice with the lead man of each team, he became constricted. Choking, he whipped out his issue switchblade and cut himself free.

A cool, serious-minded athlete, pipe smoking and rugby playing and more British in demeanor than most of us, Carson had signaled his distress. But there had been a moment's hesitation about what to do: pull him back up or let him down rapidly? Nobody knows exactly whether Carson fell fifty or seventy feet. Whatever, he lay motionless and bleeding at the bottom of the Seven Sisters cliff. All of us were shocked into momentary paralysis, all except Gerald Nichols (Nell), who rushed over and picked him up.

Between Cuckmore Haven and Birling Gap, there is no way up the cliff at the Seven Sisters. The only way out is by sea: from dinghy to dory to MTB. Nichols carried Carson out into the surf, concentrating on keeping his balance as he waded into the foaming, dark water. He lowered Carson slowly into the black rubber dinghy and paddled out to the dory, which then took them in tow. But when they pulled alongside the MTB, it was decided not to move Carson at all. Instead, a derrick pulled up the dinghy, with Carson still unconscious in it. He was covered with warm blankets and left swinging there, as in a hammock. We all boarded as quickly as possible and sat glumly around the radio in the hold while the craft's radio operator arranged for an ambulance at Newhaven. I recall it vividly, the wireless giving the MTB's call letters: "Seagull Six Zero, Seagull Six Zero. Seagull Six Zero calling Newhaven . . ."

Nobody thought that Carson would live, but miraculously he did, although he was never fit enough to return to the troop. After all our efforts, Crossbow was canceled shortly afterward. So was another operation, Coughdrop, in which we were to be parachuted into France to ride down the Blavet River in inflatable rubber dinghies to destroy the U-boat pens at Lorient.

As our training continued, we found other risks connected to rappelling down a cliff or quarry. The beginner has a human but detrimental tendency to want to hug the cliff when he should do the opposite. He should lean back with legs astride, both feet braced horizontally against the cliff face. A few leaps will easily cover a descent of a hundred feet if he pays out enough rope each time. Apart from a slightly unpleasant sensation when going over the edge at the top, most of us found it good clean fun. If a man is bothered by vertigo, he can always look up instead of down. After a little experience we used to put down several ropes alongside each other and a few yards apart and race each other down.

When Tony Firth (Fürth) was hit on the head by a rock loosened by the jerking rope above him, he turned his misfortune into an advantage. The next day, as we were panting along on a speed march from Littlehampton through Rustington on the chilly, windswept, barbed wire–protected beach promenade, handsome Tony looked like Rudolph Valentino himself. Wearing what appeared to be a huge white turban, Tony, in his Sheik of Arabee role, had a local beauty on his arm.

Fraser (Frey) was another casualty. He was invalided out of the Army when a rock hit his knee while rappelling down the Seven Sisters cliff. Although his injury was not nearly as serious as Carson's, it was bad enough.

Mac Franklyn (Frank) a freckled, red-haired young man, had a lucky escape. He had missed the beginning of our training on the cliffs. Slightly pudgy and enormously courageous, Mac wanted to catch up with our rappelling skills as quickly as possible. On his first try he picked up the anchored rope on top of the Black Rabbit chalk stone quarry near Arundel, which had a hundred-foot drop.

"Now let's see," he said, "is this how you rope yourself in for this

thing?" He was assured that he had done it perfectly. Then, to the
horror of those present, he simply stepped off the top of the quarry
with about twenty feet of slack rope. We peered apprehensively over
the edge, fully expecting to see Mac's mangled body at the bottom.
But to our utter amazement he managed to hang on somehow, in
spite of his twenty-foot free fall. His face was as white as chalk as he
clutched the rope for dear life. It had been a miracle that he wasn't
jarred loose. We pulled him up on the rope gently but quickly, and
there he stood, trying hard to maintain his decorum. He shook himself like a dog coming in from the wet, brushed himself off, and said:
"I suppose you're meant to take up the slack first. Now, let's see . . ."
He slung the rope around himself, took up the slack, stepped off the
edge, once again, and completed his descent in perfect style.

Every now and then the Skipper would move us from the parade
ground into an improvised classroom adjacent to our troop office.
On this particular day he showed us an important new technical development that had been sent down from the War Office, a nylon
rope. It was astonishingly light. He told us that it would soon replace
the heavy hemp mountaineering ropes we carried for rappelling. He
passed the sample rope along the benches, and the last man got up
and returned it to the Skipper.

"And what is this supposed to be?" asked the Skipper when Douglas (Dungler) put a reel of khaki cotton on the desktop; it looked
like the kind of thread we used to sew on buttons and doubtlessly
came out of Douglas's Army-issue sewing kit.

"Isn't that what was passed around, sir?" said Douglas amid a background of snickers. Douglas was pointing out the concern all of us
had felt during this presentation. Could such a flimsy rope support
our weight all the way down a two hundred–foot cliff? A reassuring
label about the rope's tensile strength of several thousand pounds
was of little comfort to us. It just looked too damned thin.

"We'll try it out in the Black Rabbit quarry tomorrow," said the
Skipper. As always, the Skipper went down first. The nylon rope
worked smoothly, perfectly. Lieutenant Trefor Matthews, Royal Signals, a friend whom Hilton-Jones had only recently recruited for 3

Troop, went next. Right after Matthews stepped off the edge of the quarry, the nylon rope snapped.

Matthews fell fifty feet—halfway down—struck a ledge, and fell the rest of the way. Tommy Swinton (Schwytzer), who was among those watching, went into shock. The nylon rope had been strong enough all right, but it had been sheared through by rubbing against the rocky rim of the quarry.

Amazingly, Matthews was not only alive but conscious. When we reached him, he sighed, "I suppose somebody had better go on my date for me. I bet I don't look so pretty." Matthews lived, but his Army days were over.

This accident and Andrew Carson's on the Seven Sisters, both of them nearly fatal, gnawed at us. Many of us felt depressed by the loss of two good men. There had to be a way of avoiding the risks and yet enjoying the benefits of the new nylon rope, which would make it easier to carry on raids. Suddenly, I had the answer.

We were in the back of our truck, off to another training exercise, when it came to me, logically and clearly. I nudged Ken Bartlett (Billman) who was sitting next to me on the floor. "Ken, I've got it."

"Got what?"

"The nylon rope! The way to use it!"

"How? We could try to cushion it on the edge, where it rubs against the rock, I imagine . . ."

"The hemp mountaineering rope is safer. All we've got to do is to bring it on the boat. We're not supposed to go down the cliff until the dory is in, anyway. Right?"

"Sure. But how do we get the rope up the cliff?"

"We'll put a carabiner snap hook on one end of the nylon rope, which we'll take with us. When the dory or dinghy reaches the beach with the hemp rope, we throw the nylon one down. The snap hook will have been covered with luminous paint, so the boat crew can see it coming down. They'll attach the hemp rope, which will have a ring spliced into its end, to the carabiner, and we'll haul it up. That would take no more than a couple of minutes. And if someone is chasing us and we're in a hurry, then we can still risk cushioning the nylon rope and using it instead."

There was a brief silence. "I'll be damned if it wouldn't work," Ken said. "I'll tell the Skipper."

The next day the Skipper called another meeting. "We've all felt bad about these accidents, nobody more than I. Now Masters has come up with a simple solution." He explained it much as I had to Bartlett and the others on the truck.

At about the same time, George Saunders had invented an ingenious pretzel-shaped rope seat held by a metal D ring that would be snapped onto the hemp rope. It made rappelling much smoother. One could stop instantly at any time by a twist of the wrist, with perfect control. The Skipper explained that also.

We also developed a standard operating procedure for house clearing, using a bombed house for practice. A patrol would cautiously approach the building held by an imaginary enemy, with the intent of forcing an entry and eliminating the occupants. Two men would creep ahead of the rest. One of them would throw a 77 (phosphorus) grenade, which would explode spectacularly with fireworks of sparking stars, then finally transform into a cloud of smoke.

As soon as the smoke developed, the second man would rush through it to the nearest window, which had been chosen for the break-in. He would throw a 69 (high-explosive Bakelite) grenade through the window, duck while the grenade exploded, and jump into the house immediately after it. (Although the 69 grenade was a training device, it contained enough explosive to cause serious injury and had to be treated with care and respect.)

Once in the room, the second man would shout "Clear!" and the rest of the fighting patrol would rush in through the same window. They would throw 69 grenades into every downstairs room, then endeavor to get to the top floor as swiftly as possible, firing their tommy guns with live ammunition at cutout enemy silhouettes.

Team after team went through this sequence. My friend Gary Mason was an entry man for a team I was on when things started to go wrong. Gary threw the 69 grenade, which happened to make contact with what remained of one of the thin broken window mullions. The grenade detonated instantly, and a splinter caught Gary on the eyebrow as he was ducking for cover.

The next accident that night was entirely my fault. Having done this routine so often, I was being a little casual in its execution. The 69 grenade had a screw-top cap, which was removed before throwing it. In flight, a weight attached to the end of a white tape caused the tape to uncoil. When totally unwound, it pulled out a pin and primed the grenade, which detonated as soon as it touched anything, however lightly. If the grenade's flight was not long enough to unwind the white tape, the grenade became an unexploded dud.

It was the practice in 3 Troop to pick up grenade duds, which is possible if the mechanism is understood. By carefully holding down the grenade head to prevent the detonating mechanism from working, we could safely drop the grenade into a ditch, preferably a deep one, or over a wall. It was not a pleasant task. To avoid having too many duds, we would unwind a few lengths of the tape if the grenade's flight was expected to be short, as when it was thrown into a room. Again, it had to be done carefully.

This time, however, I decided to unwind the tape of my 69 grenade while I was running, spinning it with its weighted end like a cowboy about to throw a lariat. I threw the grenade into the room while I dashed past the door rather than tossing it into the doorway just before reaching it. Bang! Something kicked my right buttock. I ran upstairs for my next task. There I fired my tommy gun into the moonlit room, where the targets were propped against some sandbags in the corner. As I returned down the stairs, my buttock itched, and I reached my free hand to the seat of my pants. It was soaked with blood, and I felt a hole there big enough to insert my thumb, not only in my pants but in me. Our medic, Max Laddy, fished out the splinter with a pair of scissors after I had passed out from delayed shock. "Didn't want to waste the natural anesthetic," he growled.

The wound took a month to heal. Every day a Canadian medical officer replaced a strip of gauze inserted into it, sometimes touching a nerve so that I jumped even out of my prone position on his cot. Every day I begged to be put back on full duty. Vegetating as telephone orderly in the barren downstairs office of our headquarters was dreary and boring. I did have access to the unit's passes and rubber stamps, but once I had written myself a sufficient supply of weekend passes (the legitimate ones were strictly rationed), and faked the signature of some unknown officer, there wasn't much else to do. Finally, I recovered sufficiently to persuade the medical officer to put me back among the living. I decided to utilize one of my fake passes to meet a long-desired date in London, at the same time testing whether my physical condition was up to dancing and other exercises. The rendezvous proceeded as planned, and my luscious date was in a romantic mood. But just as I was getting another round of drinks at the downstairs bar at the Cumberland Hotel, Marble Arch, I nearly came to grief. I had just inquired about the availability of rooms. The hotel was totally booked up, but they gave me a double in a Bayswater rooming house they used as an annex.

A mustachioed major who was behind me in the line for the bar struck up a conversation.

"In town on a pass?"

"Sort of . . . not exactly," I replied confidingly. In the breast pocket of my battle dress was my homemade document. I almost told him all about it.

"What do you mean?" he asked. "What if the military police check you?"

"Well," I said a little haughtily, "they hardly bother us Commandos, you know," implying that mere police held us in some awe. I looked at him a little more closely. He wore the insignia of a Home County regiment and a London division. Only then did I notice an armband on his sleeve. Good Lord! The letters *PM* were on it, not *MP* for military police. I didn't know what the large letters on a red and black background stood for.

"Don't you realize you're being checked now? I'm the provost marshal of the city of London. May I see your pass?"

I suddenly remembered that in a fit of flamboyance I had printed an excess of stamps onto it. Not only "Confidential" but also "Top Secret" and maybe one or two others for good measure. It might have done for a rank-and-file military policeman but hardly for the city's top police dog. I stammered something to the effect that whereas I had a pass, of course, I had meant that I really was on special assignment. He scanned my homemade product with an eagle eye while fear-of-RTU shivers ran down my spine. Then he looked me straight in the face.

"This seems to be in perfect order," he said in a measured, emphatic way that convinced me that he knew full well what the facts really were. "It must be lovely not to be bothered by the military police. Have a good weekend."

I still shivered a little while lounging with my date in front of the romantic fake electric fireplace in the hotel annex room, and not just because I had nothing on.

10 Plymouth: Fit for a Prince

Training intensified. In June 1943, 3 Troop was sent on a boating course to Plymouth in the west of England, to train with assault landing craft and practice wet landings and wet reembarkations. I was sent ahead alone to arrange for billets in private homes for our week's stay. I arranged it so that I could have dinner with my mother in London between trains. I had my satchel of documents marked "Secret" under my seat in the Soho restaurant and a loaded pistol in my belt to guard whatever was in the satchel, probably ration cards.

On arrival in Plymouth I went to the neighborhood where we were to stay and made an impromptu reconnaissance of the available digs. I developed a code as I marked down each address where the inhabitants were willing to take in one or two of us.

"Nice room" was one of my symbols, "good bath" another. The most important ones were "close to the parade point" and "pretty daughter" or "pretty landlady."

During my billet search, my top priority had been to find a place where Barnes (Baumwollspinner: literally spinner of cotton) and I could stay together, not far from where our morning formations were to be. Barnes was an engineer by training and was a Bren gunner for this course, and I was his assistant. We knew we would have to do a lot of Bren gun cleaning, what with the daily saltwater immersions. Barnes was meticulous in caring for his weapon. It came first, no matter what. So I had given up several voluptuous landladies and some gorgeous daughters, just to satisfy more important conditions.

I found a U-shaped housing complex precisely embracing the parade ground, but no one wanted to board more than one Commando. Barnes and I had to settle for living opposite each other in the two arms of the U. Both our landladies were rather plain by our tastes, and both had husbands who worked late into the night in the turbine plant on the Plymouth docks. It became immediately clear that both of the wives considered their live-in Commandos an exciting diversion during the doldrums of the war and that they were entirely willing, nay eager, for extramarital adventures. Because we spent twenty-seven hours cleaning our gun in that one week, the luckless ladies would have had to be vastly more seductive to keep us awake, let alone to perform additional nightly duties. Even Betty Grable, Lana Turner, Linda Darnell, and Dorothy Lamour—separately or jointly—would have failed to lead us astray. So we chaperoned each other as best we could and secluded ourselves behind locked doors the rest of the time.

To make matters worse, both husbands evidently were intensely jealous of their wives. Each one had asked the other man's wife to keep an eye on his—much to their mutual amusement. But all along we Commandos were fighting for virtue and celibacy. Ah, the toughening process.

On the third day we were briefed during the morning formation. The Norwegian troop was coming down to join us for an opposed wet landing for the benefit of their Crown Prince Olaf, King Haakon's son. We were to be the enemy. They were to fire smoke mortar shells from the landing craft while running in, then land and vanquish the enemy—us—after fierce and noisy resistance. It had been found that the 2-inch mortars could not lay down an effective smoke screen as it usually came out far too thin and volatile. We would have to conceal ourselves in the bushes around the landing beach. As soon as the mortar shells began to explode, we were to sneak out carrying bigger smoke canisters, ignite them, and vanish swiftly to begin our violent opposition. We were not to prolong the fighting. After all, the crown prince didn't have all day, and it was no big deal to be brave with blank ammunition. We were to be spectacularly violent, then surrender.

The smoke boosting worked like a charm, although it wasn't amusing to dart around between the sizzling crashing mortar shells. True, better to do it among smoke rounds than high explosives, but if one should clunk you on the head it might not make much difference. We boosted the smoke beautifully, aiding and abetting our

Norwegian enemy, until the flotilla was practically upon us. We faded away only when we could see the white of the crown prince's eyes. Then we yelled and huzzahed like banshees, firing our blanks with superb dash before surrendering meekly.

All except Jock MacGregor, that is.

Jock had entered into the spirit of the exercise with great dedication. He simply could not find it in his heart to come out with his hands up. Besides, he had climbed a tree that was ideal for his purpose. It had thick, concealing foliage underneath and a grand field of fire from a solid fork in the upper branches. How could he give up that, and himself?

"Oh, come on, Jock, pack it in," we called up to his perch. But he went on firing from his practically impenetrable position. Meanwhile, we were all lolling around with our hands up for the benefit of royalty, and our arms were getting tired. Being trained for initiative, we pointed out to our Norwegian comrades that as their prisoners we really had no business carrying our own weapons; they had to disarm us. When they displayed a reluctance to do so, we festooned them with our rifles, tommy guns, and Brens, with a couple of mortars and PIAT (projector infantry antitank, the main British antitank infantry weapon) thrown in. They looked like walking arsenals. When MacGregor saw them, even he came down and hung his rifle over one of them.

In formation one day, an officer from another Commando unit, unfamiliar with Barnes's perfectionist character, conducted a weapons inspection.

"There's oil in the breech of this machine gun; that won't do." This was no way to talk to Barnes about his Bren. He drew himself up to an even more upright position of attention than the one he had already assumed.

"Sir, the Bren machine gun is a machine, as the name implies. A machine must be lubricated, with oil. This oil has to be wiped dry before parade."

"And so?"

"This is a rather fine day, isn't it, sir?"

"Indeed."

"On a warm day the elevated temperature will cause a properly lubricated machine to ooze the oil from its recesses. If it remained dry, the machine would have to have been improperly lubricated in the first place. Sir!"

The officer took hasty flight.

11 3 Troop in Early Action

A few of 3 Troop had in fact already been in action along the Channel coast of occupied France. According to the records, the first five troop members in combat were "Bubi" Platt, Maurice Latimer, Rice, Bate, and Smith. All had taken part in the ill-fated Dieppe raid in August 1942. Bate was the first troop member to be killed, and Rice and Smith were taken prisoner and never heard from again. Platt, whom Latimer always teasingly called *"Sudeten-Deutscher Volksverräter"* (traitor of the Sudeten-German populace) was wounded in the left leg. He rarely spoke of his Dieppe experiences. Maurice Latimer, the old soldier who had fought in the Spanish war, never mentioned the Dieppe raid, either. A wiry, taciturn little man, he was incredibly quick when it came to taking action but slow when it concerned talking. He didn't chat.

Others disappeared from the troop periodically, allegedly to attend a course in something or other but in reality to train for some operation. One of the earliest to do so was Harry Drew. He was chosen to train with a 12 Commando force in 1943 under their Capt. O. B. (Mickey) Rooney. Harry went on one of the cross-Channel reconnaissance raids code-named Forfar, mainly designed to test the feasibility of this kind of operation. Although his taking part fulfilled a long-held 3 Troop dream, Harry was disappointed.

"It was exciting to be on enemy-held French soil at last, but we didn't really do anything. There we were, on the beach, but there appeared to be no intention to reconnoiter inland. I suggested that it ought to be possible to use a fishermen's footpath to get a bit farther into the countryside, but that idea was rejected. I was told it was impractical and that anyway the footpath was probably mined. So we came home again."

Corporal John Wilmers (Wilmersdorfer) took part in Forfar/Item, a similar raid in the series which was mounted to reconnoiter a new searchlight installation near St.-Valéry-en-Caux. Munich born but very Anglicized, a graduate of an exclusive English public school, Wilmers was a serious and dedicated Commando soldier.

Before the Forfar raid, John and the seven No. 12 Commando members of the raiding party were sent to the quiet English village of Wherwell. Ostensibly, they were there to rest, but each night they stood by, waiting for the right weather conditions for the RAF to get them there and for the Navy to bring them back. It also had to be a moonless night. This was to be the first parachute raid of the Hard-tack series. The others had been landed by motor torpedo boat.

"It was a clear and lovely evening," Wilmers remembered. "Vaguely I realized that it might be my last, that I might not ever see England again."

Just as they were set to take off, the pilot stuck his head in from the cockpit: "You've had it. The Navy has asked for a last-minute post-ponement."

They were bitterly disappointed, and the weather got worse. But on the evening of 2 September 1943, they received another standby order, and this time it turned out to be for real. Once over their drop-ping zone, they concentrated on a quick exit to avoid being spread out too far on the ground. The eight of them exited in only nine seconds.

Wilmers was the fifth man out. It was 2205 when he landed in a stubble field near the sea cliffs, as planned. Dogs barked in a nearby village. After several anxious moments, the men located one another and set out to reconnoiter the searchlight installation under con-struction. They dumped the work crew's tools down the cliff and wrenched loose an optical instrument that looked valuable enough to take along. They also cut the telephone wires.

Looking out to sea, they saw a small enemy convoy slowly passing by. They hoped fervently that it would not stumble upon their Navy pickup party—their return ticket home and the alternative was a long, long walk to Spain.

The convoy did not spot the MTB, but the dory launched from the transport had had to turn off its engine so as not to be detected. Motorless, it drifted way off course, three miles down the coast, un-til it ran aground. By the time Wilmers and the others found the dory, it had been left high and dry by the receding tide, and they had terrible trouble refloating it. Then they found that the engine would not restart and the dory was leaking. They had to paddle for the MTB as if their life depended on it, which of course, it did. "Blokes very tired, boat slowly sinking," they signaled to the MTB. "Dory to MTB, dory to MTB. Can you see us? Can you see us?" One of the men stood in the dory's bow waving a blue pin-light signal in a slow semicircle out to sea.

"Yes, we can. Go as hard as you can. We're in as far as we can go." The MTB had come within a mile of the shore. The lighthouse at the harbor of St. Valéry was looking down threateningly on them from a few hundred yards, and it was getting light.

At last the bigger craft loomed before them in the gray dawn. Friendly sailors hauled them aboard and found them dry clothes as the MTB took off at full speed for Newhaven on the Sussex coast, where tea, rum, and blankets warmed them up.

One might think that little was achieved by raids of this kind, considering the risks. But it was important to establish that landings on enemy-held territory were possible, and even to make the point that they were the work of outside raiding forces and not the underground, for which reprisals could have been the arbitrary killing of large numbers of the local population.

Corporal Jones (Kotka) was less fortunate on the raid code-named Hardtack 11, which was mounted by members of 10 Commando's No. 1 French troop in December 1943. Its objective was to reconnoiter the beach area at Gravelines on the French coast between Calais and Dunkirk, and Jones was the signaler for the operation. As with the Item raid, the dory's engine failed; this time the boat was swamped by the heavy surf. Two of the party were drowned when they tried to swim to the MTB, and Jones was captured, but the others escaped inland.

One of the French Commandos, Madec, tried to make his way to the Paris suburb of Châttillon-sous-Bagneux, where his sister lived. He got a lift from a truckdriver, who gave him a ragged coat and took him to the railroad station. He went by train to Paris, but the coat looked so torn and bedraggled that he felt he would be better off in his battle-dress top. He had removed all insignia and shoulder flashes, of course, and it, too, was dirty, which helped to make it less recognizable. He rode the Paris Métro full of German soldiers in this battle-dress blouse, which shows that the story we had heard of the Skipper's experiment walking down Piccadilly in a German uniform was not quite as unique as we had thought. Madec made contact with the French underground in the country and participated in sabotage and armed encounters until he was finally able to join his unit after it had landed on D day.

Julian Sayers (Sauer) and Tommy Farr (Freytag) were two other 3 Troop signalers who participated in a raid with French members of 10 Commando. Code named Premium, it took place on the Dutch coast at Wassenaar on 27 February 1944. Farr and Sayers were to act as the line of communication between rubber dinghy, dory, and MTB. Sayers had been chosen because he spoke fluent French as well as German and because he had worked with the French Commandos before. He had asked for the Berlin-born Farr to be his partner; they had trained together and had confidence in each other's capabilities. Yet they had different personalities. Sayers was a fashion designer by profession, married and older than Farr, whose choice of the name of a famous boxer gives a clue to his macho, streetwise character. Sayers had chosen his name because he had been reading a Dorothy Sayers novel at the time of our troop's obligatory name change. A Hungarian by birth, he proudly wore the green medal ribbon with the narrow vertical red stripes of the French croix de guerre, which he had earned even before joining 3 Troop.

As the raiding party went ashore, flares lit up the night sky and it was clear that surprise had been compromised. The party should have aborted the mission, yet land it did. When it failed to return, the boatswain and Sayers risked waiting an extra half hour, with enemy flares dropping all around them. Then they ordered to return to the MTB, which made its way back to England before daybreak.

It was subsequently learned that the entire party had perished. Their graves described them as unknown Allied airmen. The German reports stated that their soldiers in the strongpoint had heard cries coming from the sea. A rubber dinghy with three bodies "recently deceased" had been washed ashore and attempts at resuscitation had failed. The bodies of the three members of the party were washed up later. The Germans called the dead men French Canadians because of their names, which were on their identity disks, although they buried them as unknown airmen. This leads me to suspect a cover up. It is likely that some or all were captured, interrogated, and murdered.

In April 1944, RAF Bomber Command had attacked some coastal batteries on the enemy side of the Channel. When one bomb dropped short, it set off a whole line of explosions along the water's edge by sympathetic detonation. This caused concern among the invasion planners, for an unknown weapon against landing craft at this late stage could be a grave matter indeed.

Four operations, code named Tarbrush, were immediately planned to investigate this alarming new phenomenon. The Skipper himself, now promoted to Major, was put in charge. He carefully chose a team from all available Special Service personnel. He called it "Hiltforce," and it was based at Dover.

Professor J. D. Bernal, the scientific adviser to Combined Operations headquarters, warned the Skipper and his men that they might be dealing with a new, sophisticated mine that could be magnetic, acoustic, contact, or any combination of these.

"When he had finished talking," said the Skipper, "we didn't know if the mine would go off if we merely looked at it."

The Tarbrush raids were all MTB-dory-dinghy operations, well away from the planned D day beaches. The last one, which took place at Onival, was commanded by the first member of 3 Troop to be commissioned, Lt. George Lane (Djury Lanyi), a Hungarian by birth. His dory crew consisted of two 3 Troopers: Jack Davies (Hansen), an experienced seaman, and fair-haired, chunky, Hamburg-born Ernie Norton (Ernst Nathan), one of the troop's strongest muscle men.

I remember a song in North German dialect that Ernie used to love to sing when we were both in the Old Hampshires in our pre-Commando days: *"Hei-de-witzke, Herr Kapitan! Na da wolle Boetje fahre gehen."* (Hi-ho, Captain! Let's go on a little boat trip.) It was an appropriate ditty considering that Ernie's first and long-awaited combat experience was on a little boat trip.

Previous Tarbrush raids had not found anything to corroborate the fears expressed by Professor Bernal. It seemed that the mysterious explosive device that had so perturbed the D day planners was a landing craft obstacle, a primitive construction of a roughly hewn timber or steel pole with a Teller mine attached to it. It was thought that the mines had been inadequately waterproofed and that the saltwater had eroded the firing pins, which had made the mines extrasensitive. When one was detonated, the shock wave from it was enough to start a series of sympathetic explosions.

So George Lane's raid was just a final confirmation that no secret weapon existed on any of the beaches, but he was also told to photograph with an infrared camera another type of obstacle. After landing with Lieutenant Wooldridge of the Royal Engineers, they continued inland to see whether they could find some obstacle resembling the one they had been sent to photograph. Their comrades saw a flash at about 0140. A challenge in German rang out and then came a piercing scream, as if someone had been stabbed. Three single shots followed, then all hell broke loose. Very lights illuminated the scene, including the dory near the beach and even the MTB farther out, but Lane and his companion did not return. The two 3 Troopers, Davies the coxswain and Norton on his first "little boat trip," were waiting the usual extra half hour in the dory. But when they saw Germans running down the beach toward them, they put out to sea.

"For once the bloody outboard motor started on my first try," Davies said when he told me about the events of that night.

The two NCOs reached the MTB at 0309 hours and reported to the Skipper, who characteristically decided to find Lane and Wooldridge. Their search was unsuccessful. At 0358 they reluctantly had to abort their attempt. The MTB sailed back to base, with those aboard believing that Lane and Wooldridge were dead or at least wounded and taken prisoner.

Shortly after the two officers had set off inland, it had begun to rain hard, so they did not see the flash nor hear the scream or shots. The rain slowed them down, but they continued as fast as possible toward a place called Ault, where aerial reconnaissance had indicated the presence of the obstacle they had to photograph. They continued for three-quarters of an hour, but it was getting late and they had not reached Ault nor found what they were looking for, so they decided to return.

They thought they had overshot the rendezvous point with the dinghy when they came back to the beach. They moved back along the water's edge, but found themselves between two enemy patrols and were forced to take cover. It seemed that both patrols opened fire at them, but they were probably firing at the departing dory. When the patrols passed, Lane signaled to the dory and/or the MTB that they were ready to be picked up. There was no reply, even when, disregarding caution, he shone a continuous red beam where he hoped either craft was located. When that did not succeed either, they changed position, still flashing their light beam on and off. After half an hour they came upon the dinghy.

They floated the dinghy and paddled out to sea as fast as they could, hoping that the RAF might spot them and send an air-sea rescue launch to pick them up. However, when dawn came they saw that the coast was only a mile away, so they threw all their equipment overboard except for their escape kits (concealed compasses, maps, a hidden hacksaw blade) and their pistols, and braced themselves for the inevitable. They did not have long to wait, for they soon heard the throbbing engine of a German patrol boat.

As the boat approached, the men hastily made a plan. "[We would] look destitute so when they came alongside we could overpower them, pinch their boat, and run for home. Unfortunately they were not taken in. They circled us with five Schmeisser machine guns pointing at us pretty menacingly. Fight was out of the question so we threw our pistols into the water with a somewhat theatrical gesture to show that we were ready to be rescued."

In the nearby port of Cayeux, the two soaking-wet officers were interrogated separately, with Lane worrying whether his slight Hungarian accent might show. The circumstances of their capture guaranteed great interest on the part of the Germans and resulted in a highly sophisticated interrogation. It was here that our sojourn in Aberdovey, Merionethshire, North Wales, came into its own. George Lane came up with the inspired idea to do what some of us had done playfully while training there. He faked a Welsh accent.

"I figured they might just possibly detect a Hungarian speaking English," he told me, "but never a Hungarian superimposing a Welsh accent on top of that." It worked.

Nevertheless, the two officers were told that they were to be turned over to the Gestapo to be shot, a course of action that had ample precedence. Luckily news of their capture reached the top German Army hierarchy, which decided to get as much information as possible out of them. Locked up separate from Wooldridge for the night, Lane removed a wire from a stovepipe, fashioned a key, and opened his cell door. His escape was short lived. The German sentry was stretched out across the threshold outside.

"I'd go back if I were you," he said amiably. "There's another sentry around the corner."

Days passed with a series of interrogators, some of whom pretended to be Gestapo, to intimidate the pair. Then they were packed into a car bound and blindfolded. The thought must have occurred to them that Hitler's Commando Order dated 18 October 1942 was about to be obeyed. This specifically forbade Commandos on raids being treated as prisoners of war (POWs). They were to be handed over to the Gestapo, for possible torture and certain execution.

Lane found that when he laid back his head on the backrest of the car as if he were dozing off, he could peak out from under his blindfold—and read the road signs. Just before reaching their destination, he read and memorized one: *La Petite Roche Guyon*.

Hands untied and blindfolds removed, Lane could not contain himself and exclaimed to Wooldridge: "My God, what a strange place! Just look at it!"

Prisoners are never permitted to talk to each other, so they were brusquely hustled into their new cells. A little later an officer entered and told Lane that he would meet "an extremely important person" and asked him to promise to behave like an officer and a gentleman.

George Lane replied: "I always do."

He was escorted into the next room, where a high-ranking, elegant-looking officer told him that he was about to meet none other than Field-Marshal Erwin Rommel. Evidently, the famous soldier wanted to see for himself what a Commando looked like. Lane was then escorted into a beautiful large room, richly carpeted and furnished and embellished with ornate Orientalia. Rommel rose and came toward him to greet and scrutinize the tall, handsome, fair-haired Commando officer.

"So you are one of those gangster Commandos," Rommel mused through an interpreter.

"I do not know what the field-marshal means when he says that; there are no gangster Commandos," countered George, "Of course I am a Commando. The best soldiers in the world."

Rommel could not suppress a smile. "Perhaps you are not a gangster, but we have had some bad experiences concerning Commandos. They have behaved very badly on several occasions."

Lane expressed disbelief, and Rommel changed the subject. "Do you realize that you have been taken prisoner in very strange circumstances?"

"I hardly think they were strange. More unfortunate and unhappy."

"Do you understand that you gave the impression of being a saboteur?" Rommel continued. "You know what we do with saboteurs here, don't you?"

Lane replied calmly: "If the field-marshal took me for a saboteur, I would hardly have been invited here."

Rommel smiled again. "So you look upon this as an invitation?"

"Yes, of course. I am very honored."

More smiles, this time joined by all at the table. The atmosphere in the field-marshal's study mellowed considerably. Tea was served. Lane had a chance to study the man across the table. He found him shorter than he had expected, dapper, with closely cropped hair and steel gray eyes. Around his neck he wore the blue and gold Maltese cross of the Pour le Mérite medal with the Iron Cross above it at his throat. His high cheekbones accentuated the intense look of his clean-shaven face. He was downright affable now: "And how is my old friend Montgomery?"

"Very well, sir, as far as I know."

"You really think there is going to be an invasion?"

"So I read in *The Times*, sir . . ."

The interview ended amicably, but there were further attempts at interrogation after the two officers were sent to Paris. The Gestapo had a go at them also but were obviously restrained by an order of Rommel's that guaranteed their safe conduct and survival. Both ended up as POWs until the end of the war. Both were decorated with the Military Cross, as was Hilton-Jones for his "outstanding leadership and organizing ability." They were the first decorations awarded to 3 Troop but by no means the last.

Before this final Tarbrush raid was mounted, 3 Troop received orders that we were going on "extended maneuvers" in full FSMO with weapons and ammunition. Other 10 Commando units were to participate, among them a new Yugoslav troop. We were to live under canvas awaiting further orders. The rumor went around at once that "the pigeons had arrived." Surely this was going to be it.

The choice of the Dover area lent credence to the belief that the invasion of France was imminent. As we expected, we encamped on an estate near what we thought would be our embarkation port. Our tents were pitched beneath tall trees along one of the elegant driveways, an almost solid avenue of thirty-foot-high foliage, dark blue-green against the cloudy sky. The landed gentry of Britain frequently gave the War Office free reign over their real estate, doing their bit for the war effort, just like our landladies.

To pass the time, we ran obstacle courses, built rope-bridges, and swung over ravines. We had expected to outclass the Yugoslavs, who were in our eyes Johnny-come-latelies; we were shocked to find these newcomers every bit as fit as we were. Some boxing matches were also arranged. We were surprised to witness the debut of Walter Hepworth (Herschthal), whom some of us had considered to be one of 3 Troop's more timid members. Though badly mauled, he turned out to be intrepid. But we had looked forward with the keenest anticipation to Dicky Arlen coming out of his announced retirement. We had to persuade him to represent us ("Gee, chaps, I've hung up my gloves, you know . . ."), but finally he relented.

As the bout began, there was no such thing as Dicky feeling out his opponent. From the opening bell he allowed his luckless adversary no letup. He was like a mechanically driven sledgehammer—punch, punch, punch—until the bell. Next round, same thing. He won easily. Dicky was our hero of the day.

The next afternoon, after the usual workouts and exercises, I sat in my tent writing a letter home, thinking that it was perhaps my last one. Suddenly, I heard a loud crash coming from the trees above me.

I jumped up and ran out and there was George Saunders in midair, coming down fast. On landing—appearing a lot less shaken than one would have expected—he explained that he had wanted to see whether he could climb to the top of one of the avenue's trees and then jump to the top of the next one. Had it worked, he would have continued down the entire row of trees. It would, he said, have dispelled the boredom of waiting for action. George had attended Gordonstoun School, as had Prince Philip. Its principal, Kurt Hahn, had been imprisoned by the Nazis himself before transferring his exclusive school to Britain. Traditionally, he summed up his students' performance in one quintessential profound sentence. Here is George's, right on the mark: "George is a cow who gives excellent milk—and then proceeds to kick the bucket over." (Like the time he cycled me onto the parade ground!)

That night we were going to embark. Troop Sergeant-Major O'Neill marched us down to a pier. We believed that this was going to be the real thing because of his most unusual (in fact totally unprecedented) action. He distributed cigarettes (his own cigarettes!) to everybody.

But at the end of the pier we were ordered to about-face. Disappointed, we marched back to camp.

Now that this had turned out to be just another token exercise we felt that O'Neill would have liked his cigarettes back. Recognizing that this was impossible, he simply vented his chagrin by being particularly regimental. He snapped commands at us and called us nasty names: "You march like a worn out bunch of lazy bastards, and you haven't done a damned thing yet!"

It was easy to conclude that he didn't like us—any of us, except for Arlen, whom he admired greatly. We were all aware of Arlen's peculiar personality, which he exhibited on the next training exercise. We went to a railway yard to learn how to drive steam and electric locomotives, just in case we ever had to steal one in combat. Under the tutelage of some railroad personnel we took turns moving the trains up and down the yard. We also discussed the brake systems and how to do the maximum damage with explosives in order to sabotage the enemy's communications and supplies. We knew that the Germans had a machine that could tear up rails as they withdrew.

We had also learned that the demolition of rails by the French resistance generally had little effect because the enemy was very proficient in making rapid repairs.

During the briefing, the high-voltage electric rail was pointed out to us so that we would be sure to keep away from it. But Dicky Arlen thought that our rubber-soled boots would insulate us against the current of the live rail. He fearlessly stepped onto it just to confirm his belief. A terrific jolt sent him straight into the air to a surprising height. He came down looking shaken and a good deal paler than before, but probably wiser.

12 Husky, and Points East

Some 3 Troopers were considered lucky and envied by the rest of us. On 9 and 10 July 1943, four members of 3 Troop landed unscathed in and around Pachino, at the southernmost tip of Sicily: Paul Streeten (Hornig), Colin Anson (Ascher), Mac Franklyn (Frank), and Vernon Nelson (Zweig). They would see their first action well before most of us, except for those who had participated in raids. Code named Operation Husky, this landing in Sicily was to be the first recapture of European territory.

Streeten was born in Vienna into a middle-class family just before the demise of the Austro-Hungarian monarchy. The stimulating atmosphere of his intellectually and politically active home shaped him from childhood into being an activist.

I am five years younger than Paul, and my apolitical parents allowed me to become only a Boy Scout. Paul had joined the Red Falcons, a Socialist youth movement, and demonstrated, carrying flags and banners, and singing protest songs from the age of ten. Ironically, when the Nazis came into power in 1938, they persecuted both groups equally, for to them the internationalism of the Boy Scouts was as bad as the politics of the Red Falcons.

The Skipper accepted Paul into 3 Troop largely, Paul believes, because he had distinguished himself as a long-distance runner.

On 14 June 1943 Paul was attached to 41 Royal Marine Commando for the invasion of Sicily. An expatriate for five years, Paul told me that landing in Sicily was nostalgic for him. "The sun shone, the scent of spices was in the air, the fields were full of melons to which we helped ourselves freely, there were abandoned large barrels of wine, and the forsaken bays were lovely for swimming." Though Mussolini was Hitler's ally, the local population genuinely appeared to welcome the invaders. While waiting for the next action, Paul organized theatricals with "multitudes of grubby children, whose dramatic sense was delightful when they acted out roles of passion, romance, love, and sacrifice in the beautiful settings of the Sicilian landscape."

This idyllic life came to an abrupt halt at the end of July. Now 40 and 41 Royal Marine Commandos were to land behind the lines on the road and railway line from Catania to Messina. The Commandos were to interdict the enemy's evacuation of men and heavy equipment northward by establishing a bridgehead at Scaletta, a town near the northeastern end of the island.

The newly promoted Sgt. Paul Streeten recounts: "On the evening before the landing . . . I was still walking through the streets of Catania in full possession of all the powers of my limbs." The next thing he knew was that he "could see the pyramids and on the other side eucalyptus trees and the Nile . . . from my hospital bed."

He had set up a position on a railroad platform when an 88mm shell explosion threw him into a delirium and ended, among other things, his exceptional talent as a long-distance runner. "Never after was I to have the full . . . use of my left foot and my left arm; no more . . . rock climbing, skiing, running. . . . I still carry pieces of shrapnel in my neck, skull, and arm. . . ."

A less serious wound was sustained by tall, dark-haired Vernon Nelson. He carried the bullet that struck him as a good-luck charm around his neck ever after. The chubby, red-haired Mac Franklyn was seriously wounded around the same time.

Colin Anson (Ascher) was aboard the *Queen Emma,* a Channel packet steamer promoted to an assault ship with approximately 800 men. When the Germans mounted a dive-bomber attack, the *Queen Emma* laid down a smoke screen, which may have saved her from severe damage, but there were plenty of near misses and some direct hits.

Colin recalled the occasion: "The heat was so oppressive that I had decided to spend the night in a hammock on deck. Suddenly I heard a long drawn-out whistle, like from a passing express train, except it was coming nearer and nearer. Not only did it hit the deck below mine, but our hand grenades exploded by sympathetic detonation. Both the ship's medical officer and our own M.O. were killed. The Commando medical sergeant and his orderlies did an outstanding job tending the many wounded. It was a long night."

The Germans attacked yet again. One of the men of 40 Commando was wounded, and Colin helped lay him on a stretcher in the open until someone could carry him below. Colin put his own steel helmet over the man's face. "When they came for him I took my helmet back. I had heard no more bombs coming down and thought it was over. Strange, though, when I put it back on, my head and hand felt wet. Someone came around and offered me some rum . . . I began to feel rather sick. It was hard to believe. I had been wounded without realizing it. The medics came and went, carrying away other casualties but leaving me behind. I thought that was because I was not so seriously hurt. In fact it was because they thought I wouldn't survive anyway."

A splinter had entered his head and slithered around until it lodged, encapsulated, in the back of his skull. At first landfall, a field ambulance took him to a three-ton truck that served as an operating theater, with white sheets and Canadian nurses in light blue uniforms. Colin arrived and passed out.

When he came to, he was wearing what looked and felt like a plaster helmet. After half an hour he stopped breathing. His heart was massaged back to life from cardiac arrest, and he was evacuated on a hospital ship.

After long hospital stays in Tripoli and Cairo, Anson was released to an infantry reinforcement depot, but his skull had still not healed. In December 1943 he was readmitted to the hospital and was told that his skull would be patched with a piece of someone else's, "someone who doesn't need it anymore."

In a few months, Colin was pronounced fit. While waiting to join the unit to which he had been assigned, he was made temporary postal orderly in what he described as "a depressing bullshit infantry depot." On his rounds he came upon a trail of footsteps, with the imprint of so-called SV boots, which at that time nobody but 3 Troopers wore. He followed them excitedly and found that they led to red-haired Mac Franklyn, who had also been wounded in Sicily and was now recuperating in Cairo. Mac explained that he was determined to return to Britain in time to participate in the D day landings in France if it were the last thing he did.

Arnold and Hermine Metzger, author's grandfather and grandmother, Vienna circa 1910.

Author's father, Oberleutnant Arany (second left, standing) on Field-Marshal Mackensen's staff, World War I.

Pioneer Corps—author on right, Marischka lighting up. Between them, the clarinetist Salinger who was later killed in the tank corps.

Pioneer Corps—author on right.

The Skipper: Hilton-Jones, a man among men.

The 3 Troop detachment to land with 6 Commando on D day: from bottom left, Corporal Mason, Corporal McGregor, Corporal Nichols, Corporal Drew, Lance Corporal Masters.

Author (left) and Leslie Wallen on the Ydwal Slabs in Wales.

Andrew Carson on "the Slabs," rock climbing training in Wales.

On the Slabs: Author (left on top), Mason, Carson, Firth, Wallen, Gilbert, and Villiers (in front).

D day: LCIs (Landing Craft Infantry) at sea. Preparing to disembark. Commandos don't wear steel helmets.

Normandy: 6 Commando hitting the beach. Note full-size picks and shovels.

Bicycle troop disembarking from landing craft.

Sayers of 3 Troop on beach; bicycle troop disembarking in back.

Bicycle troop rushing to get off the beach in Normandy.

Heavy equipment arriving in Normandy over the beach.

Normandy: Moody (center) and Envers (right front) get information from French civilians.

Griffith's temporary grave, proving his cover story to be intact.

German propaganda leaflet: Designed to intimidate, it amused the troops.

A German leaflet threatening the invading British soldiers with rocket weapons against their families at home.

Hell-Dogs
over England !

For two years Allied bombers tried to wipe out one German city after the other, killing or wounding millions of innocent women and children. In spite of all German warnings and the confession by responsible Anglo-American authorities, that German industries could not be stopped to increase their output steadily, the massacre was continued.

Now it's our turn !

Since midnight June 15th/16th a new German long-range weapon of most terrible explosive effect is continuously engaged in massed large-scale raids over London and South-East England. We hate this war against the defenceless population, but you have forced this fight upon us.

These raids will be continued until a decisive military goal is reached.

Statement of an American radio-reporter, broadcasted on June 16th from U. S. A. :

> *"The new German secret weapon is, there is no doubt about it, the beginning of a new aera in war-history of the world."*

S W 18.

Back of German leaflet.

Latimer taking prisoners, Walcheren, November 1944.

Corporal Tom Spencer in Neustadt-Holstein, June 1945.

1st. Lt. Masters on Isle of Wight: Last leave before being demobilized.

Ron Gilbert (Gutman) on right in rare photo during a secret mission in which he met a former German pilot whom he later arrested for illicit underground activity. Gilbert was awarded the MBE.

Author (left foreground) at the annual D day Anniversary Banquet at Saulnier Farm. Ian Harris is at author's left across from Colonel Beattie, Brigade Signals.

Ian Harris, MM, (Hans Hajos) being introduced to Queen Elizabeth II at a ceremony honoring heroes of World War II.

13 Ex-European Commandos Return to Europe

In Italy our 3 Troopers were to be attached to the Belgian and Polish troops of No. 10 Commando (our own) and No. 9 Commando, as well as to No. 40 Royal Marine Commando. While preparing in Algeria for the assault landings on the Italian coast, Steve Ross contacted his friend Leslie Scott in a tone of urgency:

"I found out an important item from native sources," he said. "We can get a dozen eggs in exchange for one razor blade." That sounded like a good deal to them, so Leslie and he decided to contribute one blade each, to get *two* dozen eggs. It worked as advertised. "We made the biggest damn omelet in all of Africa. Not having seen that many eggs together during rationing in England in the last few years, we ate it all in one go and were sick for two days. We barely recovered in time for embarkation."

The 3 Troopers were happy to land on the continent from which many had barely escaped with their lives four, five, or six years previously. Now they were the spearhead of an advancing army. But there were casualties. On 19 January 1944 the popular, quietly earnest Peter Wells (Auerhahn) was killed by a shoe mine, a hard-to-detect wood-encased explosive device. He was 3 Troop's first fatality since the Dieppe raid.

A number of us were also wounded in Italy. Sergeant Brian Groves (Goldschmidt) was one of them. He had chosen his name to honor a friend at Cambridge who had been killed in action. His friend's parents were displeased, however, shocked that anyone, a foreigner yet, should take their son's name. The well-intentioned, ever-considerate Groves yielded to their sentiment and changed his name again, to Brian Grant.

Grant participated in Operation Partridge, a successful raid behind enemy lines on the far side of the Garigliano River, but the next day he was sent back with another party to retrieve the bodies of those killed the night before. It turned out to be a costly venture. He was hit by a mortar barrage and was wounded in the left wrist and left foot so badly that his foot had to be amputated. Thus 3 Troop lost one of its ablest sergeants. Barnes, the excellent Bren gunner and engineer who had inspired me when we were in digs together in Plymouth, was hit when 9 and 43 Commandos were sent to capture rocky hills that offered no cover and hardly any opportunity to dig in. George "Knobby" Kendall (Knobloch) reported on his participation in this night attack:

> I was there on Monte Inga when Barnes was wounded—multiple mortar wounds from an almost direct hit which killed the regimental sergeant-major. Later that night I went to a sheepcote on the mountain where the surgeon and his corporal had set themselves up under candlelight. I asked for Barnes. The corporal consulted a battered notebook and pointed to a manger up on the wall where some form huddled up in a gas cape was lying motionless.
>
> "Have you seen to him?" I asked.
>
> "Not yet," said the corporal. "Triage, you know. We've got to treat the ones with the best chance of survival first."
>
> "Please," I said, "he's my pal." I stuck with him until two days later when we went off the mountain, Barnes on a mule. I gave him my last lollypop from my twenty-four-hour ration. At the time I was convinced that this was the most altruistic act I had ever performed. Barnes did survive the war, although he was left severely handicapped.

Meanwhile, Steve Ross was interrogating prisoners after the Garigliano crossing. One of them, a very soft-spoken man, surprised me. "*Mein feldwebel* has very good ears and he is out there, quite nearby. So please don't talk so loud or he'll shoot both of us."

Just then, Ross was knocked out by a shell splinter. When he came to he was in shock, not only from being hit but also because of what he saw through his half-closed eyes. He was surrounded by Germans. He was certain that he was facing the miserable life of a POW, but luckily he was mistaken. "It soon became clear to me that *they* wanted to surrender to *me.*" He graciously accepted and directed them to take him down the mountain to the Commando's lines. They were going to put him on a mule. I had no confidence in that type of transportation on those steep slopes, so I ordered them to carry me.

As soon as Ross had halfway recovered, 9 Commando was ordered back to Anzio, the famous invasion site designed to hasten the advance to Rome. Here Field-Marshal Kesselring's concern to stem the allied advance motivated him to mount a fierce counterattack on the beachhead.

Ross was wounded once again during a clash with an enemy patrol. He emptied his tommy-gun magazine at an advancing German; mortally wounded, Ross's adversary fell forward. The dead man's bayonet struck Ross as they both went down, and Ross was hospitalized for a month.

Also going to Italy with Ross, Kendall, Groves (Grant), Barnes, and Wells was Michael Merton (Blumenfeld), Hugh Patrick Miles (Hubertus Levin), Leslie Scott, Steve Hudson (Hirsch), and Allan Marshall (Wolff). All had sailed from the Clyde in Scotland to Algeria by the long sea route around Ireland.

Reaching Italy via Malta, Merton was attached to 10 Commando's Polish troop, which later helped to capture Monte Cassino, the monastery perched on top of sheer rocks. It was one of the bloodiest battles of the Italian campaign. The troop suffered heavy casualties for a small unit: two killed and thirty-four wounded.

The pressure on the German Army mounted. Kesselring was pushed back toward Rome at the end of May, and in the first week of June Rome fell to the Allies. Then came the long-awaited news: D day.

The 3 Troopers in Italy were well aware that the bulk of the troop they had left behind in Britain was bound to have participated in that momentous assault. But news of how their comrades had fared, how many had been killed or wounded, did not reach them until weeks later. They anxiously followed all the news as it became available.

Anson (Ascher) had been wounded, as described earlier, in Sicily and was posted to No. 2 Commando Brigade on the Yugoslav island of Vis after his recovery. He spent the best part of the summer of 1944 here, just out of artillery range from the nearby enemy-held islands of Brac, Hvar, and Mljet. The brigade's mission was to interrupt German supplies, raid German bases, and support the local partisans who were working with the partisans of the *Dalmatinska Brigada*. It was a pirate's existence, an exciting private war, riding gunboats and MTBs as boarding parties and sinking a food convoy with the help of a light RAF regiment's 3.7-inch antiaircraft gun.

Merton and Scott were also sent to the island of Vis, where they encountered unexpected problems with the partisans. Scott felt that it was often not an easy cooperation.

"Their methodology and ethics were not at all in keeping with ours. Not only were they unwilling or unable to keep to a battle plan timetable, which caused them much grief as they tended to run into supporting artillery barrages, but they would use tactics such as driving civilians in front of them during an attack. This shield would include women and children. We Commandos tried in vain to dissuade them from this unsavory practice."

When the Allies decided to switch their support from Mihailovic to Tito, Scott was to go with an advance party to make overtures to Tito. "We wondered and sought guidance how to dress for this unusual mission. We were told that we were going to meet a man whom we had to treat as a head of state. Therefore we should not wear battle dress, but come as close to field service uniform as we could, since dress uniform was unattainable. We did our best. It turned out that Tito also wondered what he should wear. We and he had reliable sources in each other's camp. His reported to him that we were coming as dressed up as we could manage. So Tito summoned a partisan tailor and ordered him to create an elaborately gold-embroidered uniform practically overnight, rather like the princess in the fairy tale of Rumpelstiltskin, who had to spin straw into gold before dawn broke. Thereafter, Marshal Tito was always seen in this grand uniform, or one like it, though until that time he had never worn anything but a white shirt and breeches tucked into riding boots."

Colin Anson's sojourn on Vis ended in the last days of August 1944. He was posted back to the Italian mainland and from there almost immediately with 2 Commando to Albania, an evil place in his memory. The jagged landscape strewn with little gray pinnacles of volcanic rock didn't improve under the constant torrential downpour. The jutting stones tore the Commandos' plastic rain capes to shreds when they were on the move, and the rain soaked them to the skin. It was as if the ground under their feet had teeth; sharp, triangular, cutting shark's teeth that could get a person stuck if he tried to step between them, and impale him if he trod on the points.

What made matters worse was the thought of the enemy opposite them, comfortably dug in on softer ground, in positions prepared long ago, luxuriating bone dry under waterproof head cover, shelling the miserable Commandos at will. Half the Commandos became casualties from exposure to the weather. Had they been less hardy, they would have perished.

The Commandos encountered another difficulty. The mules that were provided to carry their heavy weapons simply could not negotiate the forbidding crags. The Raiding Support Regiment, with which the Commandos were working, came to the rescue. They brought up 4.5-inch mortars and 75mm howitzers—by hand. Eventually, a battery of twenty-five-pounders (albeit still qualitatively inferior to the heavier enemy artillery), an RAF company, and medical personnel were landed. With this reinforcement, and naval support from destroyers, the playing field became more level. The Germans, realizing that they were outgunned, began to evacuate their forces. They foresaw that, should the port of Sarande be taken, their garrison on Corfu would be totally cut off. Sarande fell on 9 October.

This ended the Albanian war, but it was rumored there were still some Germans on Corfu. Anson and a few men of a Royal Marine Commando jumped aboard a gunboat to have a look for themselves. But when they pulled into the old harbor of Corfu to make inquiries of the local population, the craft took off without warning and left them there.

The next moment brought an even greater surprise. They were surrounded instantly, not by Germans but by the populace in the vicinity. It turned out that they were the first Allied troops the Greek islanders had seen after four years of occupation. Bearded Greek sea captains feted them in one taverna after another. The rest of the unit soon joined them to occupy the friendly island. Anson was billeted in the Greek king's summer palace, the birthplace of Prince Philip. British Army rations were scorned for most of their stay of several weeks, as turkeys and lobsters were the daily fare presented by their generous hosts. They acquired a chef named Spiro, a name he shared with virtually all the males on Corfu, in honor of their patron saint St. Spiridon. Spiro could produce a gourmet meal even with Army bully-beef and biscuits, if there was a momentary lapse in the supply of the aforementioned luxuries. In contrast with barren Albania, Corfu's lush vegetation was an added joy. The locals were such Anglophiles that there was even a Corfu Cricket Club. In the middle of a bloody war, it was a wonderful holiday, the best Colin had enjoyed since leaving Bad Homburg, his hometown in Germany.

Then came the anticlimax. Colin returned to Italy, with a new rank and a new job. As a sergeant he was to train a new 3 Troop group of volunteers raised from refugees in Palestine, the French Foreign Legion, and from British units in North Africa. But by then the war was practically over in northern Italy.

14 Our Turn

We heard fragmentary reports about the exploits of our friends in Sicily and Italy. But when would *our* long-awaited turn come?

In April the Skipper divided those of 3 Troop who were not already abroad into teams of five. Each team was designated to join one of the eight Commando units that made up No. 1 and No. 4 Commando Brigades, now preparing for D day. (At the time, the two brigades were known as SS brigades, meaning Special Service; that was changed to the plainer title, because the initials SS had an obviously distasteful connotation.)

The Skipper announced that we could do whatever training we felt we needed most. The first request of all the detachments was identical: more shooting, particularly with tommy guns. The Thompson submachine gun, the standard Commando weapon, was loaded with a twenty-round stick magazine of .45-caliber ammunition. We had fired at man-shaped silhouettes before, during the day and at night. Now one of us invented a new target: bottles!

We collected empty bottles of all shapes, colors, and sizes and took them to the beach in an old knapsack. We lined them up on the seawall. Then, from different distances we fired bursts of automatic fire to shoot them down. This method of target practice had one tremendous advantage. A man could see his hits immediately and make instant corrections from any misses, whereas with the cardboard targets he had to take a close look at the results; if there were bullet holes, these had to be taped over so that the next marksman had a clean target to see his hits.

Corporal Gerald Nichols (Nell) was in charge of our No. 6 Commando detachment. I was the second-in-command, having just been promoted to lance corporal. Gerald had protested the fact that all the other seven detachments were headed by at least a sergeant, and their second-in-commands were all corporals. But the Skipper had replied that No. 6 was commanded by Derek Mills-Roberts, a tough, gray-haired, square-faced lawyer who had come to the Commandos from the Irish Guards. He had a reputation of running No. 6 as a "bullshit outfit" (a very regimental unit run by strict disciplinarians). So if we were to join No. 6 as sergeant and corporal, respectively, we would likely be busted for some reason or other within days of our arrival. We weren't satisfied, but there was no possible appeal. We figured that the Skipper had probably been given a limited number of ranks he could promote. We would just have to prove when we got there that we deserved promotion.

In the last week of May, each team was transported by truck to the Commando unit to which it was designated. My detachment went to Hove, next to Brighton in Sussex, where No. 6 had been based for training for some time. We drove up to the headquarters, a two-story house, but found that No. 6 had already left, except for a couple of men nailing shut some crates. They told us we could spend the night in the house, and then leave with them in the morning to rejoin the rest of No. 6 Commando.

There were no beds, so I decided to sleep in the tub in the upstairs bathroom. It was a most uncomfortable night.

In the morning we were driven to Southampton to a barbed wire–enclosed camp, where we were sequestered for the next two weeks, along with all of No. 1 Special Service Brigade. The time had come at last.

The camp was run by a black American unit, with a British canteen as the sole R and R facility. There was no entertainment. The days were filled with weapons cleaning, and live ammunition was issued. When that happened there was, inevitably, an occasional burst of fire. One of these ripped a spectacular dotted line of holes through the burlap sacking that had been rigged as a screen in front of the long row of toilets. One of our colonels was the sole user of the facility at the time, and he stampeded irately out of there, "bottomless" and swearing.

We played a good deal of bridge inside or in front of the large canvas tents in which we slept. Then the briefing started. There was a professional-looking model of the beach areas on which we were to land; it was constructed from aerial reconnaissance photos and extremely detailed maps. We were not given place names as yet, although 10 Commando's two French troops, attached to No. 4 Commando, made this piece of security farcical when they immediately recognized the estuary of the River Orne and its parallel canal.

Simon Fraser, the seventeenth Lord Lovat, our brigadier, was a handsome and respected man who had distinguished himself in the Dieppe raid. His rousing speech to all of us was reminiscent of Shakespeare's Henry V St. Crispian's Day speech.

"He who outlives this day, and comes safe home, will stand a tiptoe when this day is nam'd, and rouse him at the name of Crispian. He who shall live this day, and see old age, will yearly on the vigil feast his neighbours, and say 'Tomorrow is Saint Crispian.' Then will he strip his sleeve and show his scars, and say 'These wounds I had on Crispian's day.' Old men forget; Yet all shall be forgot, but he'll remember, with advantages, what feats he did that day." If I substituted D day for Crispian's, Lovat's speech would be almost identical.

Most of our time was spent waiting: more briefing, and waiting again; more bridge games, occasionally interrupted by a burst of machine-gun fire nearby followed by a shout of "Medics!" Two stretcher bearers would come doubling past us, slightly disturbing our concentration. "Too much live ammunition around," someone would mumble.

Once or twice we were taken on road marches through Southampton and its surroundings, with strict instructions: "No talking to civilians." This was undoubtedly intended to give us a glimpse of life outside, to keep fit, to relieve our boredom, and to improve morale. It caused us to reflect that the world outside had no trouble at all in going on without us.

It also made us envy all the servicemen who were promenading on the sidewalks arm in arm with their dates. Some were Americans, better dressed and better paid than we, tough dating competition even when we were not behind barbed wire. There would usually be a few heckling comments from our rear ranks, more or less good-natured: "Look at them D-plus-thirty boys," or some such. That was rather unfair, for we had no idea when it would be their turn to land. True, it would probably be later, or they hardly would have been at liberty to walk the town.

Once we passed two cigar-smoking Yanks in conversation with a little girl, perhaps five years old, at a bus stop. The gist of the talk was probably along the lines of "Any gum, chum?" which British children had learned to say to get a reward of chewing gum. "At least let them grow up," we heckled the Yanks.

Other than these passing comments, there was virtually no communication with the outside world. A rumor did spring up that one of our 3 Troopers got into a discussion with a passerby through the barbed wire fence. The latter is supposed to have said, "I know who you people really are—refugees from the Nazis." He was arrested and not released until several weeks after D day. True or not, this did not sound too unlikely.

The Southampton camp's facilities were basic, attested to by the democratic latrines in which the previously mentioned colonel was almost a precombat casualty. But being under American management, the camp did have one fringe benefit. Unlike similar British facilities, it boasted marvelously functioning hot showers. They were for officers only, but having been trained to be enterprising and daring, I thought that the right degree of undress would make it difficult to distinguish an officer from a humble lance corporal. So I visited the showers at least once a day, modestly clad in an Army-issue towel.

On one occasion I arrived to find one of the four cubicles already occupied. I scouted whether the bather was anyone I knew (or more important, anyone who might recognize me). I could just see enough of him through the steam and soapsuds—there were no curtains—to be sure that we did not know each other.

Just then two British Commando junior officers, happily also unknown to me, entered. As they undressed they noticed the other man (who was black) and commented in a startled whisper: "I say, did you see that?"

The British had always contended to be above racial discrimination. In 1944 they did not really have to deal with it; yet, a certain carryover from the colonial tradition seemed to rear its ugly head occasionally. Bathing, after all, was a private pursuit, not to be shared with enlisted men, "other ranks," or presumably other races.

"Indeed I did," replied the other second lieutenant. "Do you s'pose it's all right?"

At this juncture the object of their concern had completed his ablutions and turned off the hot water. He emerged from the stall, rubbed himself dry, and got dressed. His uniform, hung from a nail, had been covered by his big khaki bath towel. He was a full colonel. This totally changed the posture of the two young men. Naked or not, they snapped to attention. The British Army does not salute when not wearing headgear, or they would certainly have saluted. "At ease," said the colonel. He was the camp commandant.

In briefing sessions we were told more details about the forthcoming operation, code named Overlord. The first ashore would be frogmen to deal with the underwater obstacles, followed by assault infantry to secure the beach itself. Then it would be our turn, in two waves—at H hour plus sixty and seventy-five minutes, respectively, that is, at 0700 and 0715. We were surprised, initially, that we were not to be the first ashore, but it was explained that we were to push inland with as little delay as possible and to link up with the British 6th Airborne Division, whose gliders and parachutists would have preceded us by several hours and who would be anxiously awaiting our arrival.

"You will carry out this vital attack and consolidate the positions gained. You will stay for a week or two at the most, then return to Britain while regular Army troops will replace you."

"Don't you fuckin' believe it," said an old Africa-hand in 6 Commando. "What general is going to let go a couple of elite Commando brigades in the middle of a fuckin' invasion? Two weeks—not bloody likely. Make that two months, if you're lucky."

Meanwhile, preparations continued. Hand grenades packed in thick grease had to be wiped dry and clean. Someone instructed all NCOs to "dirty" their stripes. Members of 6 Commando had customarily whitened these chevrons with Blanco, circular cakes of equipment cleaner that were moistened and brushed on like paint, in keeping with that unit's reputation as a "bullshit outfit." No sooner had we accomplished the smearing of dirt to render the rank insignia more subtle, if not invisible to the naked eye, than our colonel, Derek Mills-Roberts, demanded in a fury who had given this disgraceful order.

"Damn good idea too," said another old Africa-hand of 6 Commando. "Fuckin' Jerry picks off the NCOs; snipers see them white stripes from a mile off. Besides, we know who the NCOs are."

But Mills-Roberts thought otherwise. There always was an element of bravado among Commandos to flaunt our elitism—going without overcoats no matter how cold it was, wearing green berets instead of steel helmets.

So the dirt was brushed off, which was much harder than putting it on. I was happy (at least momentarily) to have just one stripe to clean on each arm.

Finally the date was set: 5 June was to be D day, so we were to embark on the fourth. We younger ones sought out the men who had seen action. Many of us had volunteered just as soon as we were old enough; some volunteered before that by lying about our ages, such as young Upton, a slim, ginger-haired lad who looked hardly old enough to shave. I was just twenty-two myself. So we asked questions and hung on every word of the answers.

We played a last rubber of bridge, and then the weather broke—not noticeably from our point of view but unalterably in the opinion of the meteorologists. This meant for us a precarious twenty-four-hour postponement, so we were now scheduled to embark on the afternoon of 5 June and invade on the 6th.

We played another last game of bridge. Some of the men were having a raucous good-bye party in the NAAFI, which is the British post exchange, or canteen. They batted balloons from one to the other, but where did they get balloons inside the camp? They were not colorful balloons. A second look revealed them to be inflated condoms. Somebody said these had been issued to keep our watches dry. But I believe that they were private property put to this use because their owners figured they weren't going to need them for a while. This game caused considerable embarrassment to the NAAFI waitresses. Should they be shocked and blush, or should they pretend not to know what these "balloons" were?

15 D Day At Last

"You ride a bike, don't you?" said Nichols, in charge of our detachment with No. 6 Commando. "The bicycle troop, No. 1, should be the most interesting; I have to be at headquarters myself." Nichols handed me a strange-looking bike that could be folded in half by loosening a pair of wing nuts and was so light it could be lifted with one finger.

The first chance I had to use that vehicle was when we rode down to our flotilla of landing craft moored in Warsash Harbor near Southampton. Captain Robinson's 1 Troop had been training with these lightweight collapsibles for months. They were not like ordinary bicycles. There were no pedals, just stems, with a carrier in front for a rucksack, which we had been issued instead of our normal pack. We carried a lot of stuff in them, and I found that cycling with that load in front of me was difficult. On the ride down to the boats, men started to discard equipment they figured they weren't going to need, even if disposal was entirely against regulations. The hedgerow lining the way to our point of embarkation became festooned with unwanted spare equipment. One of these unpopular items was a brown pack-waistcoat combination (called an assault jerkin) with toggles instead of buttons; it was stiff and cumbersome, so most of the old soldiers threw them into the hedge.

Near the docked landing craft was a sloping meadow with Royal Navy offices in a low building nearby. The British equivalent of the American Waves, called WRNS, (pronounced "Wrens"), dressed in smart navy blue skirts and white hats and blouses, were constantly going in and out. Because we had a waiting period before boarding, we all decided to test our binoculars by looking at them, knowing that we might not see any females for a while.

Toward evening we boarded and sailed. One boat followed the other out of port, the men singing and cheering and waving to

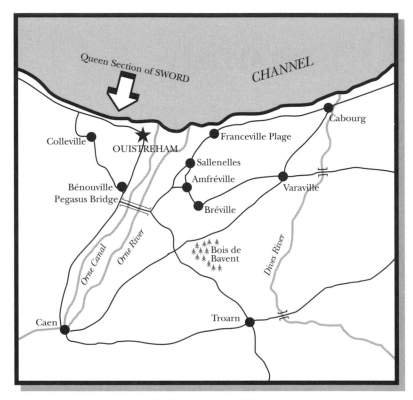

D Day 6 June 1944

neighboring craft. I wasn't really excited, and much as I tried to sense this momentous occasion, leaving English soil for who knew how long, perhaps forever, I just couldn't get worked up about it. It just seemed like a pleasant evening on the water.

We tried to get settled in the landing craft, which had one small hold forward and one aft. But first things first; someone brewed up some tea. I could not easily retrieve my enameled mug, so I had to miss out. Packing away a tea mug so that it was inaccessible could have been a terrible breach of security had someone observed it, for no British born soldier would ever have done such a thing.

Finally, we plunked down in what spaces we could find. It took a long while for all the landing craft to reach the starting gate, so to speak, and only then did we begin slowly to cross the Channel. The sea, once we got out into it, was rough. I found that I was in a tiny minority that was not seasick. Seasickness pills were dispensed, but I declined. I also refused to drink some rum; I was determined to be totally sober when landing.

We had a meal in the forward hold, but attempts at making an edible stew failed dismally. I tried to read a book but found it difficult to focus not only because of the pitching sea, but because of the thought of what tomorrow might bring.

I finally decided that the sensible thing to do was to get some sleep. After all, we were going to be out there all night and in the morning we were going to land on the Nazi held shore of Europe. I lay down in one of the white canvas hammocks strung from upright posts in the hold. There were only a few, and they belonged to the craft's crew. Some sailors came down and one snapped at me, "Get the hell out of there. The owner of this one is the Navy's heavyweight champion, and when he comes off watch soon he'll throw you out and knock your block off."

I decided that it wouldn't make sense to knock out a Commando just prior to landing on D day morning, so I faced the danger of being brutally assaulted without trepidation, with my boots on, literally.

The captain of our landing craft, an LCI/S, (landing craft infantry/small), had ordered us to stay belowdeck, to keep the decks clear for action. We were disappointed for we were eager to watch, regardless of the risks. Only when we were almost in did he let us go up on deck, where our bicycles had been stacked, to prepare to land.

The scene that presented itself 6 June was dreary. There was no sun yet. The beach and the sea were a drab, dull yellowish green. The houses on the model in the briefing tent no longer existed, so the beautiful model proved to be a wasted effort. I had the sudden realization that this might be the last thing I would ever do. I tried to look back on my past life, and I recalled vividly all the girlfriends in my life (there weren't very many), and my family paraded before my mind's eye in unprecedented peace.

I concluded that at twenty-two I had had a rich, full life and therefore could not complain if it were to end then and there. But before that, I, who had been harassed by the Nazis, intimidated, and targeted for extermination, would at long last have the opportunity to strike back. What is more, I felt well trained and definitely a better-than-even match for what I was likely to encounter. If I should survive by some chance, I would have to look upon the rest of my life as a bonus.

A vast assortment of different color flaglike wind socks was to have awaited us on the beach, and we had been told to memorize their meanings. "Mines cleared along here" was one. Another: "Mines being detonated here now. Keep down for thirty seconds and then proceed." And yet another: "Guide to the assembly point here," was a third.

That part of the master plan, however, didn't materialize. I did not see a single wind sock, although Gary Mason told me afterward that he had seen a flag with green and white stripes floating in the shallow water. This wind sock indicated where we would have found intelligence guides. It turned out that the beach master responsible for the smooth operation of our crossing the most dangerous initial enemy territory, the beach, had become aware that the wind socks were drawing an enormous amount of enemy fire. So he ordered them taken down. Alert to the confusion their absence was bound to cause, he attempted to make up for this lack by personally steering the incoming troops to the safest beach exits. In this effort he was observed and killed by a sniper.

Down went the cleated planks (the LCIs don't have ramps). I was the second person off the boat behind the bicyclists' Troop Sgt.-Maj. Titch Collins, a short, blond older man with a trim mustache. I watched him intently to see whether he would disappear under the water, in which case I would have dumped some of my load so that I wouldn't sink. I noted that he was only in about waist deep, which meant knee deep for me.

I felt better about not having to swim for it, because I carried my rucksack, tommy gun, a 30-round magazine, about 200 spare rounds (we novices were always afraid of running out of bullets at a critical time), four hand grenades (two high-explosive metal-fragmentation and two phosphorus smoke). In addition, everybody had been assigned an extra payload; mine was a 200-foot hemp rope with which to swim across the Orne canal and river, in case the enemy had blown the bridges. Others carried inflatable rubber dinghies that could then be pulled—not paddled—across the two waterways. It was planned that the entire brigade of about 2,000 men would gain the high ground on the other side in this manner. There was also the bicycle, a change of clothing, a blanket, two packs of 24-hour emergency dehydrated rations, and a full-sized pickax. Others had spades; we thought (correctly) that the entrenching tools that the Army issued us were not good enough to dig deep holes in a hurry.

One can imagine us as we staggered up the beach. With one hand I carried my tommy gun, finger on the trigger; with the other I held onto the rope rail down the plank. I also carried my bicycle. Knee deep, I waded ashore. Others had their ramps shot away, so they jumped, paddled, and swam. David Stewart (Strauss), landing with 45 Royal Marine Commando, told me later that he was hit in the face by body parts of a sailor who had been hit by a shell.

Laddy (Lewinsky) and Webster (Weinberger)—the two men who had opted not to parachute—never made it ashore. Both were killed before they even landed. For Mac Franklyn (Frank), who had been wounded in Sicily but said that he wanted to participate in D day "if it's the last thing I do," D day *was* the last thing he did. An enemy mortar felled him on the beach as he landed with No. 4 Commando. I was told he said, "Someone help me remove the brick from under my pack," and then he died. I remembered that when a tiny grenade splinter had hit my rear in the night house clearing in Littlehampton, it had felt like a brick.

We had been told to get off the beach as quickly as possible, so we moved up toward a little dune. In passing, I saw the Skipper, Hilton-Jones, who had landed next to us on the right with brigade headquarters. I couldn't think of anything better to do, so I saluted him. It must have been the only salute on the beach on D day.

I remember the charged atmosphere, the noise, the smell of things burning, and a few scenes in great detail. Some of the infantry that had preceded us were digging in behind some knocked-out, smoldering tanks. I even saw two men trying to dig in in the shallow water on the beach. Their sergeant yanked them out of their water-filled holes, yelling, "Get off the beach!" Being a greenhorn, I did not know enough to be really frightened. The noise of the whistling shells didn't mean a thing to me. I had no idea whether they were coming or going; just as well I suppose.

In a never-to-be-forgotten tragedy, I saw a wounded or dying man trying to rouse himself as in slow motion, from where he had fallen, on a slight rise above the sandy beach. As we walked across the dunes just where the white sand ended, we passed a soldier sweeping for mines with a mine detector, an oval plate with a long handle and earphones. But we could not wait for him. We had been told to get off the beach and our leader, Captain Robinson, went right past him. The mine sweeper yelled: "Hey, what are you doing?" and was told, "Sorry about that, mate, we've got to go on."

I began to wonder about the assault infantry, the East Yorks and South Lancashires of the British 3d Infantry Division, which had landed just ahead of us. They seemed to be squatting around here and there, not doing anything in particular. But I changed my mind when I heard a signaler next to me crouching in a ditch relaying a message for an officer. "Charlie Company, six men left, sir," he reported.

We crossed the road and a set of small-gauge rails. By the corner of a field, just across the little road parallel to the beach, mortar shells were exploding continuously. I hoped we would not go in that direction, but Captain Robinson aimed straight for it. Miraculously, the enemy barrage lifted as we approached, and we passed safely. We set out cross-country to get to our assembly point, clearly visible about a quarter of a mile inland—a cluster of bushy-top trees at the far end of a plowed field.

As we were crossing the road, we passed a flail tank, one of the special D day weapons, just as it beat its bundles of chains into the earth to explode mines, right next to us. Luckily, there weren't any mines in that place.

We were now off the Queen Red Sector of Sword Beach where we had landed. We lost some men, but we had been lucky, as only a few were hit. Among the missing was the PIAT man, perhaps because he could not manage to keep up with his heavy weapon, and a few medics who had stayed behind to tend the wounded. When we were a few hundred yards inland, guns and mortars opened up on the beach again. What looked like balls of fire were sailing through the sky. "Oil bombs." explained an experienced observer. These German incendiaries launched from Sobbing Sisters or Moaning Minnies, so-called because their firing made a grinding howl. Shot from rocket-fired mortars that sent up a whole frame of six shells at a time, they would ignite a large area wherever they landed.

No shells were exploding now in our path. Instead, riflemen sniped at us from the nearby woods as we were crossing the plowed field. To make matters slightly worse, several times we had to cross and recross a muddy creek. The bicycles proved difficult to grip while slipping in chest-deep brown water. A few of us managed to get across the field before the firing at us started. In front of me was a crowd of Commandos using the only furrow worth mentioning as sparse cover. I had to join the queue, but it was hard to crawl with a bicycle. Dragging it behind me proved exhausting. The only other way was to push it upright while I was well down in the furrow, showing only my arm that wheeled the bike, althought the bike itself was visible for miles. The Germans sniping at us concentrated on a crosswalk where we had to surface momentarily.

Just then some Sherman tanks came alongside us. The tank commanders were riding with their turrets open, exposing their heads and shoulders. That may have been all right in the wide no-man's-land of the African desert, but here, in the Norman *bocage,* the hedge country, it was extremely risky. But it was a boon for us at that moment. Although nothing had been said during briefing about close cooperation from them, we just whistled up at the man in the turret to give us some support. He said "OK," closed his hatch, and blazed away into the woods with his cannon and machine guns. The enemy sniping ceased while he was firing, although it started up again as soon as he stopped. I decided to make a dash for it the next time the tank started shooting. I said so to No. 6 Commando's Sergeant Harrison, the man immediately behind me in the furrow, who gave me a thumbs-up to signal his agreement. The tank opened up and I ran the remaining 200 yards to the assembly area, pushing my bicycle and running over everybody who happened to be in my way.

The first person I encountered in the assembly area was young Upton, who had been in my tent in Southampton. He was bleeding from a slight cut on his upper lip, as if he had cut himself shaving.

"Schmeisser bullet," he said, "just grazed me."

A close shave indeed; I had always thought he was too young to have a beard.

Our brigadier, Lord Lovat, was walking about in the assembly area, urging people on. He seemed to be perfectly at ease, in spite of the shooting and other noise. He carried no weapon other than his Colt .45 pistol, which was still in his holster. Instead he had a walking stick, a long, slim piece of forked wood. Later, a Scottish Highlander explained to me that it was a wading stick, used for helping to keep one's balance when fly fishing for trout or salmon.

"Good show, the Piper," Lovat said as Piper Millin, the bagpiper who had piped us ashore, came dashing up. I hadn't heard him until then, and I didn't hear him pipe even then. He was panting and catching his breath as he dragged the bagpipes as well as all his other gear.

There were a couple of prisoners at the assembly point, the first live German soldiers I had seen, and I immediately started to interrogate them. Lovat commented, "Oh, you're the chap with the languages. Ask them where their howitzers are."

So I did, but there was absolutely no reaction on the part of the Germans. I suddenly realized, looking at their paybooks, that they were not German at all but Russian and Polish.

It occurred to me that some Poles learned French in school, so I tried my high school French on the Polish soldier. His face lit up at once, and he started to talk immediately. But even the brigadier, who spoke a lot better French than I, was able to learn little from the Obergrenadier (a lance corporal like myself) Johann Kramarczyk of the Infanterie Regiment 736. He was a farmer from Odrau near Ratibor in Upper Silesia and was presumably press-ganged into the Nazi Army. In German or French, he knew next to nothing of value. I kept his paybook as a souvenir, strictly against regulations. I pushed on with 6 Commando's bicycle troop, feeling that my first encounter with a prisoner, one-on-one with the enemy, had not been a total success because it was preempted by a better linguist.

Harry Drew (Nomburg) had another kind of disappointment. Two German soldiers had surrendered to him just off the beach. Certain that they had been fed nothing but propaganda and lies, he was determined to enlighten them about their truly desperate war situation. He expected them to be devastated by the news that Allied forces were just outside Rome.

"Really? We've already heard on our radio that Rome has fallen." was their casual reply.

Harry, like I, had landed in the proximity of Lord Lovat. In fact Harry was so close to him on the beach that he had shyly touched his belt from behind, thinking that if anything happened to him, it could be said that Private Drew fell by his brigadier's side. Harry, a cynic and an unmitigated realist, did have a romantic streak.

Behind the assembly area was a country road, where at long last we mounted our bikes for the first time and cycled west through Colleville-sur-Mer (now called Colleville-Montgomery) before veering southeast and making for Bénouville. There we hoped to find that the gliderborne Oxfordshire and Buckinghamshire Light Infantry of the British 6th Airborne Division had taken intact the two bridges over the river Orne and its parallel canal. I certainly hoped they had, because it would save me swimming across with the rope and then having to help ferry the brigade across the two waterways. Once we were across the canal and the river, one way or the other, we were to cycle on to Varaville to relieve the Canadian parachutists who were to have captured it by then. The village of Varaville was so ancient that it is depicted in the Bayeux tapestry, an embroidered eleventh-century "comic strip."

The road leading to the bridges was lined with German Teller mines, but they were in little heaps, here and there, instead of being buried in the roadway. Presumably, the Germans intended to keep the coastal highways open for their own mobility and bury the mines only at the last minute. I was nevertheless puzzled that they had not found time to do so. Had they really been taken so totally by surprise?

The smooth ride got rougher as we went along. Most of us were young men who had never seen action before, and the novel experience of death all around us was very personal; we died a little with each man who fell. We were shocked to see dead parachutists hanging in the trees. Even the sight of dead cattle in the fields adjacent to our route, belly up and bloated in rigor mortis, was upsetting.

Our inexperience also had advantages. The noise of artillery and mortar shells, frightening as it was, did not scare us as much as it might have, had we understood it better. All along, our ignorance allowed us to assume optimistically that practically all the fire was to support us rather than destroy us. Only when explosions came precariously close or bullets whistled around our ears did we recognize that we were the target of an enemy who was determined to kill us.

The Skipper had impressed his expectations upon us to become involved and use our special skills—our language capabilities and knowledge of the German Army—on top of our regular Commando disciplines. "Your troop officers will be busy and have a lot on their minds, so don't come back telling me they didn't use you. Pester them until they do. Make nuisances of yourselves; I know you can be pretty damn good at that."

I did precisely that, entirely without success, at least for what seemed like a long time.

"I need a runner, quick," Captain Robinson would begin.

"May I go, sir?"

"No. Trooper Siddaway, here's what I want you to do . . ." And he would send Titch Siddaway, whom he knew and trusted from 6 Commando's desert campaign, instead of me. I think he saw me as a preposterous character with an accent whom he had only met recently, when I had been attached to the troop. Robbo, as his men called him, probably reflected that he had not even requested such reinforcement; actually the African campaign had been won without any such supposedly valuable additional help.

That scenario—my volunteering and being rejected and passed over—was repeated several times, until I could not help feeling that the captain resented my being pushy. Remembering the Skipper's instructions, I persisted, hoping that sooner or later my opportunity would come to show what I could do.

As we approached the first houses of Colleville, I was impressed by the first French civilians we had encountered since the landing. Disregarding the ongoing bombardment, a man in the light blue smock of a Normandy farmer, a navy blue beret on his head, posted a leaflet on a telegraph pole. Glancing at the headline as we rode by, I recognized a word or two: *Les Alliés, le débarquement, L'INVA-*

SION!—instructions to the local populace from the Maquis, the French resistance. Instead of taking shelter, people waved from doorways as we went by, calling out, *"Vive la France, vive les Tommies!"* The broken glass and roof tiles littering the village streets forced us to dismount and push our bikes, for fear of cutting our tires. To make matters worse, a sniper started to take potshots at us from the village steeple. Having no time to deal with him, we rushed on as quickly as possible to get out of his range. Back in the saddle, we rode through the damp, hazy Norman landscape, the road dividing grassy fields, the sun breaking through in patches. Bursts of machine-gun fire not far off, and more distant explosions, spoiled the peace of the beautiful, rustic scene.

We discovered that our rucksacks, strapped to an L-shaped carrier on the front of our handlebars, had a nasty way of sagging onto the front wheels, acting as all too efficient brakes. This inevitably seemed to happen when someone was shooting at us and we were in a hurry to pedal out of his way. The only remedy was to let go of the handlebars with one hand, free the wheel by leaning forward and lifting the heavy rucksack, and steer with the other hand, a tiring procedure. We tried tightening the leather straps that secured the rucksack, but bumping along the road soon loosened them again.

As we rode up the last hill before the open Orne river valley unfolded below, our lead cyclist was shot through the head. He was not the first casualty of the bicycle troop; several had been killed or wounded on the beach. But having been with the leading group, I had not been fully aware of what was going on behind me. Now I passed a red-haired man dead on the dusty, gritty edge of the road. One wheel of his bike was spinning in the air as if it, too, had been mortally struck.

"Deploy behind that hill," yelled Captain Robinson, and we dumped our bikes hurriedly by the roadside while he scanned ahead with his binoculars to determine where the shots had come from.

"Ah, Corporal Masters. Now there is something you can do. Go down to that village and see what's going on." He waved his arm in the direction of the first houses of Bénouville, now visible a few hundred yards down a shallow slope.

"Yes, sir! How many men do I take?"

"No, Masters, just you."

"Very good, sir." That didn't bother me. "I'll approach those houses from the left and make my way back in a sweep around the right," I told him.

"You still don't seem to understand what I want you to do. Go down this road and see what's going on in the village."

Now I understood. With a sinking feeling I realized all too clearly what he had in mind. He wanted me to draw the Germans' fire to see where they were hiding. I could not blame him for this death sentence, for I appreciated his need to know exactly where the enemy was, and his not having enough time to send out a more sophisticated reconnaissance. He had to get to the bridges, where the gliders had landed during the night and the airborne troops must be anxiously awaiting our arrival.

I looked at the scene before me. It was a wide-open landscape. No ditch lined either side of the road. Instead there was a ten-foot hedge along the left, so solid that I could not have crashed through it even to save my life. Only a shallow grass border separated it from the road's hard surface. The grass was but an inch high—no cover, whatsoever.

Five hundred yards farther down was a low parapet on the right-hand side: a stone wall, waist high, alongside the last stretch before my road ran into a T junction with the highway leading directly from Ouistreham, at the mouth of the Orne river, to the nearest big town upstream, Caen. On the far side of the road, facing that intersection, stood Bénouville's first house, built of solid Norman stone. A similar stone wall with a small iron gate enclosed a narrow front yard. The rest of the village stretched away behind it to the right.

As I began what I believed would be my last walk, my mind worked feverishly. I am not only mounting the scaffold, my head is on the block. *All that training going to waste,* I thought. Was there no way out? None. But we had also been trained to improvise. I suddenly remembered a film I had seen, I think it was "Life of a Bengal Lancer" or "Gunga Din." Errol Flynn or Cary Grant stumble upon an insurrectionist mass meeting in some Khyber Pass amphitheater. They are clearly going to be jumped and clobbered by the militant, seditious enemies of the empire when Cary Grant delivers what I have always thought of as a very funny line. "You are all under arrest!" he says with a nonchalant, debonair smile, just before he is mauled. Maybe I could try that.

I walked smack down the middle of the road. Might as well be brazen; there was no cover, anyway.

I began to shout at the top of my voice. "*Ergebt Euch alle! Alle 'raus! Ihr seid vollkommen umzingelt—Ihr habt keine Chance. Werft Eure Waffen fort und kommt mit den Händen hoch 'raus wenn Ihr weiter leben wollt. Der Krieg ist aus für Euch!*" (Surrender, all of you! Come out! You are completely surrounded—you don't have a chance. Throw away your weapons and come out with your hands up if you want to go on living. The war is over for you!)

I tried to sound as German as possible, rather than Austrian, having learned the appropriate pronunciation from my German fellow internees when we were incarcerated together.

No one came out. It was silent. On the credit side of the ledger, nobody shot at me either. With my finger on the trigger of my tommy gun, I concentrated as hard as I could on what might come to pass before me. There was some movement in one of the houses farther back on the right. Someone was waving a yellow recognition scarf from an upstairs window. All of us had been issued these bright fluorescent tie-on scarves to avoid being targeted by our own side. I wore one myself, under my camouflage parachute smock.

I turned my head briefly—the compulsion to keep my eyes glued to see my executioner was overwhelming—and pointed out this new development to my leader.

From behind his hill, he signaled with a forward motion of an outstretched arm to keep going. He had not yet seen what he wanted. I continued walking and yelling. Then it happened: a German popped up behind the parapet to my right front, firing a machine carbine at me from his midriff. Either he had been ordered to shoot me because I was getting too close for comfort, or, seeing me come nearer and nearer, he simply decided to shoot.

Why had they not killed me as soon as I appeared, simply pick me off with a fusillade of machine guns and small arms? One has to understand what it must have looked like from their point of view. First, some cyclists appear on the horizon. They kill one as soon as he comes over the crest of the hill. A momentary silence follows, then a solitary enemy starts marching toward them, urging them to surrender in a loud voice in fluent colloquial German. A lunatic? A suicidal madman? Surely no one would be that crazy—not unless he had an armored division to support him right behind the hill. In any case why not wait to see what happens, especially because he can be wiped out at will at any time of their choice?

I saw the German the instant he stood up. Instinctively, I went down on one knee as I pressed my trigger. He missed. I missed. My gun fired one shot—and jammed. He ducked for cover. I went through the prescribed "immediate action" to clear my jammed weapon and then cocked it. He reappeared and missed with another burst. I took aim, but there was only a click as I pressed the trigger.

By this time I was lying flat in one inch of grass, trying to present the smallest possible target. The next immediate action we had been trained to do was to remove the magazine, clear the gun by pressing the trigger again, replace the magazine, cock the gun, and then continue to fire. This meant taking my eyes off my adversary, or from the spot where he kept reappearing. It flashed through my mind that he was poorly trained, that he should have changed positions. I found it almost impossible to look away. The compulsion to look at one's nemesis *is* overwhelming.

At the same time I said to myself that he can't keep missing me. So I wrenched my eyes down to look at my tommy gun, and I saw that there were two or three rounds of ammunition hanging crumpled up in the breech. I ripped them out, replaced the magazine, cocked the gun, flipped up and set the sights. I had to shoot him before he finally succeeded in shooting me.

Then I heard a noise from my right rear and turned my head. The entire troop was galloping down the road toward me. Apparently, Robbo had seen what he was looking for and had immediately ordered his men to fix bayonets and charge. In the lead was Cpl. George Thompson, a former Grenadier Guardsman, firing his Bren machine gun from the shoulder instead of from the hip—the usual method while running. He sprayed the low wall to discourage my personal enemy, or anyone else for that matter, from firing.

For a few moments I just lay there, gratefully watching and reflecting on the miracle of still being among the living. As I picked myself up, I saw Thompson suddenly swivel ninety degrees to his left and fire his entire magazine at a low target I could not as yet see, practically at his feet.

I ran down the road after the others and looked over the parapet, half expecting to see my opponent killed or wounded, but there was no trace of him or anybody else. The only time he could have escaped was while I had looked down at my tommy gun or when I had turned my head to look at the approaching troop.

Then I saw Thompson's target. Just around the corner of the Ouistreham-Caen road were two enemy soldiers, each with a formidable belt-fed German machine gun. Thompson had shot both of them as they lay in the shallow ditch that ran along the left side of the road. They were way out of position, for they clearly should have been at the junction, covering both approaches. Had they been there, I would most certainly have been killed. A cross fire from just one of them in support of the man with the machine carbine would have sliced me in two.

Why had they not been where they belonged?

I guessed that they were the ones who had killed the luckless cyclist in what was probably one of their first combat encounters. Traumatized and scared of what would happen to them now that the invasion was clearly under way, they had instinctively pulled back a few feet from the corner in the direction of Ouistreham. Both of them looked appallingly young. Both were alive, though one of them just barely. I interrogated the less seriously wounded one, an Austrian from Graz, in Styria. He said they were seventeen and fifteen years old.

"We didn't fire a shot," the Austrian said so emphatically that I was convinced they had killed our cyclist, even before I noticed their half empty machine gun belts. "The *feldwebel* told us to stay here and hold out while he went to get reinforcements. We haven't seen him since."

I became aware that someone was looking over my shoulder. Corporal Thompson had come back after the troop had charged into the walled courtyard of the first house at the intersection. They had been fired upon from upstairs windows, and hand grenades had been lobbed down. The grenades did surprisingly little damage, though one splinter caught Troop Sergeant-Major Collins in the rear end; he carried on gamely.

Thompson, young, tall, with short-cropped ginger hair, looked distressed and embarrassed. "I have never shot anyone," he said. "How do you say 'I'm sorry' in German?"

"*Verzeihung—es tut mir leid,*" I replied. He repeated after me as best he could.

"We didn't shoot at all," repeated the Austrian, as if that mattered. "Can we be evacuated right away?"

"Give us a chance," I replied. "We've just got here. You'll be taken care of as soon as possible."

"Move my bread bag. It hurts. Why can't we be transported on those vehicles?"

"What vehicles?"

"Can't you hear them?"

I listened. I heard tanks. *Bad news,* I thought. As far as I knew, none of ours were this far inland yet.

As I crouched down in anticipation, the tanks appeared down the same road on which I had just come. They were ours—two Sherman tanks, a beautiful sight. They lingered for a few moments while we rushed to get our bicycles. Then we pointed out the house where the grenade throwers presumably still lurked upstairs.

The lead tank commander was riding high out of his turret. We got a thumbs-up sign before he closed his turret and swung his cannon around until its muzzle was no more than a foot from the second-story wall of the house we had indicated. He fired a couple of rounds, tearing a ragged hole as big as an automobile wheel in the side of the house. All was quiet inside. We rode past the smoldering shell hole, having no time to check on what had happened inside.

Around the next corner was the *mairie,* Bénouville's town hall, and the first bridge. The lead glider of D Company of the Oxfordshire and Buckinghamshire Light Infantry had crash-landed practically on the bridge. Several of the other gliders were not far away, nor were the bodies of some of the bridge's German defenders. It was as if the drama of the earliest hours of D day had been depicted by Madame Tussaud. The waxen-looking corpses of the enemy soldiers added to the effect.

Here we met the first of our brothers with red berets (maroon, really), dug in on the approaches to the bridge, cheering us on as we advanced. Their task had been to try to take the bridges intact, before the enemy could set off the demolition charges doubtlessly prepared to deny the invasion of the essential high ground. Only from this high ground could observed fire on the beach area be effective. If the Germans had continued to hold the high ground, the success of the Allied landing could have been jeopardized.

But the Ox and Bucks had been spectacularly successful. In what Air Chief Marshal Leigh Mallory of the RAF later described as the greatest feat of flying of World War II, the pilots of the Glider Pilot Regiment had landed three of the six Horsa gliders next to the bridges and the remaining three also landed near enough to contribute to the fighting. Deliberately made of flimsy plywood to facilitate a quick exit, the gliders practically disintegrated on landing, stunning the passengers momentarily in several instances. Undaunted, they overpowered the defenders with great spirit and a minimum of casualties. Then there was only one more thing to do. Wait for the Commandos to arrive.

"Give 'em hell," the airborne men yelled at us as we rode and pushed our bikes by their positions. I remember thinking that this was a bit overly dramatic. We simply intended to get to our destination, and to attack anyone trying to stop us from doing so.

"Hurry up; there are snipers around," somebody shouted, and at that moment we could hear bullets zinging off the steel girders of the bridge on either side of us. It was a powerful incentive to get out of there, across to the other side of the Canal and on to the river bridge.

I had dumped my coiled 200-foot mountaineering rope by the bank, delighted to be rid of the extra load. There it would remain, to be used in case of subsequent damage to either bridge by shelling or aerial bombardment.

At the top of a rise in the road, we came upon a house with a garden full of pottery animal figures and urns, apparently some sort of cottage industry. A matronly woman in a well-washed blue dress, carrying a huge pitcher of the same appearance as the items on the lawn, beckoned us into her garden to have some *cidre*, (fermented apple juice). We decided to take a short break, now noticing how parched our throats had become.

Refreshed, we continued. The two-man slit trenches with cheering airborne or parachutists became fewer and farther between. Often the road would cease abruptly, cut by huge bomb craters, and we would have to dismount and push our bikes around them into the fields. Now and then we would be fired upon, but generally imprecisely from a considerable distance. Our reaction was simply to cycle faster, to get out of range. Finally, in the early afternoon, we approached Varaville, our destination.

We heard intense firing ahead of us. The Canadian parachute unit that had landed in this area during the night, the farthest inland penetration of D day, had not yet captured the whole village. They politely declined Captain Robinson's offer of help in their battle, assuring him that they would be finished shortly. We welcomed the opportunity to rest awhile, as it had been an exhausting day, physically and emotionally. We had not consumed anything except the cider and a rib or two of the bitter chocolate bar that came with our twenty-four-hour dehydrated emergency ration packs.

We pulled into a long driveway of a farm on the left-hand side of the road, lowered our bicycles onto the grass, and lounged near them in the shade. Only about thirty men of the bicycle troop to which I was attached had made it this far. Happily, a few more stragglers arrived later; some had had flat tires or minor injuries. Some turned up on any bicycle they had been able to "borrow" or steal: heavy black German Army bikes and dainty ladies bikes. Most locking chains were no match for the wire cutters we carried. These straggler cyclists knew that they had to make it to Varaville.

At last I had the opportunity to examine my tommy gun more carefully and to clean it after its exposure to sea and sand. One round had stuck halfway up the barrel. The pull-through provided for cleaning would not go through, and I had to push out the round with a pencil. I shudder to think what would have happened to me if I had fired another shot at that German behind the parapet.

It turned out that the well-meaning soul whose idea it was to issue us these special thirty-round magazines, to give us extra firepower instead of the shorter, lighter twenty-round ones, almost did us in. For the larger magazine not only caused double feeds and jammed rounds but was simply too heavy for the magazine catch, so that the slightest movement caused the long black magazine to fall clattering to the ground, as happened to Harry Drew when landing.

The T junction of the road between Cabourg on the coast and Troarn, our objective for the night, lay less than a mile ahead. Because of the tactical importance of this juction, the Germans had fortified it and were fighting hard to retain possession.

My rest on the grass did not last long. I received word that there was a wounded German officer bedded down in one of the barns of the farm, so I rushed over to interrogate him.

The dark-haired young lieutenant lay unguarded because, although he seemed in fairly good shape, he was deemed not fit enough to run away. I searched him routinely and found a list of his unit's personnel and armament, as well as a strange-looking propelling pencil. Being new at my job, I was determined to be as thorough and cautious as my training had taught me. I took the pencil completely apart and found it to be . . . a pencil.

"Afraid it's loaded?" asked the prisoner sarcastically.

"*Vorsicht ist die Mutter der Weisheit,*" I responded, which is an old German proverb: "Caution is the mother of wisdom." Surely he knew that one, I said.

Then he asked a question I was to hear again and again:"How come you speak such perfect German?"

I answered it as I always would on future occasions: "I'm the one who asks the questions here."

By this time, the Canadian parachutists had won their battle. They marched away in great spirits in the direction from which we had just come, to rejoin their 6th Airborne Division. With them were forty-five prisoners they had taken, a sullen, disheveled lot who would probably have given up much sooner had it not been for the tenacious attitude of their commander. This officer fought literally to his last bullet. A White Russian, wearing a green German medal ribbon unknown to me, he had been so seriously wounded that the medics urged me not to interrogate him. He stood his ground as long as he could stand at all, firing several weapons that his little teenage orderly loaded for him. Miraculously, the youngster didn't have a scratch, but my efforts at interrogating him came to naught, because he spoke only Russian. His boss was rushed away by some French civilian Samaritans in an ancient blue car bearing a hastily painted red cross.

The Canadians had obviously been told, as we had, that once they had accomplished their tasks, they would be returning to England. So, thinking that they were marching off to their reembarkation point, they threw their Sweet Caporal cigarettes to us as we watched them pull out, cheering them on from the side of the road.

We took over what had been the German positions. Because the enemy knew exactly where and what these positions were, we generally didn't like to do that. The positions consisted of a command dugout from which a circular firing trench curled like the curve on a snail shell. At one point it was connected to additional trenches on the other side of the road leading to Troarn. In fact it tunneled under the road, so we could reach each position from the other without being observed. This second stronghold was equipped with three old German Maxim machine guns with drum magazines, a welcome addition to our scanty firepower. But the greatest prize of all was a 3.7-inch Pak *(Panzer Abwehr Kanone)* antitank gun, mounted on a dug-in electrically operated circular stand. This weapon, which the Germans had failed to demolish, undoubtedly saved our lives. There was ammunition galore, although all of it was of the armor-piercing variety. Obviously, the enemy had expected an attack by our tanks rather than an assault by special forces.

I examined the small artillery piece closely. We had learned about it in training, but this was the first time I had seen a real so-called *Festungs-Pak* (fortification antitank gun). The Germans had followed one of their favorite routine practices. On little metal vignettes were complete directions for its use. Around the inside of the turret were drawings of every feature of the surrounding scenery with the precisely measured distance lettered next to it. A tall, solitary tree, for instance, neatly drawn, was noted at 624 meters. The Germans had used their years of preparation for an Allied invasion most constructively, for us, as it turned out.

Then we had another stroke of luck. British Army Commandos all wear their former unit's cap badges on their green berets. I had noticed one stocky, oval-faced, fair-haired lad wearing the badge of the Royal Artillery, the brass side view of a cannon, with the regiment's motto *Ubique* (being everywhere) under it. It was, to my mind at that moment, a wonderful thing to behold. *Ubique* indeed!

Here was my chance. I translated the German inscriptions word for word while Bombardier Richardson listened attentively. He decided to ask Captain Robinson if he and his mate could fire the gun. "Are you out of your minds?" replied Robinson "Do you want to bring down all the available counterbattery fire of the Germans on our heads? Keep practicing dry runs, and if and when an emergency arises, I'll give you the order to fire. You two are excused from all duties so you can practice. Carry on."

At last we had a chance to do what the British soldiers had been yearning to do all day long. Brew up some tea and even eat our dehydrated porridge or soup. It was hard to tell by the taste which was which.

It was beginning to get dark. Our elation about having the gun and gunners to use was ended suddenly by several pieces of bad news. First, the other units to our right and left had not contacted us, nor could we elicit any radio response from them. We therefore had to assume that they had not made it to their respective objectives. We were alone.

Second, our signaler could not receive 6 Commando headquarters on his No. 18 wireless set, and they, presumably, couldn't hear him either. The set worked all right, but there was much activity on the airwaves. Allied units, German communications—all frequencies seemed abuzz with messages of varying degrees of urgency. We were the farthest ones away and were therefore unable to hear or be heard. Being out of communication with the outside world made us wonder if perhaps the whole invasion had been repulsed and we were the only Allied troops still ashore. In the words of Queen Victoria, we were "not interested in the possibilities of defeat: they do not exist." But still, the thought occurred.

We actually occupied only the westernmost end of the village, the T junction in the road beyond the first houses. Some 200 yards southwest of our position was a château, a medium-sized two-story mansion. It seemed deserted.

We had to demolish two small bridges across culverts to protect us from any armored thrust, and the explosions aroused the curiosity of some of the villagers. They came out to take a look at us newcomers. Some of them told a story of a downed plane or glider a little distance away, only one and a half kilometers, perhaps. Some twenty soldiers were there, apparently unhurt and as yet unmolested by the Germans. Could we not go and get them? We thought it would be a good idea, especially because we were understrength and were bound to be counterattacked sooner or later. I asked Captain Robinson.

"No, I'm afraid we can't," he said. "Our orders are to stay in Varaville and hold it until further notice. I cannot risk jeopardizing the lives of the men here by sending them out on uncertain adventures."

Then he gave me my second assignment: "Tell these people," he said, waving a hand in the general direction of the sight-seeing villagers, "that if they walk about after dark they will be shot. I can't have my field of fire obstructed, and during the night we won't be able to tell who is who."

He assumed of course that I spoke French, on the premise that anyone who spoke German must surely speak all European languages. The responsibility of imparting this important message in my schoolboy French weighed heavily upon me. I didn't want to be the cause of civilian deaths in Varaville, so I asked the nearest civilian bystander where the local priest lived.

There was hardly a glimmer of daylight left when I breathlessly arrived at the house of the local parish priest. A tall, pink-faced man barely thirty years old, with a receding hairline, answered my knock.

"*Ah, monsieur-le-Curé,*" I began.

"*Vous parlez français,*" he exclaimed joyfully. I begged him to pay attention since I had a very important message from the British commandant.

But he spoke first. "I have a most important question to ask of you. How fortunate that you know our language. Do you think it is safe here in Varaville? Would I be better off if I cycled to Troarn?"

"My dear Father, please pay attention to what I have to tell you." And I told him that I couldn't answer his question. I had no idea in whose hands Troarn was at that moment. Moreover, even if I had known I would not have been allowed to tell him. And if I had known, and we had been permitted to tell him the disposition of the Allied forces, I could not have advised him where he would be safer. That would depend on the developments of the next few days, who prevailed, where, and when. "My advice, Monsieur, is that you take sufficient food and go into your cellar and stay there for the next few days, then come out cautiously, to see what has happened."

He looked unhappy. "One problem: we have no cellars here. Normandy is too wet."

"Then go into the sturdiest building you can find, probably the church, and stay there. But I have the most important order for you and all the village." I told him about being shot. "Please go from house to house posthaste to ensure the safety of all the inhabitants."

He still looked unhappy. "My housekeeper and I could be in Troarn in fifteen minutes. . . ." Forlorn, he ambled off on his mission, shaking his head.

At 2130 our wireless operator happened upon a BBC broadcast: the Eisenhower proclamation about D day and its success so far—in German. This laid to rest what apprehensions we might have had about being alone. I instantly translated what the supreme commander said, and my British comrades cheered.

D day was coming to a close, at long last.

That was when the counterattack began.

16 Posted Missing in Action

The château a couple of hundred yards behind us was the first to be hit when the shelling began. It burst into flames; apparently, it had served as an ammunition dump for the enemy. When the artillery shell struck what must have been stacked crates of ammunition, it set off not only a blaze that lit up the mellow, hedge-hemmed countryside, but also spectacular and actually rather beautiful fireworks. Minor explosions alternated with dash lines of luminous orange tracer bullets streaming off into the blue darkness of the night.

Whether the Germans destroyed the château deliberately or whether they did so ranging for our position, I don't know; but it became obvious that they had heard of the loss of their fortified strongpoint and that they were doing their damnedest to dislodge us with a massive barrage of medium artillery, to be inevitably followed by a night or dawn infantry counterattack.

Luckily, the screaming shells sailed over our heads to explode in a field right behind us. Then there was silence, eerie quiet. The Germans must have concluded that they had not yet softened us up sufficiently, because the ground assault that surely had to follow did not follow. In the meantime our radio operator continued to try to call up our headquarters to ask what had happened to the units on either side of us that were supposed to contact us and strengthen our front. No answer. We were supposed to hold Varaville until further orders. But the radio batteries were running low. In anticipation of the most likely orders we could receive if we lived long enough, we had laid our bicycles by the side of the road at nightfall, ready for us to jump on them. Our signaler was now on emergency procedure, to preserve what little power he had left in his set, our lifeline. He switched it on only every hour on the hour for two minutes. No answer and therefore no indication that he had been heard. There were only about thirty of us, and we were feeling progressively glum.

How on earth were we going to be able to withstand the enemy's absolutely certain onslaught? Then the mortars opened up on us. They sounded like wood being chopped somewhere in the night. The rounds sailed down in high, sizzling arcs, landing close by and exploding with ear-shattering bangs. There was an iron bed with naked wire springs in the main dugout, where some of us had tried earlier to get a little sleep. But now that the enemy assault was imminent, each member of the bicycle troop in the main command post was standing-to in the firing trench outside, our guns cocked, and at the ready. So were those of our men on the other side of the Cabourg-Varaville-Troarn road, in those German-dug firing trenches connected to ours by a narrow tunnel under the highway.

The first we knew of the beginning of the German infantry attack was when that position came under machine-gun fire from the east. We retaliated, probably too quickly, with bursts of Bren-gun fire and more prolonged fire from the captured old Maxims. As soon as the enemy gunners saw where our fire was coming from, they responded with witheringly accurate bursts of machine-gun fire. Four of our men were hit instantly.

Captain Robinson now gave the order to Bombardier Richardson to let loose with our captured antitank gun. It seemed to me that the first few rounds chipped a few buildings almost forty-five degrees farther to the south than where I believed the enemy was lurking. But Richardson soon corrected his aim, and in the knowledge that he had plenty of ammunition he continued to pump away.

Counterbattery fire by the enemy's mortars followed immediately. They knew precisely where their 3.7-inch Pak was; it must have been clearly marked on their maps. They hardly needed to range to find their target, but range they did, rapidly. There was one explosion just beyond the gun, then one in the tiny space between it and us in the command post. A third explosion was a direct hit. A cloud of dust hung over the spot where it and Bombardier Richardson and his mate had been.

We thought it was all over for us. How could our meager garrison hope to hold out against what sounded like a battalion-strength enemy attack? With the cannon and all that ammo, we had had a chance. But now?

Then Bombardier Richardson resumed firing.

He told us afterward that he had heard the mortar round coming, so he and his friend threw themselves down, lying on top of each other in the tiny turret. When the shell exploded on its rim, they thought they'd be goners, but to their amazement they found they weren't even wounded. Realizing how vital it was to stop the Germans forming up for their attack, they jumped up and continued to fire, to load, and fire yet again.

There is no doubt that our miniartillery saved the day: by dawn not a single German had made it into our position. But we knew full well that we could not last much longer, especially if they brought up additional forces or if they succeeded in bringing even one tank across the culverts where we had blown up the bridges.

Our radio operator continued to turn on his nearly defunct set every hour on the hour for just two minutes. At 0600 another miracle occurred. "Calling 1 Troop, 6 Commando: this is Sunray. If you receive this, return to HQ immediately. Avoid Bréville on your way back. It has been retaken by the enemy. Repeat, return immediately."

Captain Robinson told us to retrieve the weapons, maps, and binoculars of our casualties. We ran to get some of these items, and as the faint light of day broke, our first small batch dashed for their bikes by the roadside, covered by the rest of us. Then they threw themselves down there, covering the next bunch making their way to the road. Our gunners were the last to leave. Varaville soon lay far behind us. We were able to do this because our fire had so discouraged the Germans that they temporarily abandoned their aggressive actions.

When we approached Bréville, we left the road and pushed our bicycles across a field to an abandoned farm. We saw chickens and found some eggs, which we ate raw while taking a short rest. Then we braved a huge, open stubble field, traversing it diagonally in single file. Suddenly, a battery of German 88mm guns began to range on our line of bike pushers, striking short of us, then beyond us, finally precisely in the middle of us. Three men fell. I had been ordered to bring up the rear to help the radio operator with his heavy set if necessary. When the third burst of shells exploded, he and I had thrown ourselves to the ground. Unfortunately, this did not agree with his radio. It now lay here and there in several pieces. We reassembled them hastily.

The troop was spread out widely, so before we made a run for it, we used our binoculars to see if the three men who had been hit showed any signs of life. None of them stirred. We were just about to take off when we noticed a group of men advancing toward us from the direction of the gunfire. They were coming from the east, silhouetted against the sun—little black figures dotting the far rim of the yellow field—so we could not determine whether they were friend or foe. We felt that discretion was indicated and took a dive into some prickly underbrush. The radio fell apart again. We left it and the bikes where they had fallen and crawled deeper into the patch of shrubbery. There we lay perfectly still, facedown, as the men came closer. We strained our ears over the sound of the crackling stubble to hear whose side they were on. Whoever they were, they passed without noticing us, and we scrambled out again, assembled the radio, strapped it to the signaler's bike, and checked the three fallen men again with our binoculars. None moved.

Then we made our run. Just as we took off, we saw to our initial alarm and subsequent pleasant surprise that a vehicle was speeding toward the fallen men from the opposite direction. It turned out to be a jeep flying a huge Red Cross flag. The field ambulance was obviously dispatched by Robbo when he had reached comparative safety.

The jeep pulled up where the men lay motionless. As we ran toward them, we were startled to see all of them sit up. They had shammed death so as to promote the notion of a cease-fire by the enemy. The medics packed them onto the ambulance stretchers, for all of them were indeed wounded.

We asked the ambulance men where we would find the rest of the troop and were told that we would find headquarters at Amfréville le Plein, half a mile down the road at the end of the field.

After a few encouraging words to the wounded, we doubled across the second half of the yellow stubble field. There, indeed, was the road. We mounted our bikes and were soon cycling hard past the outlying walled farmyards of Amfréville, anxious to rejoin the others.

We encountered no one at first, but when we turned a corner a familiar figure came into view, striding rapidly toward us. "Peter, thank God you're alive." It was Gerald Nichols, who had heard that the bicycle troop had returned from Varaville, so he had hurried out immediately to see if I were among them. "You were all posted as missing."

We had made it back to the fold, but we were not able to rest for long. We were dispatched down a small, sloping, tree-lined country road to Sallenelles, a little village near the sea on the left flank of our beachhead. There we were to back up No. 45 Royal Marine Commando in Franceville Plage. Before we took up our position, I was able to do a little reconnaissance in the tiny village. To my great surprise I found at the only intersection a bar that was open and doing business. The patrons were all local citizens who were excited about the possibility of communicating a piece of vital military intelligence to me.

"*Le blockhaus!*" they yelled almost in unison, "*Le Blockhaus—Il faut capturer le Blockhaus tout de suite.*" (You must capture the blockhouse right away.)

A jeep screeched to a halt outside the open front door and out jumped the second green beret customer ever to enter that Sallenelles bar, George Saunders. He was the only 3 Trooper I had encountered so far, apart from the brief meeting with Nichols. This called for a drink, but I had never ordered one in French. How to translate *Scotch?* It had never occured to me that *Scotch* in French is *Scotch.*

"*Un verre d'Écosse, s'il vous plaît,*" I said to the young barkeeper, trying to invent a word, but he didn't answer. Most local men within walking distance were having a drink that day, a Calvados or some *cidre,* and telling the others their hair-raising experiences since the *débarquement* yesterday morning. The mustachioed owner was in the midst of them, so busy talking that the young man behind the bar, who wore the typical local light blue smock and dark blue beret, had his hands full taking orders, pouring drinks, and washing glasses.

I repeated: "*Un verre d'Écosse, s'il vous plaît—pardon, deux verres d'Écosse.*" I was going to treat George Saunders to a drink. The barkeeper looked puzzled. "Huh?"

I struggled yet once more with my request. He wrinkled his brow quizzically, leaned forward, and whispered confidingly, "Look here, mate, why don't you tell me in plain English what you want and I'll give it to you."

I was astonished. "All right. Scotch for me and my friend. And who are you?" I asked as he poured us a couple of generous helpings of whiskey.

"Ninth Para Battalion. I was dropped quite a ways from my outfit, and these good people hid me and gave me these clothes while Jerry was still here. Now I'm helping them out. Fair enough."

"The airborne troops are right next to us," I said. "I can show you the way so you can rejoin them."

"Not so fast, mate. I like this job. I think I'll stay for a while and see how things go."

We drank to the success of the invasion and to each other's health. George and I figured out that *le Blockhaus* (the one to be captured at all costs) was a heavy German artillery emplacement in a massive concrete bunker at Merville, beyond Franceville Plage. It was to give us trouble for weeks, for it was impervious to whatever we could throw at it. The barrel was retractable, and it would poke out only at certain times each day, fire a few heavy rounds at our beaches, and disappear. Then the steel doors would slam shut until the next time. The crew was invulnerable also: twelve feet of concrete protected them at work and at home. The locals' advice to get rid of *le Blockhaus* was sound enough, but it would have to wait.

Somewhat revived by the Scotch, I asked the parachutist whether he thought his French friends would mind if I washed and shaved somewhere in the house.

"The best place would be the *boulangerie* next door. Just walk in there and ask the baker's wife."

That kind woman was agreeable at once and sent me upstairs with an old-fashioned china pitcher full of hot water. I emptied it into its matching bowl on the washstand in the sunny front bedroom with flowery wallpaper. I stripped to the waist and looked into the mirror. An intense, haggard, haunted face was looking at me in surprised bewilderment. I had difficulty recognizing it as my own.

George drove off, and we didn't meet again. He was taken prisoner that very day, on 7 June, after suffering a leg wound. He was put in a German ambulance loaded with wounded. When they came to a crossroads, he noted that the German driver was worried about traversing it. George suggested that he could go and check it out, claiming that he was familiar with the lay of the land in general and this crossroads in particular. He reassured the driver that he need not fear he would escape, as he could hardly walk with his wounded leg. The driver agreed, and off George limped, but when he got to the thickest hedgerow he was off like a shot for his life and freedom. He jumped into a pond and at first escaped detection. When he was recaptured, he was hastily dispatched by train to the security of a prisoner-of-war camp far removed from the front. There he survived the war.

At Sallenelles we began to dig in behind some houses on the road sloping down into the village. With 45 Royal Marine Commando in front of us in Franceville Plage, we were preparing positions in which we could rest below ground for protection from mortar or artillery bombardment. Then, an increasing number of French civilians began moving up the hill, pushing handcarts and baby carriages, lugging suitcases and bundles, panting under their weight, all rushing to get away from Sallenelles. I asked them what was causing this sudden exodus. They replied: *"Les Boches! Ils retournerant!"*

It turned out that 45 Commando was withdrawing from Franceville Plage to a location behind us. The fact that it had been able to get out of Franceville Plage almost unscathed was, we later heard, in no small measure due to two members of 3 Troop, Dave Stewart and Percy Shelley (Strauss and Samson). Stewart, an owlish little man, was one of the superior intellects of 3 Troop. Older than some of the others, with a small, squarely built figure, he was every bit as tough as the bigger men. He had dark hair, a wrinkled forehead, and a wide, smiling mouth from which one could expect a wise opinion, or a wisecrack. Shelley was of average size with a triangular face under wavy, light-brown hair. The scion of a wealthy Jewish banking family in Hamburg, he was given to some eccentricities. The choice of his nom de guerre was significant. I don't think he actually chose the name "Percy," but it came with his last name, automatically; we called him that, and it didn't seem to bother him. On D day, 45 Commando found itself in a precarious position in Franceville Plage. Hard pressed by vastly superior numbers of advancing Germans, they were beleaguered in one of those typical Norman quadrangle farm complexes, stone walls all around, in which an imposing entrance gate served as the only interruption.

The enemy had grown bolder. Closing in from all sides, they had begun to toss their stick and egg grenades over the walls and inflicted several casualties. The natural desire among those within was to seek cover. There was no telling where the next hand grenade from an invisible enemy was going to come over the wall. But Stewart's logical mind assessed the situation accurately. If they could throw grenades in, the Commandos could throw them out. If they were close enough to clear the wall with their grenades, then they were close enough to be hit by any thrown by the Commandos, especially because there was even less cover outside than there was inside.

Rather than trying to organize a grenade-throwing posse, which would have taken precious time and explanations, the two friends moved swiftly around the various places under and behind which the men had taken shelter and collected from them as many grenades as they could carry. Then they pulled out their pins and lobbed them over the walls, concentrating on the areas from which most had been coming in. There was a notable lull outside following the thuds of the grenades exploding.

Then the two men worked their way around to the entrance gate, which was being sprayed by occasional German machine-gun fire to discourage any attempts to leave by the only possible escape route. Applying the same principle as before, Stewart and Shelley borrowed a couple of Bren guns and crept forward to the corners of the gateway. They poked out the muzzles of the guns without exposing themselves. Swinging the weapons right and left as much as possible, they fired a few intermittent bursts at the unseen enemy. Not surprisingly, the incoming fire ceased, at least while the two 3 Troopers were shooting.

Gratified by their success, they suggested to the commanding officer that all the men inside the complex should poise themselves for a sudden exit, spearheaded by a phalanx of automatic weapons, and covered by the two Brens. This idea worked very well indeed, and the Commando withdrew with a minimum of casualties.

The movement of 45 Commando meant that we were in the front line once again. We *were* the front line. Clearly this required a totally different form of defense. So we dug slit trenches hard by the road with a field of fire that covered the route that the returning enemy was bound to use. I tried to determine how far the Germans were behind the fleeing villagers. My breathless sources assured me that they were right behind them, hot on their heels. They would come into view any minute.

Captain Robinson decided that he needed a little more time and space if he were to stem a powerful advance with our handful of tired men. We moved a few hundred yards higher up the slope, where an open meadow with small clusters of underbrush opened north of the road. There we dug in once again so that we would be able to engage the enemy as he advanced up the hill in front of the last house in Sallenelles, a stately two-story villa.

Then Robbo sent out two of his trusted men to discover how close the Germans really were. An eerie silence had settled over the rolling Norman countryside. Not a shot was heard as darkness began to fall. When the two men did not return, Robinson ordered me forward to some bushes where I would be able to see the road better. "Report back at once if you notice anything, or when it gets so dark that observation becomes impossible."

I rushed over and lay down among the prickly greenery. I scanned the road and surroundings with my binoculars and saw nothing. The men did not return. It soon got so dark that I began to fear that an enemy patrol might get between me and my unit unseen. Feeling that I was no longer useful in my observation spot, I hurried back, glad to rejoin the troop.

The illusion of comparative comfort did not last long, however; the enemy began to advance, surprisingly noisily, on the road across from our meadow. Clanking weapons clearly indicated that they were moving into the villa in considerable numbers. It was a mere couple of hundred yards from us.

Intrepidly, Captain Robinson ordered our mortar man to engage them. The little 2-inch mortar barked a few times with devastating effect. It seemed that the mortar man had managed to drop one of his shells into an upstairs window, or it exploded on the windowsill. That's what it looked like to us who were watching anxiously. Blood-curdling screams cut into the night. Several machine guns responded at once, and the mortar man was killed instantly.

Seeing our position compromised, Robinson moved us fifty yards, and we dug in chest deep for the fourth time that night. The remaining hours passed uneasily with sporadic bursts of fire. As dawn broke, we needed reinforcements and food. Instead, headquarters came on our revitalized radio and requested medal recommendations from all troops, posthaste. When our signaler relayed the message, Robinson's answer was: "Tell them we're busy."

A few minutes later, brigade headquarters repeated the demand, more urgently. "This is an order; if you fail to respond, you will simply be passed over."

Reluctantly, Robinson drew up a list. It bore the names of some of his dead, plus a few others.

The radio came on again about a half hour later, but our situation had worsened in the meantime. The message to all units said: "Submit a curtailed list." Robinson was furious.

"Don't they have anything else to do back there?" However, he had to comply with the order.

The radio came on again: "You must shorten your lists much more severely."

By now our position had again deteriorated. An attack could come at any moment, and we were too thin on the ground to have any hope of delaying it much, not to mention stopping it.

Robinson grabbed the mike. "Now look here," he said into it, "if you're not too busy polishing brass buttons, or making lists, or whatever you're doing, why don't you bloody well get your asses over here and give us a hand?"*

At last we were withdrawn and had to abandon our bicycles. Tom Bell of 1 Troop, 6 Commando, who had good reason to remember

---

*The explanation was that medals awarded had to be rationed. Recommendations for the Victoria Cross (Britain's highest medal) had already exceeded the total of such awards during all of World War I.

that day well, said that we were going to be sent back to infiltrate and torch Sallenelles that night, after a rest. We certainly needed one. A nondescript, boiled-up dehydrated meal was listlessly consumed; then we climbed up a steep ladder to the loft of a small granary. There we flopped down on a thin layer of hay and were fast asleep in no time at all, but not for long!

Our next-door neighbors, No. 4 Commando, had come under heavy attack. It was the beginning of the enemy's determined efforts to dislodge the spearhead of the Normandy invasion. The initial counterattack caused such concern that we were pressed into action once again. The call went out, "Help Number Four," and we tumbled helter-skelter down the ladder after what must have been a mere catnap. Captain Robinson led us around a wooded slope and into an apple orchard bordered by a hedgerow. With his most experienced sergeants by his side, men decorated in the North African desert (one of them had won the Military Medal twice), he ordered, "Fix bayonets!" and we charged into the shallow valley.

The enemy had probably about six machine guns well dug into the opposite slope, but half that number would have sufficed to doom Robbo's dashing assault. No question about his courage. With hindsight, however, one can but wonder about his tactics. Perhaps he believed that the very brashness of his attack would intimidate the Germans and enable us to overwhelm them. But when all the leading men of such a charge are cut down at once, it is well nigh impossible, despite the example of the Light Brigade at Balaclava, to get those following to continue it.

The well-trained Commando soldier tends to be too intelligent not to recognize the hopelessness of a situation. He will take cover and try to extricate himself with all the ingenuity he can muster. This may be a distinct disadvantage for the kind of operation that demands blind obedience; on the other hand, individual initiative and independent thinking often save the day.

Robinson was hit immediately, the sergeant to his left was killed outright, and the sergeant to his right was wounded so severely that he was invalided out of the Army. Corporal Thompson, the Grenadier Guardsman who had come to my rescue when we approached the bridge at Bénouville two days earlier, firing his Bren gun from the shoulder, led the charge. He was hit in the stomach and died hours later. Nobody apologized to him as he had apologized to the Germans he had hit. George Thompson was a brave and sensitive man.

Tom Bell of Robbo's troop was hit in the head as soon as he broke through the hedge at the beginning of the attack. He said he remembers thinking, as the rapidly firing German light machine-gun (LMG) bullets whistled around his ears: "Christ, it's like a bloody swarm of bees."

Then he went down, and out. But he came to apparently almost immediately, although he didn't know how long he had been unconscious. "I found myself crawling around the ground when I came across Captain Robinson with his hand smashed; between us I managed to get a tourniquet on his arm. He didn't recognize me, as my head was covered with so much blood."

Troop Sergeant-Major Collins, Titch Siddaway (the captain's favorite runner), and two other men were seriously wounded. In spite of his condition, Tom Bell tried to help one of them. "He was in a helluva mess. He had shrapnel wounds to his head so that his right eye was practically hanging over his cheek. Somehow I managed to part carry and part drag him back to our lines."

While all this was going on, "Tiny" Struthers, a lanky, dark-haired sergeant, had been ordered to bring up the rear with his section, to which I had been attached. As we were running forward along the shoulder of the slope, he turned a corner. He saw the carnage in front of him and yelled, "Down!"

All those behind him, perhaps six or seven of us, threw ourselves down to take cover.

"Medics!" The shout came from ahead, just beyond and out of our sight. Stretcher bearers rushed past us and, moments later, returned carrying Lieutenant Billington, another of the wounded. We realized, since we had become aware of Captain Robinson's and Troop Sergeant-Major Collins's fate, that 1 Troop, 6 Commando now had no officers and no sergeant-major. The only other officer had been one of the four men killed the night of D day at Varaville.

During the day the enemy's counterattacks gathered momentum. Officerless, No. 1 Troop, 6 Commando was again hurriedly detailed to fill a gap in 4 Commando's line. A captain from No. 4 rushed us to a stretch on the upper Sallenelles-Amfréville road, much higher up than where our previous stand had been attempted. We took over foxholes along a line of tall coniferous trees, hard by the road just in front of the tiny village of Hauger. We occupied this line so hastily that we took no rations with us. This did not become troublesome until the next day, for we were so busy that we had no time to notice how hungry we were.

Another night descended upon us, and once again we were in the front line keeping watch for the next effort by the German units opposite us to destroy our hold on the shrinking territory we had gained. Fortunately for us, they committed no tanks to our particular area as yet, and attempted to dislodge us only with second-rate infantry. This was part of the so-called "Ost Battalion," consisting of Poles and Russians who had been press-ganged into the German Army. There were some German officers and noncoms, and their mortar crews and their artillery (particularly their 88mm guns) were first class, so normally even second-rate troops would have been a serious threat to our tired, lightly armed Commandos and airborne assault forces. However, we 3 Troopers learned from interrogating prisoners that the enemy was as tired as we were, for they had just completed a two-week exercise with limited rations. Some brilliant strategic mind on their side had concocted the exercise, despite knowing that an invasion was imminent. In fact, prisoners told us they had been briefed that we were likely to come when we did, within a two-week time span. In addition, they had just been exposed to heavy bombardment by air and sea preceding our landing.

Of course, their high command did not know exactly where our landing was going to be and whether it was the main one or just a diversion. This uncertainty stood us in good stead, for it made them reluctant to commit their reserves until they could be sure. That, no doubt, was why we had not yet seen any tanks.

Meanwhile, there was no telling that the next noise might not be the churning of tank tracks on the road or the sound of running jack-boots in a bayonet charge. Three two-man slit trenches had been assigned to me because of my lofty rank of lance corporal. It was my job to ensure that a watch was kept on the road and the open field beyond. My problem with this simple task soon became apparent: as soon as I made my first rounds, I found all my charges fast asleep, including the team on full alert duty. I started to chew them out but realized that an efficient watch was what was needed, not criticism, recrimination, and punishment.

I gathered them together and made a short but poignant speech. "You understand that you *are* our front line. There is nobody in front of you except an enemy determined to kill you. If you fall asleep you are quite likely to wake up with a bayonet sticking in your gut. Therefore, we are shortening the guard shifts to one hour only. Stay awake, stay alive."

I shortened their shifts to half an hour when I found all of them asleep again at the end of the first hour. When they were all asleep even after just half an hour, I invented a new system. Instead of two men keeping watch together, I had one man in each slit trench stand astride his partner, who would now sleep legitimately at the bottom of the trench. My theory was that if the standing man were to fall asleep, he would collapse on top of the sleeping man and wake him up. Half an hour later, I discovered all of them asleep again, on top of each other.

It occurred to me that the very fear that I had hoped would keep them awake was having the reverse effect. They escaped their frightening thoughts by sleeping. In desperation I announced: "All right, all of you go to sleep. I'll keep watch the rest of the night myself."

And I did just that, almost. The tree stumps seemed to metamorphose into enemy soldiers creeping up on me, and the bushes were suspect as they seemed to move ever closer to me. I caught myself dozing off time and again, then waking up with a start and a chill of fright. In an effort to stay awake, I reflected on a slogan we had learned in bayonet training: "The Germans don't like cold steel." I found it difficult to picture *anyone* at the potential receiving end not being kept awake by the thought of cold steel, and yet I kept dozing off.

Dawn came at last without an enemy attack, perhaps because one would have been too difficult to mount with the poor quality of infantry that the Germans had available. However, as soon as it was light, their artillery preparation began in earnest. It appeared at first that they were firing air-burst shells, but we soon realized that they were really conventional ones that hit the fir trees immediately above us. What was raining down were branches and twigs with just an occasional chunk of shrapnel.

Now that it was daylight, I knew that it was even more imperative to scan the field that stretched from the road in front of us to the edge of a wood. I could see farthest when standing erect on top of my trench, a position I was reluctant to maintain while debris was flying around. A new method needed to be invented. I stood upright, legs astride my slit trench, but I hugged the trunk of the substantial tree that grew right next to it. Thus positioned, I scanned the landscape in front of me with my binoculars for any movement. As soon as I heard the whistle of an approaching shell, I simply closed my legs and dropped into my hole. After the shell exploded, I checked that I was still among the living and climbed out again to resume my observation. Because the enemy was firing regularly with very short gaps in between, I got a lot of exercise.

In between I had time to reflect on my life expectancy. A week? What, I wondered, was all that nonsense about people not wanting to live if they lost a limb? Which limb? Which part of my body would I be unwilling to give up in return for life itself? True, I was likely to become a casualty fairly soon, but not necessarily a dead one. For surely there would be somebody left alive when all this was over and done with. Who knows, it might even be me. Then came the next salvo, and down I would drop into my trench again.

As the day wore on, the bombardment intensified. In spite of our situation we began to notice that we were getting hungry. Realizing our predicament, someone from the rear had rushed up as close to us as he dared and tossed a sack of canned Army rations in our direction. There it lay for the longest time, as nobody wanted to be killed getting to it while shrapnel was pouring down on us. Finally, one particularly brave and hungry soul made a dash for it, crouched down, and threw a tin can or two toward every one of our slit trenches. Food at last!

Our can turned out to be the dreaded "M & V" (meat and vegetables, chunks of inedible, unidentifiable matter packed in what we knew to be monkey grease). We all carried a small folding metal cooker into which we inserted a white tablet of dry, smokeless fuel. A match and a mess tin would have warmed up the fiendish concoction, but that day we ate it cold.

Suddenly, an extraordinary man appeared on the scene who was to lift our flagging spirits. Advancing upright through the underbrush behind us was a slim, young captain of 4 Commando, their mortar officer, Knyvet Carr. Tall and fair, his arm in a bloodied sling, his longish face white as the proverbial sheet, he scanned the horizon with his binoculars. While the enemy shells exploded around us, he calmly called six-figure map references to his radio operator, who had taken cover behind us. I wondered whether the young captain was really seeing the enemy, and felt greatly reassured when, after some initial ranging, he ordered his mortars: "On target. Repeat."

There was an anxious moment when the signaler called out, "Mortars running low on ammunition, sir. Mortars requiring change of position because of counterbattery fire, sir."

We heard later that our brigadier, Lord Lovat, had massed together all brigade's larger mortars, "brigaded" them, as it was called, so as to increase the firepower that could be brought to bear on any one target. This had the desired effect of breaking up the Germans' attack before it could leave the jumping-off position. Two more attempts by the enemy followed—one aimed at No. 3 Commando and the other at No. 4, to our right.

The first was repelled by Colonel Young. He did this by pooling all his automatic weapons and having those equipped with them charge the attackers. The surprise of this bold action worked perfectly. In the second attempt, the enemy had the misfortune to attack the exact spot where No. 4 Commando had placed its Heavy Weapons Troop, armed with Vickers medium machine guns and K guns (a very fast-firing machine gun recently added to our weaponry). Number 4 Commando's gunners held their fire until the Germans were almost upon them ("Wait until you can see the whites of their eyes") and then cut them down. All was quiet on our front after that. For a while.

Our troop was eventually pulled back, or rather over to the other end of the brigade's line, into No. 6 Commando's main position in and around Monsieur Saulnier's farm in Amfréville.

Amfréville is a little village with a cross-shaped church in the center, the main aisle representing the vertical shaft of the cross and the two chapels forming its arms. The church stands on a large, rectangular grassy village green with paths leading to its front and rear entrances. Because parishioners habitually took shortcuts from their homes that bordered the village green, well-trodden additional paths had been established from all sides and from every corner diagonally toward the church. In an aerial view, Amfréville therefore resembles the Union Jack (the British flag), with the church at the main intersection. The villages of Hauger and Sallenelles lie to the northeast, the Saulnier farm lies to the southwest.

The small triangular green in front of the farm's entrance soon was to become the stage of high drama affecting us all. For the time being, however, it was merely a convenient temporary grave site, as I noticed with some shock after I had taken up residence in one of the farm's several straw-strewn barns. Two German soldiers had been among those killed when our brigade had first taken Amfréville on the afternoon of D day. Their corpses had been lying in the sun ever since, for everyone was either too busy or too tired to see to their burial. At the same time and in the same spot, an unlucky donkey had lost its life, and it also lay there, flies swarming on its brown carcass. Looking out through the big doors of the farmyard, I saw two Commandos digging one big hole—for all three bodies. When I made some remark about the lack of reverence, which bothered me, I was assured that the procedure was merely practical and temporary. "What's more, none of these three is likely to complain."

Three days later, the entire Commando brigade began to be harassed by a roving German semitracked vehicle, a so-called Sdkfz (*Sonderkraftfahrzeug*) 251 or special motorized vehicle. This formidable mobile half-track would trudge along the tall Norman double hedgerows and fire its mortars and machine guns. The mortar it used was a sophisticated German invention: the *Nebelwefer*. Its six barrels would shoot off in quick succession, accompanied by a horrible banshee sound. Every Allied soldier soon grew to know and hate these Moaning Minnies, or Sobbing Sisters, which we had already encountered on the beach. Before any retaliatory action could zero in on the disagreeable Sdkfz 251, it would move rapidly to another position and resume its bombardment.

Stewart and Shelley volunteered to deal with this menace. They stalked it along a hedge-lined country lane and managed to throw hand grenades into the monster's open superstructure, killing all its occupants. For this and the previous action both Stewart and Shelley were given commissions in the field, although it took a few months for the pip insignia to arrive for their epaulets.

On one of my first patrols into no-man's-land in Normandy, I climbed up to the attic of a small farmhouse where I could get a better view of the surrounding landscape through holes in the roof. Someone who had already done the same thing had conveniently left a chair below the best of these observation holes. A khaki British pack was leaning against the hind legs of this chair. Ever wary of booby traps, I gingerly felt all around the apparently abandoned piece of equipment with a thin, straight twig and my fingertips. When I was reasonably sure that it was safe, I opened it. In it I found a heavy marble-columned mantle clock. Obviously, its most recent owner had been forced to leave his loot behind when making a hurried exit. He had wisely preferred to travel light when leaving the premises and to rely on his wristwatch for telling the time of day.

A custom had soon sprung up in Normandy that disturbed those of us ingrained with a sense of etiquette. Tired of the aluminum taste imparted to all our meals by the British Army-issue mess tin, some Commandos had acquired china or lovely ceramic country plates from vacant houses. The food tasted twice as good on Limoges and the like, but some individuals would throw the beautiful plates over their shoulders as soon as they had finished a meal. They claimed that it beats washing up. "And you can't take it with you anyway."

One of our lads, Tom Spencer (Stein), attached to 3 Commando, was not only tired of the mess tin but also of the dreary fare it usually contained. So he decided to forage the countryside to improve his diet, although there was a strict order in force not to interfere with the food available to civilians. But when two Commando brigades, whose supplies are designed for the initial assault, find themselves retained in extended battle, something has to give.

One day Tom was spotted driving a jeep into 3 Commando lines, laden with the carcass of a cow. The commanding officer saw him also and had him appear before him forthwith. Colonel Peter Young had great respect for Spencer, for he was an excellent, daring soldier. Tom spoke English with a pronounced accent, so much so that he could not pronounce his chosen name. Colonel Young called him "Mr. Spennser," which was a close approximation of how it sounded when Tom said it, and Tom called Young "Kollonell" and not "sir," as everyone else did.

But on that occasion Colonel Young was so furious that he did not call Tom "Mr. Spennser." For here seemed to be a flagrant disobedience of an order. "What is the meaning of this, Corporal?"

Tom reached into his pocket and produced a handful of shrapnel, the kind of jagged metal fragments that were littering the countryside everywhere. He held out his open palm toward the colonel's astonished face. "I found this in her. Poor injured animal. I kill her with my tommy gun, quick."

"A likely story. Can anyone corroborate this tall tale?"

"Sure, Kollonell, the second-in-command was right there."

The colonel sent for Major Bartholomew. "I understand that you witnessed Lance Corporal Spencer's mercy killing of this cow. Is that correct?"

Major Bartholomew hesitated. "Who, me, sir? Witnessed? Oh, yes, quite so. Saw the whole thing. Yes, sir."

Now it was Young's turn to be surprised.

"Well, I suppose that's all right. You may fall out, Mr. Spennser."

The way this scam had been perpetrated was quite simple. When Spencer's jeep had passed the second-in-command's trench, Tom had called out: "Major Bartholomew, sir, I'm taking some steaks to Kollonell Young. Can I cut a half dozen for you and your boys also?"

"Sure thing," had been the reply. "That's very nice of you."

Mr. Spencer, who had been a butcher in civilian life in Germany, certainly knew how to carve a steak.

Two days later, I had the opportunity to improve my own food and drink intake. In the early morning I noticed a slight commotion at the far end of 6 Commando's position, the Saulnier farmyard. The family still lived in one corner, in spite of the shooting war virtually at their doorstep. When I went to investigate, in yet another exercise of my one year of junior high school French, I discovered that the central figure of the excitement was an elderly woman. She had apparently moved to the more solid stone walls of the farm for shelter during one of the bombardments, in the front line.

I guessed that she must have hidden her life's savings under her mattress, for she wanted to go to her house most urgently to see whether it had survived the bombing and shelling, and if it had been looted. Her house was a quarter of a mile back, towards Bénouville. Could I take her there, *s'il vous plaît, Monsieur Tommy*, because civilian movement was restricted, and in any case she would be too frightened to go by herself. *"C'est impossible pour nous, vous comprenez . . ."*

We started out, I with my tommy gun, and the lady dressed in the obligatory long black cotton dress of the Norman peasant women, a gaunt figure with surprisingly bright orange hair. It was a sunny June morning, with distant machine-gun fire disturbing the peace only slightly. I walked with some caution, enough to be alert but carefully avoiding any dramatic movements that might alarm her.

Suddenly, we came upon the Sdkfz 251 that Stewart and Shelley had put out of action two days previously. I had heard about it, but I had had no idea of its exact location. It was not a fit sight for my gentle companion, who was traipsing along at my heels in her black high-button shoes. Several corpses lay sprawled in and around the vehicle, most prominently a blond young German who was hanging upside down from the top of the machine, with no visible wounds disrupting the waxen pallor of his face and hands.

I hastened the lady past the macabre scene and asked her to crouch down by a fence for a moment while I returned to examine the vehicle more closely. It seemed that Stewart and Shelley had not had time to search their conquest, for I found a mess tin, one of the beige kidney-shaped German Army–issue ones. It was full of delicious Normandy butter. A quick taste proved that it was not yet rancid and was good enough to eat by the spoonful. I also found two bottles of exquisite Bordeaux wine.

Later, after the butter was eaten up by me and some of my "special friends," as Hamilton would have called them, I kept the mess tin, which had the name *Hock* scratched into its lid, and threw mine away; the German model was far superior. I decided to keep it until the end of the campaign. It was not quite as good as eating from the purloined china, but it was more durable.

When we came to the French woman's house, she was delighted to find it scarred but standing. There were whole hunks of it missing, however, and the kitchen ceiling lay largely on the tiled floor. I wanted to accompany her on an inspection tour of the rest of the premises but she bade me wait in the kitchen while she went to the bedroom alone. Whatever she was looking for, she wanted to find in privacy. I was left standing around, kicking a tile or a chunk of plaster to pass the time. Doing that, I came upon two or three small coins in the white dust, and I picked them up. When she returned, I presented them to her, and she thanked me profusely.

On the way back, just before the Sdkfz, there was a far-off rumble, and a cluster of enemy shells exploded just beyond our hedgerow. We took cover briefly in a ditch, and I comforted her by explaining: "That was nothing, madame, just our artillery practicing."

As soon as there was a lull in the firing, we continued back to the farm, where a small crowd of her friends had gathered to hear an account of her adventures. Before I knew what was happening, I had become the unexpected hero of the moment: "And Monsieur found the money—and gave it to *me!* How unlike the *Boche!*"

Generally speaking, I have always believed that elite troops behave more ethically than the rank and file from conventional units. From the latter, one would often hear extravagant statements such as "we never take prisoners," implying that they were fierce and macho and killed all the enemy they encountered. On closer examination, I almost always discovered the reason that made their claim less of a lie than I had at first suspected. They never took any prisoners because they never got close enough to where there were any prisoners to be taken.

Yet, once in a while atrocities did occur, even among elite troops. Usually, these were caused by an exceptionally strong motivation, real or perceived, or by someone losing his cool. One such event came about during the massive enemy counterattacks in the early days in Normandy. A 3 Troop sergeant, a friend who shall remain nameless for obvious reasons, asked me what I thought of his colonel—the CO of the Commando to which he was attached.

I replied, "He's OK as far as I know. Why?"

"I hate the bastard because of what he made me do. We had these three SS prisoners in his headquarters when the counterattack was closing in on us. He told me that no one could be spared to guard them and he couldn't risk them escaping, as it would compromise the unit's position. So he told me to shoot them. 'Shoot them now,' he repeated. 'That's an order!' When I still hesitated he drew his pistol and pointed it at my head. 'You have the tommy gun, so do it quick. Or I'll be forced to shoot you for refusing an order under fire.' So I shot them. The worst of it was that my gun jammed as I was shooting the first one and I had to reload."

This account bothered me for a long time. I have no reason to doubt my friend's story; why would he have invented it? Clearly it was painful to him. I debated with myself on what I would have done, just as a person who had not been in a concentration camp may wonder whether he would have killed a guard even if it meant certain death, or staged a rebellion, or tried to escape. Granted, dreams of this nature came to us after Commando training, totally forgetting the simple fact that starved, demoralized humans are generally incapable of any such actions. Anyone who has ever fasted for 24 hours on Yom Kippur knows full well that weak feeling towards the end of the fast, and that is after only one day. What about being starved for a week, a month, or years? It is amazing that some concentration camp inmates *did* manage to overpower guards, stage rebellions, and plot escapes in their dreadfully debilitated condition.

Whenever I thought back to that day in Normandy, I like to think that I would have shot the colonel.

17 Summer in Normandy

Gradually, we of 3 Troop came into our own as we interrogated more captured prisoners and deserters and were able to provide instant intelligence information. Normally, prisoners are questioned behind the lines, and relevant facts reached the frontline units three to four days later, at best. When we captured a German Panzer division's reconnaissance soldier, a 3 Trooper knew at once that this man's unit had its reconnaissance out four and a half hours ahead of its main body. This demanded that an immediate alarm be sounded to prepare for an imminent armored attack. Such information days later would obviously have been useless.

We were much in demand for our other specialty, reconnaissance. Whenever any patrol was sent out, even if it had nothing to do with our knowledge of German, commanders wanted one or two of us along, and we competed with one another to go. We developed a feel for the enemy's tactics, helped by our familiarity with men who might have been our high school classmates. We young Jews had experienced life under the Nazis, so it was natural for us to push ourselves forward whenever anything needed to be done. Although all Army Commandos were volunteers, we volunteered on top of volunteering. In our case, when straws were drawn, it was the man who drew the short straw who didn't get to go on a hazardous mission. Our more dangerous undertakings were often entirely self-motivated; nobody had to give us orders to do what we did. If we felt that something needed to be done, we did it, and luckily we had the necessary freedom to act this way. This keen spirit, combined with the efficiency with which we carried out our tasks, built us a considerable reputation. It sometimes astonished us that we, who came from somewhat sedate middle class Jewish backgrounds, had developed what could only be described as a "cowboy mentality."

A week after D day, we heard what had happened to some of our friends in 3 Troop who had been attached to all eight Commando units in No. 1 and No. 4 Commando Brigades. We already knew that Laddy and Webster, the only two men of 3 Troop who had refused to volunteer to parachute, had been killed on their landing craft, and Franklyn (Frank) had been killed on the beach. Now we learned that Eric Howarth had been severely wounded shortly after landing.

Arlen, the prizefighter poet who had stolen my name and who had vowed that he would get a Victoria Cross or die in the attempt, succeeded in part of that ambition. He had gone out toward the German line with an improvised flag, a white handkerchief on a stick, to parley with the enemy to convince them that, in view of their hopeless situation, they should surrender. The problem was, the situation at that time indicated that it should be Arlen's unit, 45 Royal Marine Commando, that should be surrendering. In the circumstances Arlen's act was certainly a courageous and worthwhile try, but the response was a burst of machine-gun fire, barely missing Arlen, who beat a hasty retreat. This infuriated him so much that he traded his symbol of peace for his tommy gun. Blazing away, he advanced toward the Germans for a second time, just as he had done on so many training exercises. This time they did not miss.

When I heard this account, it bothered me that the Germans would shoot so blatantly at a white flag, not that such treachery was unprecedented. Still, in this case it seemed uncalled for. We debated the point and came up with a possible explanation. With 45 Commando hard pressed, an approaching vehicle had been heard out in no-man's-land. Shortly afterward it appeared surrounded by a cloud of dust, which made identification impossible. Fearing a tank or half-track, the Marine Commandos opened fire. As the vehicle turned to escape, it became evident that it was an ambulance. When the ambulance reported that they had come under fire, the enemy may well have decided to retaliate.

Our detachments with No. 4 Special Service Brigade also suffered heavy casualties. With 41 Royal Marine Commando, Troop Sgt. Maj. Oscar O'Neill (Hentschel), Maurice Latimer (Levy), Tommy Swinton (Schwytzer), and Freddy Gray (Manfred Gans) were all wounded; only Gray managed to avoid being evacuated, although he had been hit five times.

Latimer was injured while stalking the outpost of an enemy strongpoint. He approached a German sentry, unseen and unheard. To put the sentry out of action without noise, Latimer pushed aside the man's steel helmet with one hand and swiftly hit him over the head with his Colt .45 with the other. He did this with such force that he broke his finger in the trigger guard of his pistol, but he was not evacuated. Two other casualties were Andrews and Terry, who had gotten themselves a "blighty" (a wound serious enough to be evacuated to Britain), and that is where they were sent. However, both were back in action before the end of June.

For the troop, 13 June was a bleak day indeed. Norton, the man who had been on the raid when George Lane had tea with Rommel, and Moody, the superb athlete and sports quiz enthusiast who had felt insufficiently recovered from his parachuting accident on Salisbury Plain to participate in D day, were killed together in their slit trench by a direct hit of a mortar shell. Broadman (Sruh), the judo expert, was wounded at the same time, and Envers (Engel) came close. He had left the same position to check out some information at headquarters two minutes before it was hit.

Three days later, Didi Fuller was killed: wily Didi who always knew the answer to any problem or he would invent a better one, devil-may-care Didi who never lost his sense of humor. In keeping with our 3 Troop tradition, he had volunteered to go out and direct an air strike on a troublesome enemy artillery piece, the one in the blockhouse that had been problematic all along. American Martin Marauders were going to try to destroy it, once it had been pinpointed by Fuller, who was hiding in an abandoned nearby farm with a radio. He had reached his hideout by crawling unseen across swampy ground. The farm had been deemed a safe distance from the target, but one of the Marauders' bombs happened to fall short.

On the night of 11 June, Gerald Nichols had been sent on a reconnaissance from Amfréville-le Plein to Bréville. Harry Drew had been with 6 Commando's 3 Troop when they took that little village on D day, but their troop commander, Captain Pyman, had been killed, and they had been forced to withdraw from the important high ground overlooking the landing beach a few miles away. This was the reason why we had to skirt Bréville on D+1 when our bicycle troop returned from Varaville.

Nichols had been charged particularly to ascertain if the enemy had any tanks in Bréville before 6 Commando attacked to recapture it the next day, 12 June. He reported that he had seen none. Because he was an extremely conscientious soldier, I am certain that he made as sure as was humanly possible that his report was correct.

At the very last moment, word came down that a parachute battalion was better rested than we were, and that they would mount the attack instead. My friend Gerald Nichols was clearly disappointed. "Since they've taken this job away from us, let's at least go and watch them do it," he said.

"Do you think that's a smart idea?" I replied. "That fellow Dunlop was killed yesterday when one of our guns fired short. How do we know something like this won't happen again?"

"Look who's standing over there," Nichols said as we came out of Monsieur Saulnier's farm onto the little triangular green. Two brigadiers. [Lord Lovat had been joined by the commander of the airborne force, Brigadier Kindersley, who had clearly also come to watch the attack go in.] Now don't you suppose they know all about that gun firing short? They wouldn't be standing around there if they hadn't taken care of it."

"You have a point," I conceded. "Let's watch."

Nichols and I came out of the main gate set in the archway of the Saulnier farm, which always reminded 6 Commando's Col. Derek Mills-Roberts of Hougemont Farm at Waterloo. We watched the parachutists take a left turn up the leafy lane past the cemetery to the Bréville road, hardly more than 150 yards away. After another left turn, the village of Bréville was no more than 400 yards up the wide-open, very slightly uphill country road, with fields and meadows to the right and left.

It was the route followed by the airborne soldiers as the artillery opened up. Nichols and I were standing just a few feet from the two brigadiers on the patch of grass outside the farm when, with tremendous noise, shells suddenly started to explode all around us. Lovat and Kindersley were both hit—killed I thought. It was not immediately clear whether it was the Germans firing at the most likely as-sembly area or delinquent twenty-five-pounder shells exploding. We rushed for cover in the sturdily built Saulnier farm house, but in the archway entrance the adjutant, Captain Powell, called out "We need wire cutters, quick."

"I'll get mine from the barn, sir," I said, and at that moment two shells hit the barn, both on our side. One exploded on the reverse slope of the roof and the other high up on the thick stone wall, col-lapsing it, precisely onto my rucksack. Had Powell not delayed me for a split second, I would have been under those heavy Norman boulder stones. It took hours to dig out my belongings. The barn did not look attractive as a shelter then, so I ran across the court-yard to dive into a shed opposite it. As I opened the door, a gaggle of noisy geese, panicked by the shelling, emerged like white bats out of hell.

Hell, it seemed, had been let loose all around us. Nichols made a wild dash through the archway to where our brigadier was lying, motionless and bleeding from abdominal wounds. Nichols picked him up, forked walking stick and all, slung him over his shoulder, and, staggering under his weight—Lovat was a big man—reentered the courtyard. Shells were still bursting all around, and to bring in a dead brigadier seemed foolhardy at best. Why not wait until the shelling had stopped? But two of us ran to help Nichols, for he looked as if he were about to fall. He put Lovat down then and shouted for the medical officer, who was taking prudent shelter di-agonally across the long yard under some cider barrels.

Nichols ran across to fetch him, darting past the captured Sdkfz 251 half-track that had been moved into the farmyard and was now sheltering a number of people under it. Cover was hard to come by, as every available space was crowded. Someone said, "Don't get the MO out. We'll need him later with all the casualties we're taking."

"But the brigadier needs him now," Nichols snapped back, and I saw him pull the doctor by the hand back across the yard.

We kidded Nichols about it later. "What some people won't do to get promoted. You probably realized somehow that Lovat was still alive, and you saw your opportunity."

Lovat was given first aid and loaded on a stretcher, as was Brigadier Kindersley. A hastily summoned jeep tore off at high speed, the driver no doubt delighted to get out of there. Meanwhile, more shells were bursting. The airborne battalion's commanding officer, Colonel Johnson, came running into the farm, his right arm dangling by a thread.

"Someone give me a tourniquet," he yelled, and I went across and helped hold his arm while his bandage was tightened. As did everyone in 3 Troop, I carried morphine tablets. I thought I would give him some, although we were supposed to use them only for ourselves, but a new series of explosions spilled them—and me—into the mud.

Nichols and I agreed to go to see Captain Brown. Surely he would be able to stop the battery from firing short.

From the explosions we had seen, Nichols and I were convinced that most of the shells were coming from behind us, from one gun or one battery with faulty data. That's why we decided to find Captain Brown, the 6th Airborne Division's forward observation officer in our sector of the line. We knew him well because we always told him what we had seen of the enemy when out on patrol. He was located at the far end of the farmyard, just past the shed with the cider barrels. His jeep was parked under the roof of a shed open to the farmyard at its western end.

"I know . . . I know," he said, "but I can't do a damned thing about it. All I could do is to stop the whole bombardment, but I can't isolate one gun or battery. Nor can I let the attack, which seems to have bogged down, go in unsupported."

There was, he said, only one thing to do. Get the attack going and then he could stop the shelling. He pulled out in his jeep, his signaler at the wheel, with Nichols running along one side and I on the other. We held on to the jeep's sides, jogging to keep up with it, until we came to the attacking paratroopers, who were lying on both sides of the road. We urged them to get up and at them, to get out from under the faulty barrage. But it is impossible to crank up an attack from behind; you have to get to the front of the halted assault yourself.

We were halfway to Bréville when Captain Brown said: "Look here, this isn't your show. You Commandos better go back now." We remonstrated that we wanted to stay and help. "I can't take the responsibility. You don't want me to have to order you back. But there is one more thing you can do. Take this chap away. He's upsetting everybody. That will be a most valuable contribution."

Brown pointed to a paratrooper with a particularly bad foot wound. His boot was slashed and bloody, hanging down in strips, and he was hopping around on the other foot and hollering with pain. We took him between us, his arms around our shoulders, holding him by the wrists. We shoved a cigarette in his mouth to take his mind off things and to keep him quiet. Supporting and dragging him, we doubled back to the Saulnier farm.

An instant later the jeep that had been clearly visible from the German positions in Bréville received a direct hit, which killed the brave captain and his driver.

What had slowed the attack, apart from the delinquent battery firing short, was a strange coincidence. The Germans had decided to attack at the same time. They had brought up tanks during the night, a few Mark IVs and some 75mm guns mounted on Czech T-38 chassis. Their infantry troops were told that they would be opposed only by a few snipers, and that their assault was sure to drive us back into the sea because it would be supported by Stuka dive-bombers and surfacing U-boats. All this was romantic fiction, but they did mount a spirited attack before our artillery barrage caught them in the open, just as it had caught our men. One German whom I interrogated had run all the way from outside Bréville to surrender with about a pound of flesh slashed out of his right thigh by a shell splinter.

When we got back to the farmyard, the disillusioned Germans were beginning to come in. As I interrogated the first one in the entranceway of our cookhouse and adjacent armory, the building blew up and burst into flames. My prisoner's back was burned—he smelled like a freshly singed chicken. Some thought he had thrown a hand grenade into the cooking fuel. But I had searched him thoroughly while having him hold both his hands on his steel helmet, so he had no way of concealing a weapon or of throwing anything. The explosion must have been caused by a high-trajectory shell (from one side or the other) entering through the roof. Inside, 6 Commando's armorer sergeant and the film sergeant with all his cameras and films were burned to death.* I realized, as more and more prisoners poured into the yard, that they were adding greatly to the confusion. Fires blazed, shell bursts ripped the air, machine-gun fire rattled in the background, and the smell of smoke and gunpowder was everywhere. Bodies on stretchers, some stirring, some still, littered the yard. I felt I had to get the prisoners out of there, to brigade headquarters. I formed them into a platoon with the correct sharp German words of command that we had learned in our specialized training. I told them that we would double-time in formation to their next destination and that anyone taking cover or even breaking ranks without my express permission would be shot on the spot.

"*Verstanden? Das ganze links um. Linksschwenken im Laufschritt, Marsch-marsch!*" They performed like a drill team. Thus, all thirty to forty of them were moved with only two of us acting as escort at either end.

It turned out that some of our troops, still wisely under cover, heard my German commands as they peered out and saw German jackboots marching around them. Three officers and eleven men thought it judicious to surrender and came out with their hands up.

---

*There are very few pictures of Commandos in action in Normandy, for that reason.

18 On Patrol with the Skipper

We herded all the prisoners into a large barn near brigade headquarters. Yet more came in from all directions, usually escorted by a 3 Troop member. We were doing our best to take aside one at a time for interrogation but we were overwhelmed by their numbers. Meanwhile, the bombardment continued. The sound of loud explosions nearby caused me to look up at the ceiling of the barn, wondering whether the roof would come crashing down. That possibility did not seem too far-fetched, so I reached out to the nearest prisoner and took the heavy German steel helmet off his head and put it on mine. Commandos did not wear helmets in action, because we didn't put much faith in the clumsy things, but I felt that being shelled in a building created a scenario that warranted an exception. Another half dozen prisoners had just entered, and I was yelling instructions at them when a voice rang out from someone behind them.

"Sprechen mit einander ist verboten." (Speaking to each other is prohibited.) It turned out to be W. G. Thompson (Zadik), the Jewish ex-German schoolteacher of our troop. "Sorry, Masters," he continued. "Take that damn hat off—I took you for one of them."

The next day—13 June—we received bad news about Ken Graham (Gumpertz). The lanky, hapless fellow, whom I had known in the Old Hampshires, had had a series of unhappy love affairs and always seemed to be depressed. In the Pioneer Corps he had lost out in love a couple of times to his rival, the charismatic Zwetschi Marischka, the mentor and Svengali of my early sex life, who would nonchalantly waltz off with the objects of Ken's affections. But Graham had met Michael Merton's sister when both he and Merton were on leave together, and with the newly found self-confidence of being a Commando soldier and Marischka being nowhere

198

around, he had truly fallen in love. He courted Ms. Blumenfeld, and she reciprocated his feelings. They intended to get married upon his return from Normandy.

We heard that Graham died from a shrapnel wound in his thigh, which we had never suspected to be life threatening. That left only Sayers and Thompson in the 3 Troop detachment with 4 Commando. The next day Sayers was hit in the chest and arm and had to be evacuated to England. That left only one.

On the evening of that day, the Skipper requested Stewart and Shelley from 45 Royal Marine Commando and Nichols, Drew, and me from 6 Commando for a special and unusual patrol. We gathered on a little green at the northeast corner of Amfréville to be briefed. I was surprised to see a large assembly awaiting us, mainly members of the French Commandos. There were also three civilians: a small, dark-haired man of about forty, wearing the typical light blue smock of the local Norman farmers, and two younger men in light shirts, one tall and a bit gawky, the other of medium build. They were introduced as members of the Maquis, the local resistance.

Our task was to lead them through the enemy lines to Varaville, the village I had reached on D day. We were to infiltrate unseen and unheard, and to leave them there. If we did not arrive until close to daybreak, Nichols, Drew, and I were to lay up there in hiding throughout the next day and return under cover of darkness the following night.

One spectacular presence at the briefing was René de Naurois, the French Commando padre—a bearded young priest, he always carried a huge crucifix, which was attached to his belt, and a tommy gun. Presumably, he had come to the same conclusion as many of us 3 Troopers: that this was the last (or perhaps the first?) truly holy war. Be that as it may, he blessed us as we prepared to go on our way.

Percy Shelley had decided to carry a captured German machine carbine, an MP40, or Schmeisser, as his personal weapon on this patrol. He thought that if he were forced to break the desired silence of this operation and fire at the enemy, the sound of this weapon would draw less attention than the deeper reports of our tommy guns. Shelley was a competent individualist. He wore a positively nonregulation light blue silk scarf cut from a parachute that had been used for dropping supplies. It looked like an elegant cravat tucked into the zippered neckline of the camouflage parachute smock that we 3 Troopers (and at the time only we) wore with no rank insignia. Shelley and Stewart had received their commissions in the field, so he was a corporal at that stage.

One had to admit that Percy cut a strange and distinguished figure. A few days previously, the newly promoted and very regimental brigadier of No. 1 Special Service Brigade, Derek Mills-Roberts, had encountered Percy strolling along the north side of Amfréville's village green. He had his jeep halted at the sight of this strange apparition, for most men were more or less confined to their slit trenches. Members of 3 Troop were allowed to move around somewhat so that we could compare notes on information we had gathered on patrol or from prisoners—a great luxury as far as we were concerned.

"And who might you be?" asked the brigadier.

Barely breaking his stride, and with a casual salute, Percy shrugged and answered, "Shelley!" in such a nonchalant tone and manner that the brigadier was taken aback.

"Oh . . . ," he said with uncharacteristic calm. "Carry on."

As soon as Shelley arrived for the Skipper's patrol briefing, he squatted down with the rest of us in the center of the green. We were surrounded by a dozen or so French Commandos and headquarters personnel who were there to help communicate with the three Maquis, none of whom spoke a word of English.

Suddenly, there was the rat-tat-tat of a burst of fire right in the middle of us. The butt of Shelley's Schmeisser had hit the ground as he knelt down, and it had gone off—a runaway gun. Miraculously, no one was hit. The bullets found a gap in the crowd and sailed harmlessly off into the summer sky.

We were clearly embarking on a risky venture, the more so because of its illicit nature. Had we been caught trying to smuggle "civilian spies" through enemy lines, we would probably have been executed, legitimately. That thought never occurred to us. Certainly it was not mentioned by any of the participants. Nor were we told why it was imperative to get the three men to their destination. We set out as soon as it was dark enough, the Skipper in the lead.

It became painfully obvious that our charges did not know how to conduct themselves on a night patrol. They probably knew the way to Varaville better than we did, but they had no idea how to infiltrate among the Germans deployed all over the countryside. As soon as we had advanced past our forward positions, they stretched out prone on the ground and wanted to crawl. I told them to get up and do whatever we did as best they could—stop when we stopped, move cautiously forward when we moved forward, step where we had stepped, and keep totally silent at all times. They were to spread out just far enough to be able to see the person in front of them and avoid bunching, so that they would not all be wiped out together by one burst of machine-gun fire or a single hand grenade. Crawl on the ground by all means, but only when that became necessary.

"But how do you know when it is necessary?" they whispered in French. It was a hard question to answer. It came from training and experience. If you got it wrong, you were unlikely to live long.

"Just crawl when you see us crawl" was the best I could offer them. When we did go to ground, they were quick to follow, but then they would not get up again. They said they felt safer down there. But we had miles to go. Whenever we had to cross a barbed wire fence (not an enemy one, just a farm fence), through which we would normally run without breaking step, we would have to hold the strands of wire wide apart for them and lift their legs through one at a time.

The Skipper moved ahead at a steady pace, and we shepherded our charges along as silently and expeditiously as possible. But he had to halt and then change directions when we clearly heard the enemy digging in directly ahead of us. Trying another route, we were stopped again by the unmistakable sound of pick and shovel. The Skipper attempted a third direction, with the same frustrating result. That slowed us down badly, but what was happening made sense to us. For until that time the enemy had been strung out loosely with wide gaps in their lines. Now they were closing the gaps, one of which we had hoped to pass through on the way out and on the way back.

It now looked as if it were virtually impossible to get through to Varaville, especially for the nine of us.

But the Skipper was not one to give up. He told Nichols to take charge of the two young Maquisards and, together with Drew and me, skirt to the left while he, Stewart, and Shelley would attempt the right with the older Frenchman. Off they went. No more than fifteen minutes later, we heard a lot of machine-gun fire from the direction in which they had gone. We feared for them, but we had our hands full trying to get our two charges through another farm fence.

By this time they were exhausted from the exertions and from what to them was unaccustomed activity and excitement. Whenever we were working with one of them, the other one would fall asleep. The gunfire we had heard had really shaken them up and proved to be the last straw. So when we heard the enemy digging in ahead of us again, the two young men signaled to me that they wanted to talk. This was not easy, for we were so close to the Germans that we had to be extremely careful, especially with the added obstacle of us trying to understand barely audible French whispers. We managed it, lying next to each other and cupping hands between my ear and the speaker's mouths. The gist of it was that they simply would not go on. We believed them.

"Tell them that's OK," said Nichols. "We'll go back and try again tomorrow, in another place."

They replied that they could not go back, either.

"Well, what do they want? They can't stay here."

They whispered that they wanted to do just that. They had a plan. They would lie up in some underbrush until broad daylight, then they would come out into the open and walk the short remaining distance to the German outposts with their hands up, waving and shouting. They would explain that they wanted to be on the German side of the line because they felt safer there and because the Allies had no food and there was no work for them.

"Do you really think you'll get away with this and not be shot?" I asked.

"*Bien sûr—certainement!*"

They assured us that they had done this before and that it had worked. We could not help but wonder why this option had not been considered to begin with, if it were all that easy. We suspected that it was probably a spontaneous idea on their part, which seemed to them the lesser of two evils. Reluctantly, we left them there and turned back.* We walked well spread out one behind the other in a stubble field, away from the obvious cover of a hedgerow, for we knew that the Germans were likely to position their machine guns there, aimed on fixed lines in such obvious places.

Nichols was in the lead, followed by me and then Harry. Suddenly, a solitary rifle shot rang out, apparently from a spot close by in the hedgerow. It cracked past me and whistled by Gerald Nichols's ear. We followed our ingrained standard procedure. We dashed out into the open field away from where the shot had come, spread out, and then converged again in a shallow hollow after a couple of hundred yards. Nichols told Drew that he wanted him to lead us back the rest of the way. He knew that Drew, coming from his relatively secure position in the rear, would do this simply and swiftly, whereas he and I might be a little on edge.

Confidently, Drew set a rapid pace until we had almost reached the lines of one of the two French Commando troops attached to 4 Commando, which was the point at which we were aiming to return to our position. We knew that it was not going to be easy, as the French Commandos must have heard the shooting and were probably nervous. There was also the linguistic problem of the English passwords. So we sang songs loudly when we got close, songs they were sure to know, such as "Roll Out the Barrel" and "Bless Them All." Even so, we heard them cock a Bren gun when we were arguing whether the password for that day was "bread" and the response "butter" (as we contended) or "bed" to be answered with "breakfast," as they insisted.

"Call your sergeant—*votre sergent, s'il vous plaît!*"

That did the trick, and we were let in. Heaving a sigh of relief, Nichols and I uncocked our tommy guns and took off the magazines. But I noticed that Drew did not do the same.

*According to official sources, the two men did get through the lines.

"Harry, we're home now, you can relax." Drew did not answer, nor did he unload his gun. Perhaps he had been more shaken by the night's events than he had let on, or perhaps he hadn't heard.

We tried again: "Harry, loosen up. Unload."

He looked at us, surprised. "I never cocked my gun," he said calmly.

"You never *what?*" Nichols and I had had our finger on the trigger practically all night.

"I never cocked my gun," Harry repeated, explaining as to children who are slow learners. "Don't you know that it's dangerous to walk around with a cocked gun? What if it goes off when you're out there? They'd know exactly where you are, and they'd blow you away."

"But what if you'd had to fire in a hurry?"

"How long do you suppose it would take me to cock it? Watch me." And he flicked back his cocking handle with a wave of his hand.

"That's precisely the split second I'd like to save when I hear a German cock his Schmeisser," I said.

"Well, you do it your way and I do it mine." That settled it as far as Harry Drew was concerned.

Then we heard what had happened to the other half of the patrol. They'd had the misfortune to approach a hedgerow where the Germans had completed their digging and were lying silently in wait. The Skipper was leading, as always, well ahead of the rest. As he neared a dark hedge at a right angle from an open field, several machine guns suddenly opened up straight at him.

He was hit immediately in the stomach. The others ran, dispersed, and tried to converge. But the enemy guns kept up the withering fire we had heard, and the men did not find a friendly hollow, as we had.

The Skipper nobly tried to help them: "Cease fire!" Stewart and Shelley heard him shout in his accent-free German. "I am a British officer, seriously wounded. Come out and get me in. You have nothing to fear."

Having failed to meet up, each one of the three believed himself to be the sole survivor of the action and found his way back individually. Stewart and Shelley made it, but the excitement proved too much for the Maquis leader. As he came toward the French Commando line, he realized too late that he had forgotten the password. After all, he had expected to come back with the three Britishers who were much better at remembering those funny English words. He might have been able to argue his way out of his dilemma, Frenchman to Frenchman, but he froze and remained speechless a split second too long and was shot dead.

We 3 Troopers were saddened by his death and shattered by the loss of our leader. He was seriously, perhaps fatally, wounded—a disaster that renewed our doubts about our own survival.

19 "You'll Get No Promotion..."

The battle for Bréville had left a depressing number of dead men in No. 6 Commando's orchard behind the Saulnier farm. They were carried to a field in the direction of Bénouville for temporary burial. There must have been between twenty or thirty of them and a smaller number of Germans, although more Germans had been killed and many of them had already been buried elsewhere. I did not count the exact number on either side, but it occurred to me that a comparatively small battle had killed an awful lot of people.

Stretcher bearers unloaded the bodies in the meadow, friend and foe at random, in the oppressively hot early afternoon sun. Others dug grave after grave, each to hold several bodies. Empty beer or soda bottles, each containing the dog tags of the body buried there, were inserted neck first into the ground—a simple method of identifying the bodies while protecting the dog tags from the elements.

I had been detailed to lie in the hedgerow bordering the meadow to cover the work detail and to look out for enemy snipers. I had by far the easiest job, but the heat and the smell and the cumulative exhaustion of the last few days played a weird trick with my consciousness. I must have dozed off in my hedgerow (luckily, there were no snipers), and I remember asking angrily of nobody in particular: "What's the point of wearing ourselves out burying the dead when at any moment we might need every ounce of energy to withstand further enemy counterattacks? What do these dead men care whether they're buried or not? What a frightful waste of energy. Who cares?"

In my dazed state, Dr. Meyer, the psychiatrist, answered. It was Peter Moody's father, whom I had never met.

"I care," he said. "Don't you understand? I don't want my son to lie there rotting in the sun. I want him under the ground. That's the least you can do for him." I felt thoroughly ashamed. "I'm sorry, sir. How thoughtless and insensitive of me." Then I came to with a start. The experience had seemed so real, so intense, though Moody was not among the bodies being buried in the meadow. He had died a few days earlier half a mile down the road. So many of our men were dead. Moody, Norton, Fuller. One quarter killed a mere ten days after the landing, and we still held only a narrow beachhead.

There had been one new development concerning the enemy gun that Didi Fuller had tried so hard to take out. An artillery major parked his half-track behind the church in Amfréville, snug up against the gray church wall. He told us that it was his ambition to knock out that *blockhaus* at Merville. A slim, studious-looking man, he explained his plan.

"I've got to have my shells in the air when the Germans stick out the barrel to fire. Later than that is too late. If I wait until I hear them firing, they have retracted the damn barrel by the time my shells explode, and I'll only barely chip the concrete. Ah, but they are Germans. I bet they don't fire at random times, so there has to be a timetable, a pattern. I shall be sitting on this steeple here, with my binoculars and a pencil and pad logging in when I see the flash of their gun. A couple of days to learn their schedule, that should do it. After that I intend to turn their gun into scrap metal."

He was as good as his word. On the third day his shells were in the air before their gun barrel emerged, and he hit it precisely as he predicted. We never heard the gun in *le Blockhaus* fire again. The major departed a happy man.

Feeling better also, I was walking along the village green that day, to take my dirty laundry to the Alsatian woman who was doing my washing. She was a plump, friendly soul who previously had worked for the Germans. Now that she felt more familiar with us, the new occupants of the Norman village where she had settled, she asked: "Did you have to kill those German boys?"

I thought she was talking about the two who had been buried with the donkey, when 6 Commando first took Amfréville. "Yes, we did."

"They were so nice, bringing candy to the children and giving them rides in their jeep."

"Even so. *C'est la guerre, Madame.*"

When I was on my way back across the village street, a jeep pulled up. With a start I recognized the steel-helmeted general commanding the Second British Army, Gen. Sir Miles Dempsey. I snapped to attention and saluted.

"Corporal, why are you not wearing a tin hat?"

"I'm a Commando, sir, and we don't wear them."

"Why not?"

"We think they're too clumsy, too noisy, and of not too much use. Our green berets boost our morale, sir, and diminish the enemy's."

"I understand; carry on." The jeep drove off, and he was gone.

I firmly believed what I had just told the general. The Germans had to wear not only their heavy helmets but also a gas mask plus two filter canisters. We carried no respirators at all, believing that the enemy would not dare use poison gas for fear of retaliation by the Allies' superior airpower.

I was impressed to have encountered General Dempsey. It was an unprecedented event to see such a high-ranking officer this close to the front line. But I was even more impressed the next day when he reappeared, minus his steel helmet. Instead, he wore his general's peaked cap, its scarlet red band visible from probably a mile away.

It is this kind of sensitivity that gains respect for a leader as word gets around. We thought more of Dempsey than of Montgomery, for all his showmanship, even though we understood its arguable necessity. Most soldiers in the field admired the quietly efficient, down-to-earth generals such as Omar Bradley, Alexander, and Dempsey, not to mention the diplomatic Ike. The Montys, Pattons, and MacArthurs of this world were the meat of the media, not the men in the line.

As time went by, we were getting more and more tired of our miserable food. What we missed most was bread. We dreamed of bread, with perhaps some cheese. Because we were assault troops, we were not supplied like regular field contingents by the Royal Army Service Corps. In theory we were not staying in France long enough to make that worthwhile. Therefore, no bread. Instead, big square tins would arrive with circular lids that had to be pried loose. Inside we found what all of us called dog biscuits. We soon grew to hate them passionately. But then we discovered that the French loved them. These connoisseurs of gourmet food had been deprived of their favorite baguettes, their yardstick-long crunchy white bread, because all white flour went to Germany. It was to me one of the mysteries of the war why the Germans should want white flour, because they always had preferred black bread, or at least brown. Why the French cherished our dog biscuits was another mystery. I could only suppose it was because the biscuits were white, well, whitish, and were a novelty.

Exchange is no robbery, says an English proverb. But trading or even buying food from the local farm population was strictly prohibited, at least for the first few months, presumably to conserve scarce civilian food sources. Therefore, my enterprising friend Gerald Nichols got up early each morning and wandered up the Bréville road, past the cemetery, past the sniper who was supposed to be skulking there. Then he would cut to the right, behind the last few farmhouses. Next he would enter the low stone house of the Lemoine family, by the back door.

Monsieur Lemoine was a jolly, apple-cheeked man with an imposing brown mustache and a little cap that he seemed to prefer to the usual navy blue beret. He would sit at his kitchen table and offer Gerald a glass of *cidre*. That done, Gerald would produce the big square tin of bisquits, and Madame Lemoine would give him a loaf of brown or black bread. We German and Austrian refugees had been craving such bread for the past five to six years. It was quite unlike the square white loaves (cut paper thin) usually served by our English landladies. Because the biscuit tins were so large and the biscuits so *délicieuse*, Madame would throw in a dozen eggs.

That left our unrequited desire for cheese. But here in the land of Camembert, there had to be a solution. The farmers around our area had none. A rumor sprang up that some shops had actually reopened in Ouistreham, but that meant getting a special pass. With our connections in the right places, however, and the urgent need to check some intelligence information with sources in Ouistreham (of course), I soon acquired the necessary piece of paper.

The little coastal town had barely had a chance to recover from the trauma of the invasion when I arrived on my quest for cheese. I bought up all the Camembert I could find—eighteen boxes. We didn't need that many, but we'd been promised we'd be going back to Britain any day now, and what better gift for friends or relatives than a box of Camembert.

But the days came and went, and we were still going on daily reconnaissance patrols. Bréville was taken, and after the collapse of part of Monsieur Saulnier's barn wall onto my kitbag, Gerald and I had moved to the parish church of Amfréville. We set up housekeeping in the Chapel of Ste. Thérèse de Lisieux, in the right wing of the cross-shaped building. It became the meeting place for us 3 Troopers.

It was there that we heard about Harry Andrews, the man who didn't want to look down and tell me how high we were on that first parachute jump. We had been in the same company in the Old Hampshires. Hans Arnstein had been a brash young man before he became Harry Andrews. In his hometown of Erfurt, his father was a department store tycoon who owned a famous store called *zum Römischen Kaiser* (The Roman Emperor). In late 1937 Harry and several members of his family were released after several months in a concentration camp. The incarceration had come out of the blue, for no apparent reason. At that time people still asked "why?" when they heard that someone had been arrested. They asked out of the sheer habit of law-abiding citizens.

"Because they had scrambled eggs for breakfast" was the black humor response, but not many weeks later, any kind of humor became incompatible with chilling reality. Still, in the first few years of the Nazi regime, some people were, in fact, released from camps, having been thoroughly terrorized and humiliated but more or less intact. Others had gone insane; some had committed suicide. Unlike the later brutal limbo, some families of inmates actually received urns purportedly containing the ashes of their next of kin, accompanied by notes: "Shot while trying to escape."

Andrews's parents decided that it was high time to get him out of the country. To equip him for survival in a foreign land, they dispatched him to a suburb of Berlin, a place called Niederschön-hausen, to a so-called *"umschichtungs stelle"* (a retraining camp) to learn a marketable skill. However, after the *Kristallnacht*, the staff and trainees of this establishment had to disperse to save their lives. They met up again in early January 1939, but now the emphasis was to try to get on one of the hastily arranged *kinder transporte,* the Jewish community's desperate attempt to save the children, ready or not with their new skills.

Andrews, after enduring several postponements, finally succeeded in getting on one of these special trains. It left Berlin for the Hook of Holland, and from there the youngsters went by ship to England and freedom. They were put up in a former camp of holiday chalets called Dovercourt for its proximity to Dover, of white cliffs fame, overlooking the English Channel. Next, Andrews was sent to Chiltern Emigrant Farm in Oxfordshire, where he was to learn farming.

He did not think he would ever make a farmer. Much more interested in mechanical skills, he persuaded the boss to give him the job of running and maintaining the facility's primitive power plant. In his spare time he was addicted to his only valued possession, a record player that he had brought with him from home, complete with a few popular classical records. Even more precious to him was some recently discovered jazz music. Life was not too bad: the rough and tumble of friendly horseplay among young lads, and the music. On one of his rare weekends off, his cousin had introduced him to a wonderful girl. Liesl was also a refugee from Germany, and they fell in love.

One day the big flywheel of the farm's power plant began grinding to a halt. Because Andrews was in charge, it was up to him to keep it running. But how? He flung himself on it, disregarding the likelihood of injury, and kept it in motion, pushing it, riding it, until at last it resumed its humming revolutions. He was a determined sort of guy.

When his parents finally made it out of Nazi Germany en route to Latin America, their ship docked in Southampton. They weren't allowed ashore, so Hans tried at least to see them during their brief stay, and applied for special permission to travel to that port. It was refused.

As with most of us, the Normandy landing on 6 June 1944 was Harry Andrews's first chance at combat. Action at last. He must have relished the thought thoroughly.

The messenger walked into our church at Amfréville that day and turned right into the chapel of Ste. Thérèse.

"Have you heard about Andrews?" he said.

Luck plays an enormous part in warfare. Skills are not to be belittled, but the bold and even the reckless are not necessarily the ones at greatest risk. Somebody had to go first on a reconnaissance patrol, so Harry had led the way onto a path between the Norman hedgerows sown with S mines.

The S mine was a German antipersonnel device, a little canister filled with steel ball bearings; the Americans called it a "Bouncing Betty." When it was buried, three prongs protruded out of the ground, virtually invisible to the naked eye. When stepped upon, it sprang waist high and exploded, hurling its steel balls forcefully upward at deadly speed. That's what hit Harry. He was killed instantly.

The morning light would filter in through a lovely stained glass window, set high in the massive wall, combining welcome art and aesthetics with the important feeling of relative security. That is, until our engineers and demolition experts decided to blast away some trees that interfered with observation of the enemy. Their venture was entirely successful, but the beautiful window of Ste. Thérèse went with the blast, an innocent casualty of war. Perhaps the local population was disappointed that their patron saint had not protected her window more effectively, because the chapel was rededicated to St. Hubertus, a minor and marginal saint whose specialty was the protection of hunters. I would not have permitted the switch, had it been up to me. For Ste. Thérèse, with her bouquet of roses, had watched over me, a Jewish boy from Vienna, on many a noisy night. My rucksack and wine were stored in one of her pews, and I leaned my tommy gun there before I went to sleep.

I also stashed my Camembert there. At first, the aroma of incense blended with the not unpleasant one of ripening cheese. With the passage of warm summer days, however, the smell of cheese became obnoxious. One circular box after the other had to be eaten—quickly. It was then that I invented the wine and cheese party for special friends, as Hamilton would have said.

War is hell, but not all of war.

On the afternoon of 19 June, Thompson (Zadik), our last survivor with 4 Commando, went on a two-man patrol with that Commando's Lieutenant Littlejohn in roughly the same area as that night patrol where we had lost the Skipper. Their objective was similar in that they wanted to infiltrate the enemy line to verify reports that the Germans were having severe supply problems.

By getting an early start, Littlejohn and Thompson hoped to be able to probe for the most likely spot to get through to that same Varaville crossroads where my bicycle troop had spent D day. They crawled up and down until nightfall, observing the Germans in what by now was a virtually solid line of defense positions. With foxholes no farther apart than twenty to thirty feet, this would make the Commando's task well nigh impossible.

They tried to cross the Longmare-Gonneville road but could not make it, so they stayed in a ditch throughout the next day, watching the Germans from no more than fifty yards away. It can be argued reasonably that they should have given up, but once again that occasionally counterproductive Commando trait came into play: an insurmountable reluctance to quit, a desire to do the seemingly impossible.

They tried again the following night. Littlejohn went first and suddenly faced the muzzle of a German rifle only a few inches in front of his face. He threw a grenade and made a run for cover but was shot in the leg; Thompson broke cover and dived into a bomb crater. Because Littlejohn could not run with his wounded leg, he shammed being dead. The Germans stood by for an hour before coming out to examine the body, cautiously waiting to see whether there were any more participants in what they thought was going to be a larger scale night attack. When none developed, they approached the prone figure. One of them fired a shot at Littlejohn from two yards distance, but he missed. Still uncertain, they prodded him in the face with a bayonet. Incredibly, he did not flinch.

They took his weapon, binoculars, and watch. Apparently they had also seen where Thompson had taken cover, for they went off in search of him. Shortly afterward they returned and removed Littlejohn's boots. They may have preferred them to their jackboots, although I never saw any Germans wearing our footgear. Perhaps they were sent home for future use.

Littlejohn heard them say, *"Der Eine ist gefangen, der Andere ist tot"* (one has been captured and the other one is dead). Fortunately for Littlejohn, it seems they had no immediate plans to bury him. As soon as he was reasonably sure that they had left and lost interest in him, he started the arduous task of crawling silently away. He arrived back in our lines, exhausted.

Lieutenant Littlejohn, a small, roly-poly man with short, closely cropped fair hair and a round, boyish face, received neither medal nor citation for his unbelievable courage, because nobody could corroborate his account of what had happened, as if he would take off his own boots, shoot himself in the leg, and stick a bayonet in his cheek.

Thompson was taken prisoner. Now there were no 3 Troopers left in No. 4 Commando.

"You'll have to go there and take over as a one-man detachment," Nichols said to me.

"I'm not so sure I'd like that," I replied. "After all, we've been building quite a reputation here with Number Six. I'd have to start from scratch with Number Four."

Nichols said I had nothing to worry about, because by now the 3 Troopers in No. 4 had become highly regarded, too. Anyway, he said, someone had to go, and it made sense to send someone from the 6 Commando detachment, which had come through unscathed. If I didn't want to go, he'd have to send somebody else.

So I packed up my rucksack and went over to the little château at Hauger, a few hundred yards to the northeast of the chapel that had been my home.

When the Skipper was lost, David Stewart took charge of the remaining members of 3 Troop in 1 and 4 Special Service Brigades, because he was the senior sergeant who remained unwounded. He came over to the church to meet with Nichols and me. "Gerald," he said, "you are forthwith a sergeant, and you, Peter, are a corporal."

"Thank you very much, Dave," I said, "but do you really have the power to promote us to a higher rank? A paid higher rank?"

Stewart grinned from ear to ear. "Who said anything about 'paid'?" A week after my reluctant transfer to 4 Commando, Nichols and I met again in the Amfréville church. He proposed a typical Nichols idea, "Let's cycle down near the Longmare crossroads and see what the Germans are up to."

"No way," said Stewart, who was present in the chapel when Nichols made his suggestion. "Not two of you together. Only one of you may go. We're taking too many casualties. Can't risk both of you getting hit."

We protested. Since when had there been restrictions on our movements?

"Since the brigadier ordered me to see that all 3 Troopers are strictly rationed when going on patrols. More than one may go only with his express permission. Too valuable, he says."

I told Nichols to go alone because it was his idea. I was disappointed because he and I worked well together on patrols. The most important ingredient in this hazardous activity is mutual trust. Very simple criteria came into play when choosing men for a patrol. There were only three possible answers to the question, "How about Bill?"

"Bill is all right" was an understated solid endorsement. Bill knows his stuff, and if anything happens to you, he won't abandon you if humanly possible. He'll carry you in or hasten to get help. Your life could depend on the three words, "Bill is all right."

Or there was the reply, "Bill is no good," which clearly meant the opposite of the above. This may sound harsh and brusquely judgmental. It had to be. Your life may depend on it.

Or there was the third answer: "I don't know about Bill." This meant I've never been out there with him, or only once, uneventfully. It's too soon to tell. Be careful and alert.

Just before I left 6 Commando, Nichols and I accompanied a large fighting patrol in the same general area between Bréville and Longmare. The objective had been to snatch a prisoner and to intimidate the enemy into believing that we were much stronger than we really were and that, more likely than not, we were going to mount a massive attack at any moment.

Some fifty men of 6 Commando were to move into no-man's-land unseen at dusk and take up positions with Bren guns placed at the flanks. Then three men armed mainly with hand grenades would rush forward, throw their grenades, and grab a German out of his slit trench and bring him back alive. To protect them, our Brens would open up to the right and left of the narrow lane allowed for the small party's return. The captain in charge, moreover, would have his Very signal pistol at the ready; at the appropriate moment he would fire one green Very light followed by a white. This would bring down a few minutes of intense artillery fire on the enemy's front line, facilitating our getaway.

By the time we cautiously reached our starting point, just a few hundred yards and a couple of hedgerows from the targeted German forward positions, we had to wait an interminable time for complete darkness. Some lounged around, while others slept. When it was finally time, the three chosen grenade throwers advanced and did their bit, and did it well. I stood next to the captain when the Brens opened up on the flanks. Suddenly, to my surprise he called out, "We've got to get out of here," as if reacting to the bursts of automatic fire.

"I think that's our Brens firing, sir," I said.

"Yes, I know, but we missed the right moment. Damn! I dropped the green Very light. Help me find it, quick!"

I did, after crawling and feeling around for it in the grass. He hastily fired the green and the white signal, and the three courageous men came doubling back, unfortunately without a prisoner. But they had succeeded in startling and shaking up the enemy, so much so that they had as yet not returned our fire.

The first bursts of German automatic fire rang out only when the three men had already reached us. As often happened with their belt-fed light machine guns (particularly at night), they were shooting to the right and high, well over our heads. The combined noise of the exploding grenades, the Brens' opening fire, and the Germans' response caused some young Commando reinforcements to get a bit panicky. They ran homeward, their reaction no doubt stimulated by their officer's alarmed posture.

In fact, it would not have been a bad idea to go back at this point, but less hurriedly and more calmly. There was a real danger in moving too quickly, because we had come to our assembly area via a narrow path between minefields. Now, we were about to be rushed along it by what threatened to be a stampede, the most excited men prodding anyone in their way with their bayonets.

Nichols instantly appreciated the hazardous situation. He brushed aside the bayonets and yelled: "Follow me!"

Then he picked up an unused yellow telephone cable from the ground; he had noticed it along the obviously safe path on which we had arrived on our way out. He let the cable run through his hand as he led the way back. His brilliant move doubtlessly saved lives. We suffered no casualties and were back in our lines by the time the inevitable enemy mortar barrage descended on the place we might still have been but for Nichol's presence of mind. That's the kind of man with whom one likes to go on patrol. As anyone would have said when asked the quintessential question, "Nichols is all right."

That is why I was angry when Stewart would not let Nichols and me go out on the bicycle patrol together. But the next time I saw Stewart, he told me that Nichols had been knocked off his bike by a mortar.

A splinter hit his jaw and knocked out some teeth. "I think he'll live," said Stewart, "but I probably saved your life by not letting you go with him."

There were two things I had to do for Nichols. I took Lord Lovat's wading stick from where it was leaning on Nichol's kitbag. He had been saving the stick ever since he had carried the chief of the clan Fraser into the Saulnier farm. He intended to return it to Lord Lovat if he ever came back. This task was now mine, and I kept the stick until the brigade's advance eventually forced me to leave it behind.

My second important self-assignment concerned the Lemoines. I knocked on their door the next morning to tell them that the sergeant who visited them each day would not be coming again.

"He has not been killed, has he?" the wife asked anxiously.

"No, madame, just wounded," I replied. "As they carried him away on the stretcher, he said I must promise to come by your house every day and bring you these biscuits. Then he fainted."

Thus was the French connection to obtain our precious bread and eggs maintained successfully.

Nichols's teeth and jaw were repaired back home in Britain, and he received a well-deserved instant commission, but he did not return to us.

On my way back from the Lemoines, I saw an unusual and startling sight. On the north side of the Amfréville green, adjacent to the house of my Alsatian laundress, was an unassuming one-room restaurant in a little house built on the road, like all the others. Its only distinguishing feature was a small neglected greenhouse that bridged the space between it and the house to its left. That morning there were mounds of flowers in the greenhouse, and their colorful array caught my eye. Then, I noticed something else, the soles of two Army boots sticking out toward me.

The two French troops of our No. 10 Commando were attached to 4 Commando in Normandy. They had landed on what was probably the most difficult British beach, on the extreme left flank of the entire D day invasion, and predictably suffered heavy casualties. Their spirit and morale were undaunted then and in the days that followed, for it was a homecoming for them for which they had yearned for years. We of 3 Troop had an inkling of what that must have meant for we sensed it also as Europeans returning to the Continent after six years. As Steve Ross put it: "We may not have known what we were fighting for, but we sure as hell knew what we were fighting against."

There was no question that the French landscape, the charming villages with their little stucco houses, and the meadows resplendent with summer flowers awoke a certain nostalgia in most of us. This looked quite a lot like what had been our land, taken from us by evil strangers and opportunistic neighbors, just because we were Jews. But whereas we wanted to fight our oppressors and had few illusions about returning to our countries, our French Commando comrades were liberating their homeland.

During the counterattacks, the French Commando's sector of the line had been one of those targeted by the enemy, so they had lost even more men. One young man among them had an experience that was unique among the rest. In the midst of the fighting and the bombardments, he had met a local girl and they had fallen in love. She was the daughter of the innkeeper of the little restaurant on the village green at Amfréville. Properly chaperoned, for the standards of morality were extremely strict in rural France, the romance had gently blossomed. Even though they had known each other for only a short time the soldier had asked *le patron* for his daughter's hand in marriage, pleading special circumstances—so little time, the war. The family took him in like a son, but he went on a night patrol and was killed. His comrades brought the body back, heeding the plea of the bride-to-be and her parents to hand it over to them. They felt the least they could do was to give him a decent burial, not just the usual interment in a lime-lined hole in the ground. So he was to have a proper funeral, as the village would have done in peacetime. I saw him lying in state in their greenhouse, festooned with flowers, while the war went on outside.

On 22 June, Ernest Lawrence (Lenel) went out to obtain an up-to-date identification of the German unit facing us. It was important to know whom one was facing, because a new unit might indicate an attack in the near future.

Ernest was one of many brothers of a well-to-do Darmstadt family. Their father had owned celluloid factories, among other holdings. Their main products were the plastic detachable collars on men's fashionable white shirts. His brother Victor had been my Old Hampshire corporal, the physical training addict who had taken us on cross-country runs after work, the one who had told me that his crazy young brother had joined "some suicide outfit." Ernest was an excellent Commando soldier and had been promoted to corporal and Ken Bartlett's (Billman) second-in-command of our 3 Commando detachment.

Lawrence had painstakingly approached a German outpost and had actually made it, unseen, into the German's slit trench, a believable feat only if one knew Ernest's skill and dedication. A companion of 3 Commando was with him and was close enough to observe and hear what took place next.

As Ernest jumped into the man's trench, he snapped at him in German: "Keep quiet! Do exactly as I tell you and nothing will happen to you. But one word out of you and you are dead."

The German panicked and screamed. Ernest shot him. Then, not wanting to return empty-handed, and with typical Commando confidence and optimism, he thought he had enough time to get the man's paybook out of his breast pocket in order to obtain the necessary information. However, other Germans were closer than he had calculated, and they rushed and overpowered him.

Ironically, two deserters walked into our lines the next day. I interrogated them, separately of course. My first priority was to determine their unit's identity. That was easy. Both were Poles from the same unit that had been in the line opposite us for some time. Then I focused on Ernest Lawrence. By a stroke of luck, they had come from precisely the sector of the previous day's incident.

One of the men—blond, tall, and slim with a curved pipe with a little silver lid—spoke better German than his mate.

"Did anything unusual happen in your lines yesterday?" I asked him.

"Yes, sure. I saw a prisoner being taken."

"Was he wounded?"

"Not that I could see. He was being marched right by my foxhole under his own steam."

"What did he look like?"

"He was slim, medium height, brown hair, clean shaven."

I double-checked with the second deserter. Same description.

Back to the first one. "Give me any additional information so I can tell whether you really saw what you say. Try to remember it precisely. What was he wearing, for instance?"

"That's easy: he was dressed exactly like you, not like these other ones."

The camouflage smock. Only 3 Troopers wore them at that time. I passed on the good news. Ernest was all right.

The prisoner suddenly burst out laughing.

"What's funny?" I asked.

"I was just thinking. *Feldwebel* back there comes to my hole every morning. He know I smoke the pipe, see. So I have lighter. Arrogant German bastard he not even look down at me. "Jaschinski, light me," he say. Every morning. This morning he come for sure. Nose in air. "Jaschinski, light me." But this morning, no light for him. No Jaschinski. I like see *feldwebel* face!"

It seemed a pity to have to take his precious lighter away from him, but POWs are not allowed to have potentially dangerous instruments.

Ernest Lawrence was never heard from again. No notification. No name on any casualty list. No grave. There are several possible explanations. First, there was the Hitler–von Rundstedt order to execute all Commandos as *franc-tireurs,* but we were aware that most local enemy commanders seemed to feel secure in ignoring it. Second and more likely may be that the German soldier whom Lawrence shot had not been dead and had related that Ernest had addressed him not only in flawless German but with a Darmstadt accent. That might have induced the local commanding officer to remember the Hitler order. Or it might have motivated this officer to hand over Ernest to the Gestapo representative of his division. Or, it is just possible that he was loaded onto a truck en route to further interrogation or to a POW camp, and the vehicle had been hit by a bomb or a heavy shell and blown to smithereens.

Whatever happened to Ernest, we had lost another one of our best.

20 Bréville, Yet Again

"That cadet in the green beret, you are out of step again," the Regimental sergeant-major shouted at James Griffith (Kurt Glaser) on the cadet school parade ground. It was hard for these long-serving regular soldiers to accept the notion and concept of Commandos. "I get there, though, Sergeant-Major, don't I?"

Griffith was severly censored for his rejoinder, so the sergeant-major must have been shocked when Cadet Griffith, of all people, was taken out in midcourse, commissioned, and sent to Normandy to command a unit. Not that Griffith was clumsy; quite the opposite. He was tall and elegant-looking with a high forehead and a nonconformist expression that seemed to say, I'll do it my way. Watch me. It will work.

Griffith was one of the few in 3 Troop who had succeeded in getting sent to OCTU, the Officer's Cadet Training Unit, a move roundly and sometimes a little enviously criticized by the rest of us who had landed on D day in the meantime. In fairness, the men who went with him—Firth (Fürth), Street (Barth), Dwelly (Goldschmied), and Kershaw (Kirschner)—had no way of knowing that they should not have taken the chance. Eric Howarth (Nathan) for one, didn't go, because he thought he might miss the invasion.

The higher-ups believed that someone from 3 Troop should take the Skipper's place after he had been wounded. Field commissions for Stewart, Shelley, Bartlett, Gray, and Nichols had not yet come through, so Griffith's course, much to his delight, was cut short, and he was appointed to command us.

Griffith liked to be where the action was; he was not a parade-ground bullshitter. But it was not easy for him to come and take charge. Apart from having missed D day and all the action so far, he was now to command those who remembered him as one of the troop's medical orderlies, as one of us. The British Army formality of standing at attention before an officer and calling him "sir" did not come naturally to many of us. I sympathized with his problem and resolved to help him as much as I could, as I had always liked his devil-may-care attitude. So I made a point of saluting meticulously, standing at attention, and calling him "sir" whenever anyone was within earshot.

Well aware of the difficulty in which he found himself, he wisely called all 3 Troopers together and made a short but poignant speech. "I know as well as you that I was not here when all of you landed on D day. I wish I had been here with you, but I can't change that. Since then you have been gathering vital experience, which I find myself now lacking. Therefore I appeal to you to help me catch up. Whenever any of you is sent out on a patrol by the units to which you are attached, please ask whether I can come along also. I shall always be available, and I shall be very grateful to you."

It so happened that I was scheduled to go out on a patrol the following night. It was to be a reconnaissance into a forward hedgerow, to see whether the enemy occupied it at night. The main attraction of the patrol was that it was to be led by Maj. Pat Porteous, a famous charismatic soldier who had earned a Victoria Cross on the Dieppe raid when he had led a bayonet charge one-handed, because he had been wounded in the other hand.

On this patrol he was to command the overall effort, and his lieutenant, John Hunter-Gray, was to be in charge of the reconnoitering portion. I checked and received a positive response from both these gentlemen when I asked if Griffith could come along.

I had told Griffith to come over to 4 Commando's headquarters in Monsieur Farbre's little château at Hauger toward dusk. He appeared promptly in the war room (formerly the château's dining room), where I now usually slept under the table, a common practice for protection against falling ceilings. Lieutenant Colonel Menday, wearing a khaki sweater without rank insignia, was poring over a map spread on the table. He had taken over 4 Commando when Colonel Dawson was wounded on D day. Menday was a powerfully built man with dark brown hair, an elongated head, and a small mustache. He was exceedingly deaf. Sometimes this created the impression of imperturbability, of an intrepid leader; for he would often remain upright when others ducked hastily for cover, simply because he had not heard the approaching danger or explosion.

He looked up and saw Griffith standing in front of him; Menday had not heard him enter.

"Who are you?" he asked in not exactly a friendly manner but rather as one addresses an intruder.

"I'm Lieutenant James Griffith, Number Ten Commando," he replied without saluting, since there were no crowns and pips on the other man's plain pullover. "I'm to go on a night patrol with a Mr. Hunter-Brown. Are you Hunter-Brown?"

Griffith had committed three sins in one statement, an unfortunate beginning. He had gotten Hunter-Gray's name wrong, which was bad enough, but worse than that he confused a lieutenant colonel with a junior subaltern. Worst of all he had not recognized 4 Commando's Commanding Officer, as anyone else in the unit would have done. It was a disaster.

Lieutenant Colonel Menday was not an even-tempered man. "No, I am not Hunter-Gray or Brown or any other color! I am just the CO of this bloody outfit, that's all. That's why I'm the last one to find out what's going on and who's going where. I'll tell you one thing, though, right at the start: you're going no place, not on any of my patrols. Now get the hell out of here!"

Griffith was taken aback. He seemed to have innocently walked into a hornet's nest. I was embarrassed, and my "Excuse me, sir" overlapped Griffith's "I am sorry, sir, but . . ."

Neither was necessary, for Menday was more embarrassed about his outburst than we were. "Pardon my losing my temper. Please disregard all I said. I do believe that Pat mentioned something about this to me. You must be the chap taking over Hilton-Jones's lot. Good luck on your patrol."

As soon as it was dark, Griffith and I and a few others, having been properly introduced, set out on what was Griffith's first combat patrol. Quietly and almost entirely uneventfully, we plodded out into the hedgerow no-man's-land on a beautiful summer evening. The noises we heard were the ordinary ones of a summer night, and the sights we saw fell into the same category. Griffith had known war before, when his father, the liberal Jewish Doctor Glaser, had taken him along to Spain as a teenage boy to inoculate the anti-Franco forces. But the patrol was a novel experience. It was a good initiation for Griffith and he appreciated it.

After that patrol, Griffith rapidly got used to our way of life and in no time gained the respect of both subordinates and superiors.

When the last battle for Bréville had been won, I was surprised to find people gape at me; not just gape, but subsequently greet me with more than usual enthusiasm. "Glad to see you!" they said emphatically with great heartiness. I was mystified until I saw some temporary graves that had been dug on the village green facing the the town hall, small rows of white crosses with the names of the dead neatly lettered upon them. There I found the answer. In the front row I read, "Lance Corporal Masters" on one of the crosses. My unfortunate namesake was a paratrooper killed in taking the village.

On my first visit to Bréville just after the last battle for the town had been won, I found some elaborately dug positions along the hedge bordering an orchard, complete with camouflaged roofs. Upon examination I found a regular bunk in one of them, which seemed to me luxury indeed. I made up my mind to copy this idea at the earliest opportunity. Under that roughly hewn bed, an officer's, no doubt, I found a beautiful Walther P-38 pistol in a polished black leather holster. Ever alert to the possibility of booby traps, I lifted it carefully, having felt with gentle fingers around and under it before gathering it up. I carried it as an extra personal weapon, until I lost it to Tom Spencer (Stein) in a game of blackjack.

During the same visit to Bréville, an airborne padre flagged me down while I was riding my bicycle.

"Are you going back to le Plein?" he asked.

"Yes, sir."

"Do you have a handkerchief?" I admitted as much, and he asked me to spread it out before him.

"I'm afraid this is all that's left of one of our enemies, or at any rate this is all we could find. Please give it to the Number One Brigade padre at headquarters." He dropped a small triangular piece of charred flesh onto my white handkerchief. Melted into it were German Army–issue dog tags. I completed my grisly errand without looking at the name on the tags.

I went on one more patrol out of Amfréville-le Plein. I was joined by a foreign-born corporal, not one of the French Commandos and not a 3 Trooper; he was from some Eastern European country. He and I were to examine a row of tall trees opposite the French Commando lines, where an enemy sniper was reported to have been active. I made sure that my French friends knew we were going to be out in front of them, then the corporal and I set out in daylight. When we had arrived in an area where it was prudent to move with considerable care, we took a short break among some sizable bushes.

"First of all let's have a cigarette," said my partner.

"You see that bush over there?" I answered. "The one way over there, at the other end of the field? That's where you're going if you're seriously thinking of smoking. You sure as hell aren't going to do it within a couple of hundred yards of me. Besides, I'm for checking out those trees first, in case that sniper is real and sees you light up."

"You really want to go over there? We can go back in a while and tell them we looked all over but there was no one there, can't we?"

"I most certainly mean to go over there. All the way, if possible. You don't have to come."

"Oh, all right, I'll go with you. But first I must have my cigarette."

"Over there, not here," I repeated.

He slouched off while I took good cover. When he returned, I led the way to the trees in question. We found one where the sniper had nailed cleats into the trunk, obviously to make it easier to climb to his perch. We crouched down and scanned the branches, but he was not "at home."

We returned and pointed out the tree from which he had been firing. I made a mental note that my partner of that day was definitely "no good," on that simple classification scale on which one's life often depended.

Shortly afterward 4 Commando was moved to take up defensive positions in Bréville. I lived in a standard foxhole on a strip of grass in the middle of the village. Colonel Menday had sent me out with two French Commando soldiers who had discovered a good observation post (OP) in no-man's-land, from which one could observe a sizable portion of the German line. It required a careful approach, for if we had been spotted moving into this position, we would have been in dire jeopardy. Our chosen perch point was but a few hundred yards from the German outposts but a mile or so from our most forward positions. Every day, so long as we remained in the Bréville area, I manned this OP, at first with the two Frenchmen, then sometimes with only one of them. At other times, one of 4 Commando's snipers, Sgt. Paddy Byrne, went with me. He was an Irishman whose stalking skills came in handy in the risky approach to the OP. Later, Paddy or I would go there alone, one of us in the morning and one in the afternoon, relieving each other at noon.

To get there I had to follow a procedure that was a peculiar mixture of caution and risk taking. It became part of me, and I could follow the same route practically in my sleep.

I left our lines through an orchard east of Bréville, carefully stepping over the trip wires of the magnesium flares strung in front of our positions. In daytime, those in the front line would hang white paper markers from these wires so they could be more easily avoided by our side. These would be removed at dusk so that an enemy would have no chance of seeing the hair-thin wires no matter how stealthily he approached. When triggered they would ignite flares that illuminated the entire neighborhood as bright as day, making aimed shooting easy.

Moving farther into the territory between us and the Germans along a farm field, I always passed the corpse of an enemy soldier who had been killed in the earliest fighting. He was too far out for either side to risk sending a burial party for him. Medium sized with dark hair, his body was progressively decomposing, and platoons of maggots participated in the process so effectively that bones were protruding here and there. The smell of death with which we had quickly become familiar was so intense that I habitually held my breath when passing that spot.

Beyond it I had to cross the leafy lane leading to the Longmare crossroads on the right, the same lane where the mortars had caught up with Nichols. This had to be done carefully. Although the lane was so curved that I could not be seen crossing it from more than a hundred yards on the enemy side to my right, I could never be sure that a German patrol with a machine gun had not moved up to that very point to cover the lane. Trying to get across from the bushes on this side to the bushes on the other, I would have been a perfect target. Thus it was wise to remain on my own side, scanning every bush to the right that might conceal such a patrol before dashing across to the welcome cover on the other side.

Even though nothing happened the first dozen times, I disciplined myself to be just as cautious each subsequent time as I had been the first time. There was a farm I had to pass, deserted except for a few surviving chickens. This was the Grande Ferme de Buisson, where patrols had been clashing and avoiding each other in the past. It had an access driveway off the lane to the left. It wasn't at all in the direction of our observation post, but I could not afford to approach the latter without checking out the former, because a hidden enemy patrol there would cut off my line of retreat. Tommy gun in hand, finger on the trigger, I quickly searched the buildings.

Then followed one of the riskiest parts, leaving the farm and its bordering hedge and emerging facing the enemy into an open meadow. A hedge ran along its far side. It was a scary situation: if I were to reach my objective, I would have to be in the open and chance a burst of enemy fire. Therefore, my routine was to examine that hedge minutely with my binoculars for at least five to ten minutes before coming into the open. When there were two of us, my companion would cover me by training his tommy gun on the hedge while I stepped forward. Whenever I did so, even when I went alone, I would step out slowly and deliberately. Looking over my right and left shoulders, I would always beckon an imaginary platoon to keep down, impatiently waving my outstretched arms, palms down, backward, as if to tell everybody to keep down.

If an enemy patrol were watching me, I hoped they would hesitate to open fire on what they could think was a deployed platoon. Twenty feet out, I changed directions and sprinted to my right, recrossing the lane that was no longer bordered by any bushes. The carcass of a horse lay in the curve. It had been dead so long that there was nothing left for maggots. Even so, the smell lingered here too.

On the other side of the road was a small farmhouse with a garden, where I took cover and rested. I felt relatively safe there, lying invisible between the orderly planted bushes, recovering my breath from the brisk run. There was a delicious bonus, ripe red currants and luscious gooseberries that melted in my mouth, lubricating a throat parched from tension. There was also an abundance of artichokes, but they could wait for the return trip, because they needed to be cooked.

Now came the last stretch of my hazardous journey, a quick diagonal move to the OP, approaching it from the rear, the blind side from the enemy's point of view. It was a small two-story house with an attached shed that stood a few hundred yards from the Longmare crossroads on the main country road to Varaville. Its only entrance was on the west side from a little L-shaped brick courtyard, screened from the road by a hedge. The shed, which had lost all its roof tiles in previous shellings, stood with its naked wooden A-frames facing the road. By lying flat behind the edging strips on its atticlike floor, so as not to be visible, I could get a splendid view of the enemy's front-line positions.

To remain unseen, I had to enter the courtyard from the rear. Two steps led up to the front door. Across the first one lay the bloated body of a dead yearling calf. I had to climb over it, stepping on its swollen rust and white midriff, the sweet stench of death again reminding me that all dead creatures, man and beast alike, smell about the same. Because this became a daily route, it would have been more pleasant to remove the carcass, but it was too heavy, and the process would have been too noisy.

I cautiously climbed up and around the corners of the narrow staircase until I came to one of the two most difficult parts. There was a large gaping shell hole in the brick south wall of the house, giving anyone observing the house a full view of the stairs. To make matters worse, dust from the debris lay thick on the stairs around the shell opening. But it was the only way to get up to my post, so I had to make a choice. Either I moved past the hole slowly so as not to raise a cloud of dust, but being easily visible to any observing German, or I risked moving past the gap in one swift move, which would leave a telltale plume of dust in my wake.

Sometimes I did it one way, sometimes the other, depending on my mood and the weather. It was always an anxious moment, for I could never tell whether I had been seen. I suppose I would know soon enough: the Germans would send out a patrol to capture or kill me, or they would simply kill me with one of their uncomfortably accurate mortar barrages.

After passing this spot, I came to the upstairs bedroom. At first we had been satisfied to sit on the floor far enough back from the window to keep from being seen. There we could look out with our binoculars across the road and the wide yellow wheat field beyond it to the line of tall trees at its far end, where the Germans were.

German infantrymen occasionally were visible below those tall trees when they moved from the shadows past sunlit spots as the light filtered through the green foliage. We bristled when we saw their field gray uniforms disrupting the natural colors of the Norman landscape, and we tensed like English pointer dogs when they first get a whiff of the scent of their quarry.

For frontline soldiers, they appeared surprisingly secure. We often watched them going to have lunch, walking upright carrying their mess cans, never bothering to crouch. By and by we got to recognize some of them, particularly one bald man who wore a pale blue silk scarf around his neck, a salvaged piece from a cargo parachute, just like the one our Percy Shelley was in the habit of wearing.

One of the French Commandos who used to come with me was the eagle-eyed Ducas. Small, tough, and agile, a serious man with close-cropped dark brown hair and a small French-looking mustache, he had become a reliable friend. Ducas was "all right." He had discovered two German observation outposts well in front of the enemy line. One observer was to our left, close to the crossroads where there was a hole in the hedge. One day Ducas noticed that the hole wasn't there, because the upper body of the observer had filled it. If we looked with great concentration where we knew he had to be, we could just make him out. He was chest deep in a foxhole, looking out over an orchard of young pale green apple trees that adjoined the yellow wheat stretching out before us.

The other outpost was not just hard to see, he was totally invisible. But Ducas had remembered that he had seen a yellow shell scar at the bottom of the trunk of a large tree that stood in front of the middle of the enemy's position. One day he could not find that bark-less blond gash in the usual spot. Then it reappeared, and he concluded that it had been covered up by a man standing in front of it. This observer, Ducas reckoned, must have a slit trench in front of that tree, and deep almost blue shadows below it hid him and the trench from view. One day Ducas proved to be right for we saw the man approach and leave his hiding place.

It was a long and weary watch each day, but Colonel Menday considered it so important that he told me to return and report to him personally if I saw anything the least bit unusual.

It rained most days that summer of 1944, so much so that we all agreed that we were harassed by three enemies, not one. Worst by far was the rain. It soaked us mercilessly when we were outside, and we were outside practically all the time, night and day. We had the horrible feeling that we would never be dry again, and would never again enjoy the wholesome sensation of clean warm clothing.

The second worst enemy were the mosquitoes, a familiar plague in Normandy's damp summer climate but perhaps particularly bad that year because of the boost to their diet—all those dead animals and soldiers. The Germans used such a smelly disinfectant powder that we could tell where they had recently been. Because it was really intended to combat lice and fleas, I doubt if it were any more of a deterrent to mosquitoes than the British Army gooky pink cream, which came in a round tin can like shoe polish. The mosquitoes seemed to eat the cream as a first course, then us as the second.

When my mother asked in her letters what she could send me in the field, I begged for a mosquito deterrent. A few weeks later it arrived in a well-wrapped little glass vial labeled by its manufacturer, "By Appointment to His Majesty the King." It smelled delicious but apparently not to mosquitoes. It proved marvelously effective but incredibly volatile. An application would last for a maximum of fifteen minutes. I went through my little bottle in four days.

The third worst enemy, and a poor third at that, were the Germans. They shot at us, shelled and mortared and even bombed us occasionally, luckily missing more often than not.

On one especially rainy day, I returned from my lookout post in the late afternoon to find my foxhole filled completely with water. Whatever floated, did; the rest was totally submerged. I upbraided my comrades for not salvaging at least some of my belongings, but that was no help for the moment. I demanded and received a pass and a lift to a rear area where a quartermaster store had been established in a trailer. There I convinced the bureaucrats to issue me one dry everything. Having accomplished that, I returned and moved into one of the little houses on the village square in Bréville. By now Bréville had been evacuated, understandably, in view of the repeated battles there. The house behind me, much like mine, had been designated as 4 Commando's guardroom, where a detail of six men took turns sleeping and mounting watches around 4 Commando headquarters in the town hall, the *mairie*. My own house was almost requisitioned out from under me; it was wanted to store metal boxes full of mortar shells and .303 and .45 ammunition. But enough space was found in the back room so I could have the front one, if I was crazy enough to sleep in a place that could blow me sky high if it got hit.

To me the luxury of living in comparatively civilized surroundings far outweighed the risk. I slept on a mattress, naked; reasoning that I had my tommy gun right next to me and if a surprise attack were to penetrate into Bréville (our forward positions were 150 yards away) I could shoot and make a stand, clothed or nude. There were some discomforts. The roof had many small holes, and I had to deploy eight tin cans over the red tiled floor to catch the water when it rained.

I had acquired a little basket where I kept my eggs and bread from Monsieur Lemoine's farm and a little can of butter wrapped in a wet rag in lieu of a refrigerator. I even had a pale blue enamel jug in which I kept a few of the pink rambling roses that grew in profusion along the fence.

Under the circumstances, it was an idyllic lifestyle. But it was threatened one evening when a German bomber, a rare sight, flew low over the *mairie* at dusk. Surprisingly, he took no offensive action, but he came back an hour later and dropped two bombs smack on the building, damaging it severely. Luckily, we suffered no casualties, but during the night the enemy artillery, no doubt utilizing the information with which the *Luftwaffe* had furnished them, began a sustained bombardment. I was practically propelled out of my bed by the crashing explosions. Shells sailed just over my house and hit the guardroom and killed three men as they lay sleeping on mattresses. One recent reinforcement Commando soldier on watch managed to jump up and run for the door. By reflex he grabbed his blanket, and as he dashed over the threshold he tripped and fell. This clumsy accident doubtless saved his life, for just as he went down the next salvo exploded a few yards in front of him.

In the morning, I was ordered to abandon my house and, along with a dozen others, move elsewhere. We were to dig new positions in an orchard to the east, not far from where the trip flares, now moved forward, had originally been positioned. That is when I invented "Supertrench," inspired by that German officer's built-in bunk.

I began by searching Bréville's empty houses until I found a double bed. I lugged it into the orchard meadow on my back and marked its four corners with twig pegs on my chosen real estate. Then I started to dig. When I had excavated about half my desired depth of five feet, I became aware of someone standing behind me, watching. I wiped the sweat off my brow and out of my eyes, and I recognized Regimental Sergeant-Major Morris of 4 Commando. Stern and bald, he looked puzzled, first at the bed, then at me.

"And what might that be?"

"My trench, sir," I replied.

"For how many people?"

"Just me, sir."

"I think there should be enough space for three more. I'll send them right over."

"Thank you, sir."

It was a bit of a blow. But at least I could retire from digging, having done more than my share, and concentrate on directing operations. I had my new tenants go even deeper than I had originally intended, then we dropped the bed into the hole. We fetched some of the sturdiest doors we could find in the vacant dwellings and laid them over the rectangular excavation to form a roof. Before we put all the excavated soil back on the roof, I took my helpers over to the hedgerow facing Amfréville. There, the most recent battle had left two German Mark IV tanks and a German light tank, a Czech T-38 chassis with a 75mm gun mounted on it. The latter was so totally demolished that several sheets of armor plating were either on the ground or hanging loosely down its side. We lugged these over to our new home and laid them on top of the doors, then we heaped on the soil followed by clods of grassy earth—and a fallen tree for good measure.

The rectangular hole formed the downstroke of what was essentially an L-shaped plan. A little firing trench branched off to the left to form the horizontal base. The firing position had no head cover, but we felt safe in the other part, because we believed it to be practically mortarproof. Even if one had exploded right in our firing trench (the only opening), it would not have harmed us, lying around a right-angle corner from it.

One unexpected fringe benefit fell into our lap when the regimental sergeant-major (RSM) ordained that one person per trench had to stand watch in each firing position during the night. There being four of us, we had an easy time of it. Everybody came around to admire what we had wrought, almost like a housewarming. Four other men banded together and decided to build a copy of Supertrench, fifty yards away; they asked me to draw them a plan and list the building materials. They followed the plans meticulously.

A day later the nasty bomber returned during the night and dropped one bomb practically on Supertrench II. The crater it made included one corner of the structure and blocked the exit, burying its inhabitants inside. We watched in horror when all was frighteningly quiet following the explosion. After what seemed an interminable pause, the smoke and dust cleared enough for us to see the earth stirring on the side of the crater. The tip of a shovel appeared, and then another. All four men emerged and came running over to shake my hand. They believed that Supertrench II had saved their lives, although I thought they had just been lucky.

We still mounted our observation post every day. Paddy Byrne and I were there together when we saw a German officer step forward from the middle of their line, approximately in the area of the scarred tree trunk. He stood in the open yellow wheat field studying a large map. Oddly, he wore a greatcoat in the summer heat.

"I'm gonna shoot the bugger," announced Paddy. He put the muzzle of his telescopic sniper's rifle, the one with the notches on the butt signifying kills, over the rim of the roof on which we were lying. I reminded him that we mustn't compromise our position and so lose an ideal observation post. The Germans might see where the shot had come from and send out a fighting patrol to polish us off. "Sure, sure, you're right and I know it. But this bloke is some kind of big wheel, and the opportunity is just too damn great. What do you say I kill him and we call it a day and get the hell out of here?" I agreed. It was too good an opportunity to miss. I focused my binoculars in anticipation of seeing the German drop.

Paddy aimed carefully and fired. "Got him," he said in a whisper that almost amounted to a shout. "Let's go." He was up and out and halfway down the stairs, not even caring about kicking up the debris dust, before I had time to say anything. I followed hot on his heels.

"Paddy."

"Yeah?"

"I watched carefully through my binoculars, and I hate to tell you this, but I don't think the bugger noticed being shot at. He didn't flinch."

"Perhaps he was slow falling over. That happens sometimes. I had him in my sights when I pressed the trigger. In any case we had to get outta there fast, didn't we?"

"Anyway, let's get back quickly. I must tell the CO about him and his map. Maybe they're planning an attack," I said.

When we got back I walked over to the upstairs room in the undamaged part of the *mairie* where Colonel Menday lived. Knowing about his hearing problem, I knocked loudly on the door and yelled. It opened, and the colonel stood before me.

"What the devil do you think you're doing?" he shouted, red in the face with fury. I tried to explain that I was merely following orders, his own, to report any unusual happenings immediately, but he wouldn't listen, so I left. Five minutes later he sent for me. He apologized for his outburst, just as he had done to Griffith, and listened attentively to my account. I didn't mention Paddy's shot, nor did I ever find out whether my friend cut another notch into the butt of his sniper's rifle.

No German attack materialized.

The next day I was lying on the attic floor of the shed by myself, watching the edge of the field as usual. Paddy was due to relieve me at noon. Another hour to go. Suddenly, I heard a noise close by. I remained motionless and listened. The noise—a roof tile kicked on a brick surface—had come from the brick courtyard immediately below me. I could not help thinking that my day of reckoning had come. The Germans had seen the flash and heard the sound of yesterday's shot, or some alert German had seen me sneak past the shell hole on the staircase. Now they had sent out a fighting patrol to surround the house and shed. At that moment they were probably trying to pinpoint my position.

Of course it might be an animal—a stray cow that had survived the numerous bombardments in the area, or one of the two white horses I had seen prancing around in the surrounding fields. But I had to be prepared for the worst. So I carefully took a 77 grenade out of my pocket, unscrewed the cap, and unwound several lengths of the tape that would pull out the pin in flight. We always did this when throwing the grenade a short distance, in this case just the ten foot drop to the brick floor, to make sure that it exploded on impact. I was still hoping it would turn out to be a loose farm animal when I heard another sound that eliminated that possibility. The sound was definitely and unmistakably human, that of a man clearing his throat.

My next move was clear. I would throw my phosphorus grenade into the brick courtyard to cause confusion and injury among the enemy patrol. It would also create a cloud of smoke, which would hide me from them as I jumped onto the ground at the back of the house and ran as fast as I could into the cover of the bushes of the Longmare lane. The odds were poor that I would get away with this plan, but it was my only chance.

I raised my hand to toss down my grenade, a green metal canister, which easily fit into my palm. I got ready to stand up and take the three steps to where I planned to jump from the roof. As a last measure I tried to raise my head slightly to see my target, the enemy just below me, before dropping the grenade. But the A-frames of the roof were so close together that I found it impossible to lift my head near the edging strips. I would have had to stand up to see anybody in the courtyard, and I could not risk that.

Just then there came a voice with a characteristic Irish brogue calling, "Peter."

"God help us, Paddy," I called down. "I was just going to . . . what in hell are you doing here so early? I thought you were a bunch of Jerries coming to get me."

It took a man of Paddy's skill to have come this close without my hearing him approach, especially as he had brought with him an artillery observation officer and a signaler. Phew. I wound the white tape back up and replaced the grenade's screw-on cap.

In spite of his calling, the forward observation officer, a squat Royal Artillery captain, seemed none too agile as he climbed over the dead calf, up the staircase, and past the shell hole. But Paddy Byrne managed to levitate him up on the shed attic post, and he explained the sights to him. His radio operator remained below. The captain did not take long to call down the necessary map references, and mere minutes after his arrival he ordered, "Fire."

After minimal ranging, twenty-five-pound shells began noisily crashing among the fringe of trees. He gave the order "Repeat!" twice and whooped and hollered about his success. Then he left.

The benefits of this shoot followed soon, for the next day we had a deserter, an older soldier well versed in slang, just when we badly needed another identification of who was opposite us. I learned more good German Army dialect words from him than were in the little blue instruction booklet from which we had studied back in training.

"When you Tommies unveiled your secret weapon yesterday, this *landser* decided it was time to pack it in. Man alive! It was god-awful. Shit flying all over the dump. God-awful."

Deserting is always a risky business. It was even money that you'd get shot by one side or the other. He was thrilled to have made it alive.

"How many casualties did you have in that bombardment yesterday?" I asked him.

"Casualties?"

"How many killed, how many wounded?"

"We didn't have any killed or wounded. We are well dug in."

"But you said it was god-awful. And you had no losses?"

"It *was* terrible. Stuff exploding all around on the trees, in the ground right next to my hole . . . awful. That secret weapon zeroed right in on us. No more for me, I said to myself. I pretended to take a bundle of washing back, walked sideways, changed directions, and ran."

I learned from him that the same unit we had been observing was still there.

We needed a verification of that a week later. Ducas, my old French Commando friend, and I had a plan. It was still raining, in fact it was pouring. We reasoned that the enemy would never expect any activity from us on such a dreadful day, any more than we expected any from them. We would take this chance to do something totally unprecedented: cross the road and snatch their outpost, the one on the left, the one in the hedgerow.

In order to reach it, we had to break new and unfamiliar ground from the moment we left our lookout position. We had to cross the lane again, above where it intersected the main Varaville road and advance cautiously along a hedgerow. But we had heard a rumor that this hedge and its surrounding area were mined. Because of this we had brought the top end of one of our radio aerials. Holding it lightly between two fingers, we crawled in the wet grass, always keeping the thin metal rod in front of us, feeling for trip wires. The booby traps were said to be concealed hand grenades tied to trees or bushes and connected to trip wires. A man had already been severely injured by one of these devices.

We found none. Soaking wet, we arrived at the road's edge. Looking up and down the road, lying prone in its grass margin, we saw that the most likely place for a concealed machine gun would be about 150 yards nearer Varaville, where a fallen tree lay halfway across the road. We scanned the tree for a full five minutes with our binoculars but saw nothing stir.

Now came the most hazardous part. I lay with my tommy gun pointed at the foliage of the fallen tree while Ducas dashed across the road. Nobody had been that far forward before, or at least nobody had returned to tell the tale. The grass on the other side was deplorably scant, and Ducas lay down as flat as possible and covered me as I raced across. Then together we crept through the shallow grass toward an apple tree whose narrow trunk looked inadequate to hide us. Once again we found that everything looked totally different close up than it had seemed from our observation post. We sensed that we must be close to our quarry. Ducas raised himself on his elbows and looked first but could not find him. I edged to the bottom of the slender trunk of the apple tree. I raised my head off the ground and looked through just one of my binocular lenses, because holding the binoculars horizontally would have exposed all of my head. No sooner had I focused my eye than I saw the German so big in my circular field of view that I was startled. I pushed down Ducas even flatter and pointed ahead of us.

"*Il est là-bas!*" I whispered into his ear through my cupped hands. "*Très près!*" (He's over there, very near by.)

He looked but again could not find him. I rechecked whether I had given him the right direction, but the rain got onto my lens and I could see nothing at all. I quickly wiped it with my handkerchief (the only dry thing I still carried) and looked once more—and there he was as big as ever, looking at me. It seemed surprising that he had not seen us with our scant cover. But still Ducas could not see him. I looked again, and he turned unhurriedly and left his position, not as I had expected by climbing out of it, but rather by opening a door into a bunker, which I had not noticed before. It opened right off his trench. He shut the door behind him and was gone.

I didn't like it a bit. First of all, I couldn't picture the two of us dashing over there, jumping into the trench and bursting through that door, not knowing what we would find on the other side. Second, I was concerned about the manner in which he had nonchalantly ambled away. Would a soldier in an outpost turn his back and leave his station if he were alone?

Well aware that I was not only wet and getting wetter by the minute, but that I was also getting cold feet, I suggested to Ducas that we abort the mission, and turn for home. It *was* getting late. He agreed readily. We covered each other back across the road and made far better time than we had on the way out. A little frustrated with our sudden timidity, we were at least able to report that the Bréville-Varaville road could be stealthily crossed, even in daylight, particularly in a heavy rain.

One day I was sent out to make a reconnaissance that was not dissimilar to what we had been doing, although our role as 3 Troopers had gradually undergone a change. We were meant to utilize our fluent German and our knowledge of the German Army, but our Commando superiors knew that we were well trained and eager to get out into no-man's-land. They liked to have one of our men along in case they came upon a prisoner or even a corpse. As Stewart had pointed out, Brigadier Mills-Roberts had actually rationed us. We were to go out on only important patrols, endorsed by him personally. But most of the patrol commanders dared to secretly ignore this order, employing some subterfuge that was greatly facilitated by us, because we wanted to go with them anyway. When it came to solo assignments or a small reconnaissance of just two men, it had become customary to choose a 3 Trooper.

Thus I was asked to explore how far one could advance to the northeast on the other side of Bréville, roughly on the extreme right of the familiar wheat field. A typical Norman *bocage,* a double hedge 10 feet high, with a footpath in between, led due east from our positions. A standing patrol was also positioned out there, a few hundred yards ahead of our front line. It was relieved every two hours. The parallel hedgerows turned right at a 90-degree angle about 500 yards out, so that had a patrol continued straight, they would find themselves in the open yellow field between our old daily observation post and the enemy line we had observed from there. Nobody had even been as far as this corner, and therefore we were not sure how far forward the enemy had situated his line. It was up to me to find out.

Instead of my green beret, I was wearing the beige woolen hat I had found while rock climbing on the Ydwal Slabs in North Wales. "I'm going out there and I should be back in an hour or an hour and a half," I told the standing patrol. I asked them to make sure that the relief patrol knew I would be returning the same way. They promised they would, and remarked that they thought I was crazy to go out there. I believed that their standing patrol duty was at least as dangerous as my reconnaissance, for they were liable to be shelled or mortared. I was going to be too far out and too near the enemy line to have to worry about some of these hazards. But I was familiar with that attitude. Tank troops say that anyone out in the field without the protection of armor plate must be a madman. Conversely, the foot soldier says that only lunatics would go into battle in a flammable death trap, such as a tank.

Soon after I passed the standing patrol, my field of view was so limited by the *bocage* that I had to begin to crawl, to avoid being surprised and picked off by some enemy outpost. A bloated dead white cow blocked virtually all of my path between the hedges. It smelled to high heaven, and its entire near side was crawling with maggots. I held my breath and barely managed to creep by. I studied the wheat field with my binoculars for a long time, because there were some dead tree trunks that could have hidden a machine-gun nest. When I was reasonably sure that nothing was there, I turned down a similar path on the right. The hedge on my left was getting scanty, so I had to make sure that I was not seen from that side. Happily, there was a narrow overgrown ditch along the right hedge, and I crawled into it and began inching forward. It was slow going among the brambles. After I had advanced in this manner almost halfway to the line of trees, often stopping to listen and observe, I decided that it was time to turn back. I had at least established where the enemy was not.

The return trip was, as always, much quicker; I could walk more or less upright along the path now that I had ascertained that it was secure. When it came to the left turn where I would have had to pass the dead cow again, I decided to walk on the other side of the hedge to avoid the smell and the narrow passageway. It was getting dark.

Now that I knew there were no German outposts far enough forward to pose any threat to me here, I felt perfectly safe walking upright in the meadow. I was approaching a tall bush when I suddenly saw a shadowy figure jump out from behind it, then crouch as if he were about to fire.

"Hold it," I yelled.

The soldier lowered his tommy gun. "Christ, I almost shot you."

I asked him why.

"When we relieved the standing patrol, they told us you were out there and that you'd come back on the path between the hedges. When we saw someone coming along the outside of the hedge, we were sure it was an enemy sniper."

That's how easy it is to be killed by friendly fire—not by negligence but through misunderstanding. I had meant that I'd be coming back from the same direction, and they had taken me literally, even though I was only ten feet from where I'd said I would be. So the soldier couldn't have been faulted if he had shot me.

The British were much more reasonable about friendly fire accidents. Unless gross negligence were evident, they would sensibly report "killed in action." This was a comfort to the families of the dead instead of causing pointless frustration and guilt feelings on the part of the usually innocent perpetrators.

Two days later I went out the same way with Ducas. We made better progress, because although the situation could theoretically change every day, I had been there before and we could afford to make logical assumptions and take some calculated risks.

We were well past the farthest point of my former exploits when Ducas urgently pulled me to a stop. He pointed to the bottom of a slender tree just to the right of the path. At first I could see only a small pile of dry leaves at its base. But the Frenchman's famous sharp eyes had noticed a small disk-shaped spot, light tan in color, peeking out from under the brown foliage. A small string loop stuck out from its center.

I went up to it, very carefully, for we suspected a booby trap. Despite Ducas's protests—he was in favor of leaving it strictly alone—I started to remove one leaf at a time, gingerly with two fingers. It was one of those days, one of those dangerous days, where I felt that nothing could happen to me. I told him to take cover and keep his head down in case something blew up, while I continued to clean off the leaves. I found that the disk with the loop was the base of the wooden handle of a German stick grenade. When I had almost all of the handle in the clear, I saw that the grenade's cylindrical head was enclosed in a white linen sack. I carefully inserted my hands under it from all sides until my fingers met in the middle. I was feeling for a release switch—an antilifting device that would explode the whole caboodle if its weight were removed. Finding none, I took a deep breath and raised the contraption. The bag, wired to its head, was full of egg grenades. It was obvious that the enemy connected the loop to a trip wire at night. This would set off the stick grenade and everything else by sympathetic detonation, causing a formidable explosion that could have easily eliminated an entire patrol. At night nobody would be able to spot anything, not the barely visible bottom of the stick, and certainly not the trip wire. Luckily for us, they had left it disconnected, so it would not interfere with their own patrol activities. We went only a little farther, practically to the tree line. There we found recent German newspapers used as toilet paper, evidence that the enemy had been occupying that position as a standing patrol. This was certainly worth reporting, and we turned for home.

I carried the booby trap back and took it straight to the brigade demolitions officer, who I thought would be interested in what contraptions the enemy was using. I was wrong.

"You take this damned thing right outside and put it at the bottom of the garden before it blows up," he said.

"It won't blow up unless we set it off, sir," I replied. "It hasn't so far, and I've been carrying it around with me for the past hour."

There was one more strange aftereffect of this particular reconnaissance. Apparently, one of the original soldiers of the standing patrol when I had first gone into no-man's-land was there again when Ducas and I returned two days later. He assumed that I had spent the time in between "out there." He also heard that we had been watching the Germans line up for meals, so he spread the legend that the man in the sheepskin hat (my balaclava cap-comforter) just about lived in no-man's-land, "and since he speaks fluent German, he even joins their chow line whenever he's hungry." Awed glances greeted me everywhere.

Harry Drew (Nomburg), who was attached to No. 3 Troop, 6 Commando, encountered a similar booby trap on 2 August—only his was not disconnected. He was in the lead of a two-man patrol when he tripped the almost invisible wire strung tightly across the trail.

"Get down. Booby trap!" he yelled. Sergeant Hare of 6 Commando was close behind Drew, who had flung himself to the ground. But Hare had no chance to escape the almost instantaneous explosion.

His right knee was badly torn. Drew turned back and ran to get medics with a stretcher, but Hare managed to crawl back to base under his own steam. He got there first, because Drew in his haste to get help had run into a British booby trap. It had been left behind by mistake, and its loose trip wire twisted around his ankle.

"I heard the click, but by the time I became aware of the shorter-fused British 36 fragmentation grenade at the end of this wire, it was too late. There was a tremendous explosion, which showered me with shrapnel from the waist down." It ended his time in Normandy. He joked that he was the only man who had ever set off both a German and a British booby trap on the same day.

At the beginning of August, the brigade moved at last to the Bois de Bavent. Number 4 Commando occupied a row of slit trenches just over the crest of a reverse slope, two men to a hole, sleeping head to foot. Because of the rain and enemy mortaring, we had built roofs over all these dug-in positions with sturdy branches and soil and sod piled on top. To keep out the mosquitoes, we placed a rain cape or blanket over the entrance hole.

Ingenious as these precautions were, the mosquitoes were more ingenious at getting in. My partner was a young man from the King's Liverpool Regiment, "a Kingy Boy," as he told me they are called in that port. One evening he said, "I can't face another night of being bitten to death by the little buggers. What do you say we kill ten each after we've shut the entrance hole up tight? No more can get in. That ought to do it for a good night's sleep."

I readily agreed, so we lit tapers of twisted newspaper and burned them out of the rafters. We killed ten each but heard and saw more. We killed another ten each, and yet another ten, making the score sixty mosquitoes in one small foxhole. We abandoned the hunt, not because no mosquitoes were left, but because we were exhausted. It was like surrendering to a vastly superior enemy.

If I walked about in the evening and slapped one hand on top of the beret on my head, there would be at least six dead mosquitoes there. Each tree had a tornadolike black funnel over it, a black cloud of mosquitoes. They bit through our battle dress although the material was quite thick. They would actually burrow into the cloth so deeply that their presence was not known until they bit and drew blood. They even caused casualties. Men poured all kinds of insecticides into their foxholes, and some were overcome by the fumes while the damned insects thrived. Some men set fire to flammable liquids to burn the mosquitoes out and got so careless that they suffered burns themselves.

We were being shelled increasingly by 88mm guns and mortared more and more accurately. The 88mm fired with a clearly audible sharp report, but it was not followed by a prolonged whistle, which could give one a chance to take cover. It was the briefest bang-zoom-crash and seemed to take no longer than it took to read these three words.

We did find an effective measure to avoid excessive mortar casualties, however, one so simple that we kicked ourselves for not having thought of it sooner. When the enemy mortars fired their high-trajectory shells, it sounded like distant woodcutters chopping wood. But often the sounds of other activities blocked out this vital audible warning, and the first thing anyone heard was the crunch of the exploding rounds among our positions. So we put someone with a whistle out in no-man's-land, which in the Bois de Bavent was a deciduous bushy forest. He was well dug in and concealed. He could hear the faraway chop-chop-chop much better out there, so when he blew his whistle everyone would dive headfirst for their holes.

Number 3 Commando was a ten-minute walk through the forest, bearing east. Since our move, communications and exchange of information among 3 Troopers had become much more difficult than it had been in the central location of the church at Amfréville. Therefore, I made a point of going over to see Ken Bartlett (Billman), the sergeant in charge of our 3 Commando detachment regularly. He had an elegant slit trench at their position in the middle of the woods. He was a friend from the Old Hampshires, a fine cellist born in Munich.

I would go there by a circuitous route because I had to cross a small road leading from our lines downhill directly into the German line. The Germans had a small concrete pillbox overlooking the road, so I had to cross above a bend where they could not see me.

Not necessarily to save me the inconvenience of this detour, 3 Commando's commanding officer, Col. Peter Young, invented an ingenious method to destroy the pillbox and open up the road. He procured a pair of roller skates from a village behind the line and affixed a Bangalore torpedo to them and as large a load of explosive as could be tied to this makeshift vehicle. (A Bangalore torpedo is a galvanized steel pipe filled with explosive, used to blow away enemy barbed wire.) The colonel's chief engineer and demolitions expert then calculated the length of fuse needed, based on the grade of the road and the anticipated and tested speed of the skates. That done, the fuse was lit and the contraption launched straight down the road from the bend. The Germans heard the noisy ball bearings of the skates rattling downhill. Curious, not to say anxious about what was coming toward them, they rushed out to intercept the mysterious gadget. That was when it blew up. Now I could go to see Ken much more easily.

Ken Bartlett's trench was one of a loose cluster of trenches. In their midst a radio (a regular one, not Army issue) had been fastened in the branches of a tree, and the men would turn it on to listen to the BBC News. Ken's foxhole actually sported a white lace curtain that he had liberated from a vacant house before leaving for the woods; it was fine enough to screen out the mosquitoes. When I arrived there, we'd sit and listen to how the rest of the war was going. Afterward we would usually discuss what we had heard in general, and our situation in particular. On one occasion mortar shells suddenly crashed through the trees all around us, and we had to seek hasty refuge in his luxury "home." But the radio, being tied to a tree, had no cover. It received a direct hit. That was the end of the news.

Ken Bartlett's almost attractive trench brings to mind a few prejudices regarding creature comforts in the field. These apply also to my living in the Bréville house with my blue vase of roses, and later to my Supertrench. The detractors claimed that a soldier who lived too comfortably on the front line was likely to develop a shelter complex. When the occasion demanded it, they asserted, he would be less likely to want to come out. Instead, he might want to keep hugging the imaginary security blanket of the pleasant and comfortable surroundings. They may have had a point, but I firmly believe that it does not apply to self-motivated elite troops. Quite the contrary, I'm convinced that making the most of a bad situation and living in a self-respecting environment allowed us to get better rest and boosted our morale.

This also applied to our diet. I had the greatest admiration for our 4 Commando cook (he must have volunteered for the job, for Commandos hardly had any staff, not even cooks). He would dump the dreaded M & V tins (meat and vegetables) onto a board in a little clearing in the damp forest that was our front line. Then he would pour hot leftover tea* gently over it, which would dissolve all the monkey grease and put it where it belonged, back to nature, hoping—perhaps overoptimistically—that it might be biodegradable. After that he would sort out all the mixed vegetables and sauté them separately in Normandy butter, adding some chives from a nearby meadow and some liberated seasoning. This gallant effort to improve our quality of life actually made the horrid rations palatable and even delectable.

The greatest bonus of my visits to 3 Commando was the brick pond, a short walk from Bartlett's position, where there was an abandoned brickyard factory. Behind it was a square pond used in manufacturing red bricks and roof tiles. Ken and I, dressed in our issue blue gym shorts, would go there to swim, an unbelievable luxury near the front line. To feel bathed and clean was a treasured privilege. There was one drawback. The 3 Commando 4-inch mortars were placed behind the factory next to the pond. We debated what we perceived to be a real danger. What if the enemy commenced counter-battery fire? I asked Ken: "If the shells fall into the water and explode while we're swimming, do you suppose we'd be killed, like fish when explosives are thrown into a lake?" He wasn't sure, so we would rush ashore whenever our mortars opened up.

En route to my next visit with Ken, two days after the loss of the radio, I was suddenly caught in a fearful bombardment. Shells exploded all around me. By this time I had become "an old soldier," habitually scanning the landscape for possible cover wherever I walked, in case something went bang. Whether it was an artillery or

---

*Water was in extremely short supply because the water truck had to run through a dusty stretch of road visible from the enemy side; it was risked only rarely, with artillery support. In between we washed and shaved in leftover tea.

mortar shell, a burst of machine-gun fire, a sniper's shot, or a hand grenade was irrelevant. The deliberately or accidentally targeted soldier needs cover quickly. So as soon as the first missile detonated, I found myself diving headlong under the fallen tree I had selected in advance to shelter me. There was a shallow indentation under it just big enough to get into, and I pressed myself down as low as I could to weather the storm. When it was over, I dusted myself off and continued on my way, surprised that I had not suffered a scratch. I could not help but reflect that, had I been seriously injured on this mostly unused route, it would have been a long time before anyone found me.

At the next morning's formation, there was an announcement. "The brigadier requests volunteers for a potentially hazardous mission. Those interested should come to the reverse-slope apple orchard at fifteen-thirty dressed for battle."

I did what any old soldier does on such occasions. I asked my best local sources in 4 Commando what this was all about. That got me nowhere: either they wouldn't tell me or they really didn't know. The way they acted, I believed that they were completely in the dark, so I asked Bartlett. He had access to Colonel Young, so I figured that he would know something.

"Ah, I'm so glad you came, Peter. So what's all this stuff about a dangerous mission? The colonel doesn't have an inkling, or so he says."

"Well, that leaves only one course open. Let's both of us trek down to brigade headquarters and grill our friends in brigade signals!" There our favorite contacts greeted us at the entrance to their dugout, which looked like a forest of radio antennae.

"Good to see you chaps. We were expecting you. The answer is *no*, we don't have a clue. Honest."

We turned back, disappointed and puzzled, but agreed to put our names down. "After all," said Bartlett, "we've volunteered for every damn thing so far. Why would we stop now?"

Back at 4 Commando, I put on my camouflage jumping smock and stuffed my pockets with hand grenades and spare tommy-gun magazines. I decided to wear my "sheepskin" hat. I was ready.

"And where do you think you're going?" Number 4's adjutant stopped me as I passed his slit trench.

"I'm responding to the brigadier's call for volunteers, sir."

"In that getup?"

"It said 'dressed for battle,' sir."

"You'll have to spruce up a bit. Battle or not, this is a brigadier's formation."

"Yes, sir." So I made some minimal changes in my appearance, cursed the adjutant inaudibly for messing with me about trivia, and took great care that he would not see me as I left again for the more serious business of the day.

I met Bartlett in the orchard. Many of the French Commandos had showed up also. The brigadier had not yet arrived, so we were given the order to fall out. It was a hot and humid afternoon, and we all lay down in the grass in the sparse shade of the apple trees. We picked up unripe fallen apples in the sloping meadow and munched them to quench our thirst, speculating what our mission might be.

"Fall in." We jumped to our feet and lined up randomly, because we came from an assortment of different No. 1 Brigade Commandos. A jeep carrying Brigadier Mills-Roberts and an aide drove up.

"Attention. Stand at ease. The brigadier will now brief you."

"Gentlemen," began the brigadier. He sounded like General Sturges had sounded when he had briefed our 3 Troop prior to its high-risk raid (which was subsequently aborted). The brigadier stood high up on the jeep's seat. "First of all, I must apologize, for I have no hazardous task for you. I know you're disappointed, but I was faced with a serious problem. A local French friend gave me a present, and here it is."

I noticed only now that next to him on one of the jeep's rear seats was a sizable object covered by a large brown sack. Mills-Roberts now removed this cover with a melodramatic flourish, revealing a keg of beer. He explained that there was no point in distributing the beer to everyone in the brigade, because each man would have received only a thimble full. So he decided that he might as well share it with the "most gallant Commando soldiers under my command. Come and get it. Take out your mess tins and form a line." He dispensed the beer himself, enjoying every minute of it.

When it was my turn, I held out the only mess tin I now owned, the kidney-shaped khaki German one with the name *Hock* scratched into its lid. I thought it much bigger and better than my issue one, which I had thrown away.

The brigadier looked at it with apparent amusement. "Don't come for a second helping with this one," he said, filling it to the brim.

Most of the French Commandos looked unhappy, and we heard a good deal of mumbled grumbling—not only because they would have preferred a good vintage wine to any beer, but because they felt that their manly courage had been disrespectfully used in a facetious gag. Bartlett and I could understand their sentiment, but we did not share it. We drank our beer to wash down the unripe apples and went home.

21 "Just One More Attack"

The static role of the two Commando brigades caused considerable frustration among all ranks. It was all very well to be told that we were holding the vital pivot of the entire invasion, but being a pivot (no matter how vital) meant standing still, a role that was repulsive to special forces. Moreover, we were holding our long stretch of front line with very few men—true of the whole 6th Airborne Division to which we were attached, but doubly true of the two green beret brigades. Our red beret brothers had two battalions up and one in reserve; we were all up, with no reserves. We went to great trouble to pretend that we were stronger than we were, by active patrolling and occasional hit-and-run attacks. That was costly, for it meant taking casualties, added to those caused daily by the enemy's mortars and artillery. By now the Germans had a pretty good idea where we were, so the accuracy of their bombardments kept improving.

A degree of battle fatigue set in. It was less acute for us 3 Troopers perhaps, because we were out and about, not as trench-bound as the others. However, all our trenches were small, claustrophobic, two-man foxholes, not the large, communal, downright gregarious ones of World War I. Under fire in times of stress, one looked at just one face and three dirt walls. The same face, day in, day out. Considering all this, we were remarkably cheerful.

At last, in early August, after a flood of rumors that we were going home had run off into the thin air above the Norman hedgerows, the Commando medical officers had banded together and recommended that we return to Britain to refit and replenish our depleted units.

"These men are tired and unfit for further sustained combat," they reported.

"Just one more attack" was the reply by the management, "and this time we mean an assault."

251

The news that we had permission to advance at long last was a wonderful tonic that helped us overcome our frustration and fatigue. The badly outflanked enemy was said to have withdrawn to the other side of the river Dives.

On 17 August, Colonel Dawson, who had recovered from his injuries and returned to take over for Colonel Menday, led 4 Commando's advance through the summery woods. In a cautious but flamboyant mood, he had stuck a huge light violet dahlia under his second cap badge, the escutcheon of the French Commandos attached to No. 4.

We rested near a small abandoned farm. There were two irresistible Mirabelle plum trees in its orchard, and we stuffed ourselves with the luscious greenish yellow fruit.

Suddenly, we were rudely reminded that whether the Germans were retreating or not, there was still an enemy out there. Flying so low that we could not hear them until they were upon us, two Focke-Wulf fighters, the first we had seen in weeks, appeared, seemingly skimming the treetops, machine guns blazing. They didn't score any hits, but they certainly made us jump and disturbed the idyllic scene of rustic peace. By the time we dove for cover, they were gone.

This failed aerial attack had one pleasant side effect. We could be reasonably certain that no enemy ground troops were in the immediate vicinity, for they would not have risked hitting them instead of us. Therefore, we could now simply enjoy the scenery as we advanced through the pretty woods.

On 18 August we were told that we were to attack across the next river. Modern warfare seemed to progress from one river to another. It was to be a daylight assault, crossing over the small waterway of the Dives near the village of Dozulé, which the Germans had burned down in anticipation of our arrival. The river basin was in the middle of a flat and bare landscape, but there was a high rise of grassy hills overlooking it on the far side. This meant that we would have to approach the river, cross it, and attack the hills on the far side in full view of a well-dug-in enemy.

The next rumor bore out the high regard we had for our brigadier, for he allegedly turned down the plan, an unheard-of happening as far as we knew. He said he wanted to mount a night attack instead. The bigwigs were doubtful. A night river crossing was the most difficult operation to conduct successfully, especially with tired troops. But when Mills-Roberts proudly guaranteed that his men could, and would, do it, he was allowed to go ahead.

On the night of 18–19 August, we moved out of the woods and walked along a railroad track, stepping over the cross ties. We were making such good time that we had to stop to keep from getting ahead of schedule. It seemed like an endless waiting period, everyone lolling about, sleeping if possible, wishing to get on with it.

Mills-Roberts wrote that he studied his map inside a plate layer's hut, where it was possible to use a flashlight after hanging a blanket over the sole small window. The time had almost come to give the order to attack, but he thought he should empty his bladder before that. Temporarily blinded after leaving the lighted interior, he moved only a step or two away from the hut before relieving himself.

He recounts in his book *Clash by Night* what happened next: "Some bugger's peed on my face! (said his accident victim)."

"I walked self-consciously away before the unfortunate fellow was fully awake or knew the name of his benefactor. In the distance I heard the regimental sergeant-major of 3 Commando, who was a Coldstream Guardsman and extremely regimental, saying to him, 'Now then, lad, don't say some bugger's peed on your face. It was the brigade commander who's mistakenly relieved himself on your face. You want to wake up and not be so dozy.'"

Canadian engineers had built the most primitive of bridges. Single planks, each about one inch by eight inches, were laid on top of anchored rubber dinghies. Mills-Roberts called it "a kapok assault bridge . . . part of the ordinary Royal Engineers' equipment," but to us it was a rickety improvisation at best.

To avoid losing our balance and tumbling into the river, the engineers stood waist deep in the water, and we used their uplifted arms as handrails. Actually, I don't know whether they stood on the bottom in a shallow spot or if they were lashed to the dinghies; it was too dark to tell. We reached the other bank safely and unheard, the entire brigade in single file. We had avoided roads and paths in our advance, following the railroad line most of the way. With 1,500 men on the move, "unheard" is an exaggeration. The Germans must have heard or suspected something, but they shelled the roads instead of the railroad track, and their rounds whistled harmlessly over our heads.

Mills-Roberts then had his tape-laying team mark the trail. His brilliant idea was that two men, suitably protected, would carry a roll of white tape on a stick stuck through the roll between them. With this tape, normally used to flag the boundaries of minefields, they marked a safe route that others could easily follow without the concern of stepping on mines.

When we left the bushy riverbed, mists began to rise, signaling the approaching dawn. The enemy's forward positions were silently overcome by fighting patrols who took them totally by surprise. But the Germans' biggest surprise came when they realized that an entire brigade had crossed the river without being detected and was now in their midst. We were halfway up the hills before a shot was even fired. Then there were a few brisk encounters ending with the bulk of the brigade holding firm positions on the high ground. That had been our objective, along with a lower feature to the right, which 4 Commando had branched off to occupy.

We advanced at dawn on 19 August, way past the date that our assault force had expected to be in France. We found to our surprise that we had passed unknowingly under the barrel of a heavy gun in one of these mist-draped hedges. Either the gunners had fled, or the gun was left unmanned and unguarded at night. The risk of the operation was brought home to us when 4 Commando met fierce resistance at a château nearby. After a brisk display of firepower, the enemy at the center of the château hoisted a white flag. The small party sent forward to accept the surrender was promptly cut down by German machine guns.

Although it is possible that the perpetrators of this outrage were unaware of the surrender, it inspired a furious attack by our men. The château was captured, and all its defenders poured out into the sunny morning with their arms raised high. Among the wounded was their commandant, a bookish-looking man in his midthirties, clean shaven, with unmilitary wavy graying hair. He had a bad abdominal wound.

Pale and wan, he lay on a stretcher in the grass of a meadow where our medics had deployed our casualties and theirs. Noticing that I was ordering prisoners up one at a time for interrogation, he immediately asked to speak with me. "I cannot lie here like this," he began. "I am looking ungentlemanly without my cap; I must have been careless and dropped it when I was hit. I am certain it is still lying there. Can someone go back and get it? I feel I cannot stay here, looking unmentionably sloppy."

"Tough."

"Can I at least comb my hair? Could you help me get out my comb and mirror?" I did.

Granted, he was in shock, but he also had a bent for the melodramatic. I found this both ridiculous and irritating under the circumstances: a fierce Moaning Minnie mortar attack had zeroed in on our very meadow. The mortar shells came hissing down among the motley array of stretchers lying wherever they had been hastily set down. Everyone who could move dived for the only available shallow ditch, which ran along one edge of the field.

Having been preoccupied with my prisoners, I was a fraction of a second behind the general surge for cover, and I barely managed to take a headlong dive into that ditch, already filled with my comrades in arms. I landed on top of someone who had gotten there ahead of me. The good news was that I had made it this far; the bad news was that the ditch was not deep enough, and my rear end was exposed embarrassingly above its rim. To make matters worse, the soldier on whose back I had unceremoniously come to rest started to scream hysterically. Perhaps he thought he had been hit, which of course was true in a manner of speaking. Or he was just unsettled by the noisy explosions only yards away from us. Be that as it may, it annoyed me.

"Are you stupid or something? Anything hitting you would first have to go through me. So what the hell are you carrying on about?"

Luckily, the bombardment ceased and we could all come out and brush ourselves off. Some of the casualties had been wounded anew. I resumed questioning the German officer.

Our medical officer and his medics were hopscotching from stretcher to stretcher dispensing morphine injections to friend and foe alike. When they reached the German officer, he said with a gallant flourish: "*Nein!* Not for me. Give it to my men first." In shock, he barely managed to utter this sentence between his chattering teeth. "I am ashamed," he added, "for I am showing weakness."

I explained a little unkindly that if we didn't have enough morphine to go around, he might not get any at all. The doctor was giving it to everyone who needed it without distinction; he was not going to meander selectively among the maze of stretchers.

After the officer had been jabbed by the needle, he calmed down a bit, then he raised his head as best he could. "Could I speak to my *oberfeldwebel* for a moment?"

"*Nein! Ausgeschlossen,*" I said (No, totally out of the question.)

"But I promise on my German officer's honor not to discuss anything of future military significance."

I reconsidered my refusal. I was certainly going to listen to whatever was said, and some useful information might be revealed in their present stressed state.

"Go ahead."

I called over the German sergeant-major, a squat, stocky man with wire-rimmed glasses and a cropped haircut.

"*Feldwebel* Luther."

Luther took one step forward and snapped to attention, clicking his heels. He raised his right arm to say "*Heil Hitler,*" but thought better of it halfway up and managed a military salute of sorts instead.

"Luther, I must ask you a very important question. Do you think we surrendered too easily?"

"*Nein, Herr Leutnant.*"

"Are you quite sure?"

"*Ja, Herr Leutnant.*"

"That takes a heavy burden off my mind. Dismissed, and thank you, Luther." The German sergeant-major about-faced and was marched off with the other walking prisoners. His questioner now turned once again to me.

"I am happy now that I know I have not let down the Fatherland. It lifts a stone from my heart. And I am happy to have been taken prisoner by you and not by the Russians, nor even the Americans. After all, we have always liked each other."

"We have?"

"*Natürlich!* We have bad names for all our other enemies, but not for you. We call you 'Tommy'; that's almost a term of endearment. And you feel the same way about us: you call us 'Hans'; we are, so to speak, on a first name basis."

At this profound juncture two medics picked him up, "hun" or "Hans," and carried him off to safety. I couldn't help thinking that he might well have called me *"Saujud"* (Jewish pig), had our roles been reversed and had my cover story not held.

Meanwhile, we had lost radio contact with the bulk of the brigade on their hill, so it was crucial to reestablish communications as soon as possible. A three-man patrol was dispatched to get through to them, then return and report on their status and condition. As hours wore on and the patrol did not return, our anxiety increased. Finally, 4 Commando's Major Boucher-Myers, who had recently returned after being wounded, assembled another small patrol with the same objective as the first one, plus trying to determine what had become of them. He had probably heard of my patrol experience, so he asked for me and two Bren gunners to set out with him on this task.

There was an additional fallback position should we fail in our objective. An hour and a half after our departure, a convoy of jeeps laden with the three most urgent needs, ammunition, food, and medical supplies, would drive at the highest speed possible up the road to those holding the hill. This would be a desperate attempt to crash through whatever fire or obstacles the enemy might have put in place. To improve its chance of success, our artillery would lay down a heavy barrage of smoke shells on either side of the road to hide the jeep column.

We three began our part of the operation cautiously. There was a small stream we had to cross about fifteen minutes out, with inconveniently steep banks on either side. The road crossed it over a small bridge. There we saw what had happened to our preceding patrol. They had yielded to the temptation to cross the stream over the bridge together, instead of one at a time. In the middle of the bridge all three had been caught by enemy cross fire, and their bodies, or parts of their bodies, were strewn everywhere. We saw what had happened well before we reached the bridge. We stopped immediately, deployed one Bren to one side, and stayed very still for at least ten minutes, studying every inch of the landscape in front of us through our binoculars. Then, and only then, did we dash across the bridge, one at a time.

No one shot at us. We had been correct in concluding that the enemy had abandoned their ambush position. But all this had taken time. We stepped over severed rumps, arms, and legs and moved forward along the narrow country road that led up the hill, using a shallow ditch on its left as cover. In the dusk it became difficult to discern what lay ahead. Suddenly, we were aware of someone moving on the road about a hundred yards in front of us. Boucher-Myers was in the lead and I, behind him, flattened in the ditch, as he waved the Bren gunners forward. They crept up rapidly and were about to fire when we thought we made out a green beret in the gathering darkness.

"Stop. Hey you over there. This is 4 Commando trying to make contact."

A hand waved in response, and we met a patrol from the hill trying to make contact with us. Major Boucher-Myers conferred with the commanding officer of the Commandos who had successfully captured the hill. They were, nevertheless, cut off from the rest of the Second British Army until the connecting road could be kept open.

Eventually, we set out on the return journey. As we descended from the hill, the smoke barrage started to explode on both sides of us, shrouding the country road in walls of white. This caused us some anxiety, for even though they were firing smoke shells, not high explosive, that fine distinction would have been entirely lost on us if the shells had strayed a little off target and hit us.

When we neared the bridge, we could hear the roar of the jeeps engines between the noise of the artillery. And just as we came to the bridge, the convoy roared over it. I found the spectacle particularly unnerving, for jeep after jeep drove hell for leather onto the bridge and then over the remains of the bodies of the first patrol. I knew it couldn't be helped, but it shocked me all the same.

The next day Boucher-Myers asked me to come with him on an unusual quest. Our outposts had reported seeing German shells dropping short out in no-man's-land, not high explosives nor smoke but spilling propaganda leaflets over the countryside. None of the leaflets reached us, so Boucher-Myers wanted to go have a look at them himself.

Soon after we left our lines, we came upon the paper that was littering the landscape. There were three kinds of leaflets, all couched in an incompetent mixture of American and British jargon so comical in tone and content when addressed to the likes of us that it was clearly doomed to failure. One would think that they would have better propaganda; that was supposed to be their strong suit. The major was fascinated by the leaflets. Two were printed in two colors, black and red, and illustrated with artwork.

The third one had no pictures, only text: "Welcome to the Continent!" it began. "Hullo, Boys! Here you are at last old chaps!" Under the subtitle, "Whom have you got to thank for this invasion-dinner? . . . you must eat up the soup into phich [sic] a certain Mr. Joe has crumbled your crackers for you . . . It ist [sic] this Mr. Joe from Moscow . . ." As one read on, it became obvious that this leaflet was targeting Americans, for it mentioned them specifically four times—in spite of the "old chaps" line—and it ended with the question: "Die for Stalin—and Israel?"

The two more colorful leaflets were equally pathetic, if a little more interesting to look at. One showed a sketchy view of Berlin's Brandenburg Gate diagonally opposite one of London's Tower Bridge; over both loomed a ghastly snarling skeleton, a flaming torch in hand. "BERLIN and now—LONDON," it read. On the reverse side was "Hell-Dogs over England! For two years Allied bombers tried to wipe out one German city after the other, killing or wounding millions of innocent women and children. . . . Now it's our turn! Since midnight June 15th/16th a new German long-range weapon of most terrible explosive effect is continuously engaged in massive large-scale raids over London and South-East England. We hate this war against the defenseless population, but you have forced this fight upon us. These raids will be continued until a decisive military goal is reached. . . ."

Such propaganda was enough to make any British soldier want to fight harder. But the best leaflet was the second one: entitled "When you left your wife," it showed a British corporal, his forage cap tilted over his left ear—strictly against British Army regulations—in an emotional embrace with his blond wife, dressed in a pinafore and wearing a bandanna on her head. "When you left your wife you tried to console her in the belief that by this very last, great effort of all Allies together THE WAR WILL DEFINITELY BE OVER IN A FEW MONTHS. . . . You are facing German soldiers now, defending the forefield [sic] of their home. . . ." It ended on the admonition: "Did you write home already? Do it at once! A few hours from now, it may be too late!"

Some of these leaflets had obviously been intended for earlier distribution, but I imagine that their artillery was preoccupied with other tasks. Even so, sometimes it was hard to understand the Germans, even for us 3 Troopers. Bill Boucher-Myers wanted to give each of our seven troops in 4 Commando a set of these leaflets as souvenirs. So he and I got down on our hands and knees and collected twenty-seven leaflets, three for each troop and one for him and one for me.

On our way back, I burst out laughing.

"What's funny?" he asked.

"We captured an enemy order just yesterday. It warned all their troops not to pick up *our* propaganda leaflets. It said: 'Anyone below the rank of major found with one will be summarily shot!' Isn't it ironic, sir, that here you—a major—and I have been risking our lives crawling all over no-man's-land helping the Germans deliver theirs?"

The leaflets caused 4 Commando a lot of amusement. By providing them, the enemy had boosted our morale enormously, just the opposite of what he had intended. The whole episode made it wonderfully clear to us that we were winning the war.

22 Victory for the Skipper, France, and Italy

The Germans who had shot Bryan Hilton-Jones had been too cautious to come out to bring him in during the night. We had thought he had been killed, and their leaving him out there, severely wounded, nearly did kill him. He was almost dead when they finally carried him in at dawn, and a prisoner they had caught earlier was ordered to dig a grave for him. They didn't know the Skipper as we did. He managed somehow to stay alive.

He slowly recuperated in a German military hospital in Pont L'Évêque. His German Army doctor, no doubt fascinated by the young Welsh officer's will to live and his flawless linguistic talents, took a keen interest in his treatment. He prescribed a special diet for him, which was luxurious not just by military standards, but haute cuisine even in the land of haute cuisine. They became friends.

One day the doctor had a surprise for the Skipper. He told him, confidentially, that the British were about to retake Pont L'Évêque and that the Germans were planning to evacuate the field hospital. The allied attack would doubtlessly be preceded by a fierce bombardment, but if Hilton-Jones didn't mind weathering that storm, the doctor was willing to lie and report that this particular prisoner was unfit to be moved. There was every reason to believe that he would be recaptured by his own side tomorrow or the next day.

Bryan Hilton-Jones thanked him.

The 46 Royal Marine Commando liberated Pont L'Évêque with the 6th Airborne Division, and along with it the Skipper in his hospital bed the following day.

"My diet certainly deteriorated when I fell into British hands," said the Skipper later.

I got into Pont L'Évêque with 4 Commando after the battle was won. I found a bar open in a little square opposite a church, in the center of the small provincial town.

"You must try the local Cointreau called Crystalle," someone had told me. So I ambled in, full of admiration for the French sense of priorities: a town was captured and the bars were open. I tried the Crystalle, and it tasted like fine Cointreau.

Henry Gordon (Geiser) of 3 Troop was among the Skipper's liberators. Unlike some of our men who had been unaware of the Nazi threat in their childhood and early teens (some of them even confessed admiring the trim uniformed glamor of it all at an impressionable age), Henry was brought up in a totally different milieu, one that was uniquely programmed to make him into one of the keenest volunteers to fight a familiar enemy. His great-grandfather was Wilhelm Liebknecht, the founder of the Social Democratic Party in Germany, who had been forced into exile in London after the 1848 German Socialist uprising.

Henry's great-uncle Karl Liebknecht (Wilhelm's son) had been murdered during riots in Berlin in January 1919. Henry's father, born in Berlin, had also been a Socialist union leader. Political enemies were usually killed immediately by the Nazis. Several attempts at assassination were narrowly avoided by the Geiser family. They fled, first to Berlin, then to Silesia, and then on to Brno, in the Czech Republic. The Spanish government helped Henry get a job in their Paris embassy. When the Spanish were defeated by Franco's Fascists, the defunct embassy still issued Henry a Spanish passport, and a Socialist British Member of Parliament enabled him to escape to England, where I met him in the Old Hampshires. He was still the same outstanding soccer player he had been before his odyssey, when he had been Dresden-Süd's center forward. He became one of the earliest members of 3 Troop.

After the defeat at Pont L'Évêque, the Germans continued to retreat so quickly that the Commando could not keep contact with them without using transport. I remember waiting for some British Army's Royal Army Service Corps trucks by a lonely roadside near a potato field. Quickly I lit a hard-fuel tablet in my tiny tripod cooker, dumped a fresh supply of recently traded Normandy butter into my captured German mess can, and invited everyone nearby to harvest and then peel some potatoes. Hungry stomachs stimulated willing hands. Everyone agreed that they had never eaten better french fries.

A moan of disappointment went up when our transportation arrived and we had to end our feast.

Our pivotal position was now a thing of the past, for the Americans under General Hodges and the Canadians under General Crerar had broken through at Torigni, Villers-Bocage, Évrecy, and Thury-Harcourt. General Leclerc's French armored division and Patton's armor were closing the gap at Falaise, trapping vast numbers of the enemy while the Allied air forces were pulverizing their tanks and ordnance caught therein. One of our dispatch riders returned on his motorcycle, covered in debris dust.

"I was supposed to deliver a message in a village near Falaise. I passed it three times, turning about time and again, trying to find it. But there was nothing left of it, just piles of rubble, knocked out tanks, dead horses, and dead Germans."

The roads to Paris were now open. The remaining task was to mop up pockets of resistance. At dawn one morning in the last week of August, we were approaching the little town of Beuzeville, southeast of the seaside resort of Honfleur. Colonel Dawson, the slim, fair-haired CO of 4 Commando, sent me ahead of the unit with two objectives: to see whether the enemy was still there, and, if they had pulled out, to see whether there was a place where the Commandos could rest comfortably for a week or two. This was to be the end, finally, of what was originally supposed to have been the use of the Commandos for only the initial D day assault.

Eager to see whether the coast was clear, I started out cautiously along a little country lane. Level wide-open fields were on either side bordered by the usual hedgerows. I paused now and then and scanned the gray-green morning landscape in front of me before moving on. Across a field stood an impressive little mansion, a two-story structure with bay and dormer windows, not an unlikely place for the enemy to have prepared for defense.

Suddenly, I saw some movement ahead, so I crouched down, my finger on the trigger of my tommy gun. A man had emerged from among some bushes and was coming toward me in the dim morning haze. The small, elderly man, a civilian, started to wave to me. Was he mad? To venture out between the Germans and us at the crack of dawn seemed a sure way of getting shot. We continued to walk toward each other. When we stood face to face, he embraced me and kissed me on both cheeks.

"Vous êtes les Alliés! I am the mayor of this town. Welcome! You have come at last!"

"Where are the *Boches,* Monsieur?"

"They are just leaving at the other end of town, taking a lot of things with them that don't belong to them, but never mind . . ."

He assured me that he would accommodate as many of us as I liked. There was plenty of room in his barns, and we could eat all the good ripe apples we desired.

"Thank you, monsieur. I must return at once to report to my colonel."

"No," the mayor said firmly. "I insist that first you must come with me to my house over there and meet my family and have a drink: you are the liberation."

After we had had six drinks and I had been hugged and kissed by his wife, his unbelievably beautiful daughter Olga, and the entire household, I had to explain that my colonel surely believed by now that I was no longer among the living and therefore was likely to mount an attack at any moment.

The Commandos stayed there for two weeks, enjoying the apples, resting, and exploring the beautiful coastal towns of Honfleur and Trouville. We even had the unique opportunity to spend our invasion money in these resorts, for some shops were beginning to open up. On our first outing, Gary Mason (my aphrodisiac-borrowing friend) and I saw an elderly lady struggle with the weight of a heavy black marketing bag up the hilly street to her house. We rushed over and carried the bag loaded to the brim with groceries. When we took it from her she was worried, thinking we were going to run off with all that produce, probably her first marketing trip since the town's liberation. When we delivered it, and her, safely to her home, she gratefully invited us to have dinner with her then and there. It was the best meal we had in France.

The old Africa-hands, the 6 Commando men with whom I had landed on D day, had been right when they doubted that after the initial assault we were going to stay "two weeks at the most."

Three months is what it actually turned out to be, longer than any other unit in continuous action. With no one in reserve, we were all "up," all the time; the chunk of real estate assigned to us in the beachhead had been too long to manage with any lesser number. Those Canadian parachutists who had so generously tossed us all their cigarettes on D day afternoon, believing that they had done their job and were headed home, stayed in France as long as we did.

It was the end of August 1944. We were tired but in high spirits. Going home. It felt great to be alive.

I said good-bye to the mayor and his wife and lovely Olga. Our families have been friends ever since.

One month later, in September 1944, the 3 Troopers in Italy heard all about the campaign in France firsthand when three of our own, who had been commissioned in the field in Normandy, were sent there to take charge of some reinforcements. These were Lt. Ken Bartlett, formerly attached to 3 Commando, and Lts. Percy Shelley and David Stewart, who had been attached to 45 Royal Marine Commando. Their problem of commanding their former peers was easier than that faced by Griffith in France. Whereas he had come raw out of cadet school to take charge of men who had been in combat, they were all seasoned veterans.

The 3 Troopers faced just one more action in Italy, Lake Comacchio. One thousand German prisoners were taken in that operation; disappointingly, they turned out to be Russian POWs who had volunteered or been press-ganged into the German Army as members of the 162 Turkoman Division. The flashes on their lower sleeves read "Brigade Georgia," and only one lieutenant could be found who spoke some German. These prisoners were temporarily kept in fields surrounded by barbed wire. There was a sudden stir as a German general drove up in a staff car to surrender. A scruffy-looking Sergeant Anson (unshaved from sheer lack of time) was frantically trying to deal with the huge numbers of even more disheveled enemy soldiers. The general looked around in vain for some sort of receiving line. When none materialized, he addressed Colin, looking straight ahead, past him.

"I am a general. Where is the commander?"

"You'll have to wait," Anson snapped. "We're busy with your men. They come first."

The deflated general flushed a deep purple above his gold-braided collar, whereupon some of the general's staff officers ordered their noncommissioned personnel to unload his luggage. Colin interrupted them: "Each man, regardless of rank, can take what he can carry—no more."

A new day had dawned. But in another part of the woods, the war was not nearly over.

23 Sixteen to Holland and Germany

When the 1st Commando Brigade finally returned from France, the 3 Troop detachments from it settled down in Eastbourne to replenish their decimated ranks with new soldiers.

James Griffith, now promoted to captain, was the commander of the troop, and Eric Howarth had succeeded Oscar O'Neill as the troop sergeant-major. Many of us were also given higher ranks as noncommissioned officers, so there were quite a few new lance corporals and corporals around. I became a sergeant.

If there was such a thing as the spirit of 3 Troop, Eric Howarth was it. Churchill had said in one of his wonderful wartime speeches: "We shall not flag nor fail . . ." If any of us ever had the slightest inclination to do either (and I confess there were such moments), there was Eric to set the example, calmly and cheerfully. His style was totally different from that of his predecessor. There was no trace of the stereotypical bullying that is supposed to go with the job. He achieved better results by inspiring the troop and by giving clear, precise commands. These were always reasonable and often mellowed with a touch of humor.

The son of a Jewish lawyer and a Protestant mother, Eric was born in Ulm, Württemberg, Germany, in 1922. Frau Nathan, Eric, and his sister escaped the Nazis, managing to get to England, after Nathan Senior was incarcerated in the Dachau concentration camp. Luckily, the father was able to join his family later; "the final solution," the wholesale murder of the Jews, had not yet begun.

Eric attended the London Polytechnic and King's College, Cambridge. When the internment of friendly enemy aliens started, he was shipped to Canada, one of the 2,000 or so who were kept there in several barbed wire–surrounded camps. Like many 3 Troopers, he suffered the frustration of being locked up by a

STRIKING BACK

friendly nation, aggravated by the inability to participate in the fight against Hitler.

At last there appeared to be some hope, when the Home Office sent out one Alec Paterson. He was a prison commissioner by profession, but also, and more importantly, a great humanitarian. His assignment was to determine whether any trustworthy, willing, and suitable internees might be utilized in the Allied war effort. Sir Alec found Eric Howarth to have all the required qualities, so he recommended his immediate release and had him returned to England so that Eric could fulfill his fervent wish to enlist in the British Army, albeit the Pioneer Corps.

But a shocking disappointment awaited Eric and several others who had been chosen to join His Majesty's Forces. The returnees found themselves back at square one as they were reinterned at Huyton, from where they had originally been sent to Canada, when the authorities got their signals crossed. The officials in Britain had not been instructed to guide the eager young men to the nearest recruiting office. Once he was in the Pioneer Corps, after frustrating delays, Eric volunteered for whatever came along and thus found his way into 3 Troop.

On D day, Eric had headed our ill-fated detachment with 4 Commando but he had not made it off the beach. The Commando landed at the extreme left of the entire Allied beachhead. On the narrow strip of sand on that gray morning, Eric was felled by a mortar shell even before he could reach the dune.

During his short time ashore, Eric had already taken two prisoners who turned out to be his salvation. Realizing the serious nature of his wounds and the unlikelihood of a speedy evacuation of, by his own description, a hopeless case, he ordered them to stick with him. With his chest and abdomen slashed by the metal slices of the German missile, he was hardly in a condition to command anyone to do anything, but Eric never let adversity conquer him.

Eric gave the prisoners his morphine and ordered them to administer it at regular intervals, whether he was conscious or not. He told them that he was their ticket to England and safety, so they had better keep an alert eye out for medics to evacuate him, and them, as his stretcher bearers. Then he fainted. They followed his instructions meticulously. Even so, it took them more than a day to be picked up and transported to England. By this time their charge was more dead than alive.

Seven operations later, Eric began to agitate to be returned to active duty. He did this with his usual obstinate enthusiasm. He pestered and cajoled. He ridiculed the absurdity of being invalided out of the Army, or even out of his beloved Commandos. To the surprise of none of us, he won.

Troop Sergeant-Major O'Neill had been RTUd because of what witnesses described as a grave injustice. On a patrol, he had emphatically and by all accounts wisely disputed a self-destructive course proposed by an inexperienced young officer. Eric therefore was promoted in his place when the brigade returned from France. His contribution to the breaking in of the new volunteers was superb. Eric was a shining example, confessor and counselor and friend.

When we took the new men on a strenuous rock-climbing expedition in North Wales, I asked Eric whether he had any problems with his wounds.

"It doesn't hurt that much," he said, "only when I make certain moves."

He had been urged to apply for a commission when that opportunity had first arisen. He had steadfastly refused, for he feared that he might miss combat while attending the three-month course at OCTU. He wanted to be with the rest of us when we went into action again.

We tried to train the new volunteers as rigorously as we had been trained, and we chased them all over the countryside "for their own good," as we kept telling them. I recall a speed march that took off at a particularly brisk pace, Eric in the lead. Gary Mason, as friendly and good-hearted a person as one could wish to know, was charged with bringing up the rear. Inevitably, some men faltered and threatened to drop not only back but out altogether. Gary would not countenance defeat. He did not want to let Eric down, so he pushed the stragglers with encouraging words and both his outstretched arms on their shoulders.

One novice had the poor judgment to take issue with this form of contact. "Corporal, you can't do that. You must not lay hands on me. It's not allowed."

"Gee, I'm sorry," replied Gary, "I forgot." Then he placed a well-aimed kick on the plaintiff's rear end, like the great soccer player that he was. Eric didn't see any of this, but he would have endorsed Gary's method. Nobody fell out after that.

While we were training the new recruits, 4 Commando Brigade landed on Walcheren Island in Holland at the mouth of the River Scheldt on 1 November 1944. The island dominates the approach to the important Belgian harbor of Antwerp. The Allies needed that port urgently because it was getting progressively more difficult to supply our advancing armies via the Normandy beaches, for most of the Channel ports were either still in German hands or had not yet been sufficiently repaired to receive any shipping.

For the landings on Walcheren, 4 Brigade was composed of 4 Commando with its two 10 Commando French troops, and three Royal Marine Commandos (41, 47, and 48), plus the Belgian and Norwegian troops of 10 Commando. Seven 3 Troopers took part in the landings at Flushing and Westkapelle: Sergeants Farr and Gray, Corporals Douglas, Hamilton, and Latimer, and Private Watson. Lieutenant Vernon Dwelly, one of the 3 Troopers who had opted for OCTU and who had been recently commissioned, became 4 Commando's Intelligence Officer. The mysterious Captain "Bunny" Emmet was 4 Commando's adjutant. As a lieutenant, he had been one of our 3 Troop officers. He wore a Tank Corps cap badge on his beret and sported RAF aircrew wings. He must have had a colorful career, but being a taciturn man, he never talked about it.

Walcheren, held by the German Fifteenth Army, had been thoroughly prepared for the anticipated assault. Well dug in, its troops defended a maze of concrete strongpoints in the loose sand dunes that were part of the island's dykes. The RAF had breached these dykes in several places, and flooded many of the defenses. Navy and RAF Mosquitoes and rocket-firing Typhoons softened up those not underwater. Ultimately, troops on the ground had to force the surrender of one enemy position after another.

The landing itself was accomplished with few casualties, although the naval assault force that protected the troops as they went ashore suffered heavy losses. Of the 3 Troopers, Captain Emmet was wounded, as was Watson, who helped him ashore. It was a cold and blustery day with high seas, and the disembarkation was hampered by underwater obstacles, such as steel poles with mines attached to them, similar to those encountered in Normandy but more effective. Several landing craft were stuck on them, and their occupants had to swim and wade to the beach in the icy water.

Hamilton, the jolly Austrian who had always asked me in training to share my candy or glucose tablets, was one of the few unlucky ones; he was killed instantly in the shallow surf.

Major Bill Boucher-Myers (with whom I had picked up the enemy pamphlets in no-man's-land and linked up with the Commandos on the hill in the Dives river crossing) established 4 Commando's beachhead. Freddy Gray and Maurice Latimer were at Westkapelle with 41 Commando. Enemy firing had all but ceased, except for one remnant in a tall tower at one end of the village. Freddy gave his tommy gun to Maurice and strutted down the main street conspicuously unarmed, shouting at the top of his voice: *"Ergebt Euch alle— Ihr habt keine Chance!"* (Surrender—you don't have a chance.)

In response, a *feldwebel* came out and offered conditions under which they would submit. Latimer, quick moving as always, managed to slip by him unseen while Freddy argued with him.

As a Sudeten-German Socialist, Latimer had a pragmatic populist approach to most problems. "He thought that the common man was much better than those in charge," Gray said, "so he went behind my back and, more importantly, behind the German sergeant's [back] and got the Germans in the tower to surrender without any conditions at all. He led them out the back so their sergeant wouldn't see them. Then he told the sergeant he might as well give up also as he had no troops left."

The next day the two 3 Troopers set out before dawn to infiltrate the enemy lines and stimulate further defections. They came across some German orderlies bringing coffee to their officers. When Freddy yelled *"Hände hoch!"* the coffee spilled and the mugs broke. *"Wo ist der Kommandant?"* he asked them.

"They were afraid to tell us and actually cried when I demanded an answer. While this was going on, Latimer had drifted off somewhere. Suddenly a big sleepy man surfaced from a bunker and stood there in the half light, demanding his coffee. He was clearly the man we wanted. I had just pointed my tommy gun at him when out of the sky, or so it seemed, flew Latimer, who landed on top of him."

Flattened by Latimer's vigorous tackle, the demoralized German agreed to give up his strongpoint.

By the second week of November, the Germans had surrendered on Walcheren, and before the end of the month the first cargoes were being unloaded at Antwerp.

At the beginning of January, we 3 Troopers who were training the new volunteers in Eastbourne, Sussex, were given a furlough. On 7 January I received a telegram at my mother's place in London.

> PRIORITY CPL MASTERS P F [My promotion to sergeant had not yet been officially substantiated] CLARIDA 3/5 DUKE ST LONDON W 1 =
> URGENT RECALL STOP YOU WILL REPORT BACK TO 3 TROOP HQ
> 0900 HOURS WEDNESDAY 10TH JANUARY COMMANDING 3 TROOP
> 10 COMMANDO ++

I took the night train and soon found out that the reason for the emergency was that the Germans were threatening to break through in the Ardennes and were trying to retake Antwerp. The new volunteers were not deemed ready for action, so the sixteen men of 3 Troop who boarded the ship that day were all old hands: Griffith, Howarth, Nelson, Fenton, Villiers, Harris, Mason, Seymour, Spencer, Davis, Drew, Turner, the Hepworth brothers, myself, and one of the very few genuine British 3 Troopers, Griffith's orderly, Henderson. As we sailed from Tilbury, a German V-1 chug-chugged overhead toward London. This so-called "doodlebug" was an unmanned explosive rocket designed to terrorize Britain's civilian population. It felt a bit perverse to be sailing into action but away from the dangers on the home front.

During the passage, Walter Hepworth seemed anxious; he had not been in action before. We were probably as apprehensive as he was, but that did not mean that we were gentle and understanding toward him. He finally told us what was bothering him. "There you are, chest deep in your trench; you look at the enemy across from you and you fire at them and they fire at you. And then you load and fire, load and fire, load and fire . . . always load and fire."

Walter had obviously seen too many World War I films. There followed much unkind laughter, which cheered us up more than it did Walter.

We traveled from Ostend to Eindhoven in Holland on a freezing train. We arrived in Helmond, a typically neat and spotless little Dutch country town. The windowpanes were so clean that one could see them only when they glinted in the moonlight. As we moved up to the river Maas, we heard that the German Ardennes offensive had been halted. The prevailing mood was one of disappointment. We were happy enough that the breakthrough attempt had failed, of course, but we had wanted to participate in foiling it. Our brigadier, Derek Mills-Roberts, obviously shared our sentiments: now that we were here, we should make our mark somehow and contribute something worthwhile.

We had been assigned the task of helping to clear out the enemy between the Maas and the Rhine, in preparation for the assault crossing of the latter. Mills-Roberts was shocked to learn that no patrols had ventured across the Maas to date. He therefore chose such a patrol as his brigade's inaugural effort. Information from the units that had preceded us on the wintry banks of the wide river suggested that they had seen no enemy activity on the opposite side. In fact, they speculated that the Germans may have pulled back, despite the results of a Canadian unit's experiment a couple of weeks previously. They launched an empty boat and floated it downstream, to see what reaction it would provoke. Within minutes, machine guns opened up on the far side, reducing the boat to splinters. Since then, however, they had observed no sign of life across the river.

All this was of great interest to us 3 Troopers. Because of our reputation, we were given the honor of carrying out this first patrol mission across the Maas. Three men were to row across at night, covered by two Bren guns, which were to shoot to the right and left of the boat if it came under fire on the way across or back. The boat party was to reconnoiter the opposite bank plus a strip of land in-land to check on the enemy's disposition.

There was one big problem even before we could get started: there was no boat. The one the Canadians had sacrificed was the only one moored on this side of the river. So Mills-Roberts sent out re-connaissance parties to local lakes and ponds. One team returned with a worthy craft.

Who was to go? As usual in 3 Troop, it was not a question of ask-ing for volunteers. Rather, it was who would have to stay behind. We resorted once again to the time-honored method of drawing straws.

After two winning straws were drawn, Eric Howarth annouced that the remaining place should be awarded to him. "After all, most of you went through the Normandy campaign and I had to miss it."

There was some dissent: "Whose bloody fault was it that you were so clumsy as to get yourself hit? Draw the third straw!" This was re-ally said in jest. Eric was voted an automatic "in." Had this not been agreed upon, my straw was the next best one, and I would have gone. Instead, I got the consolation prize. I was to be in charge of the machine-gun party, consisting of Drew and Mason. This having been decided, we three rushed to the bank of the Maas immediately to scan the opposite bank carefully with binoculars while we still had daylight.

On this cold and forbidding late afternoon, we approached the snowy, narrow, and gently descending slope cautiously, to avoid be-ing seen. There were no bushes for cover, so we crawled in the snow to get as close as possible. There we lay on our stomachs, our elbows propped up on the ground, studying the other bank.

We could see a small house silhouetted against the vast, flat Dutch landscape and the wide slate gray sky. Several long dark barges were tied up in the river in front of it, parallel to what appeared to be a towpath. Nothing stirred. It was getting noticeably and painfully colder. The warmth of our bodies melted the snow under us, and the dropping temperature would refreeze the mush.

"Hey! Someone's moving over there," Harry Drew whispered. "Just behind or on the second barge from the left."

Neither Gary Mason nor I had seen a thing.

Then someone sitting on the barge lit a cigarette. It seemed crazy to us that this German sentry felt sufficiently secure to smoke openly in what was, after all, the front line. True, the Maas was between him and us, but even without a telescopic sight it could have been his last action on earth, had we not been there on other business. Would a lone scout or an observer do such a foolish thing? Hardly. A solitary soldier would have been more experienced, for he would have been more carefully chosen. This looked like a haphazardly selected man from a larger unit who was doing his turn of watch duty. He must have been ordered not to smoke, but he hadn't taken it seriously because so many of his pals were nearby, and a big river divided him from the enemy. Moreover, this enemy had not been very aggressive so far, as no one had even attempted to cross the river.

This put a totally different face on the proposed operation. If the opposite bank was held by a platoon or a company, a reconnaissance patrol crossing would be suicidal. Therefore, I dispatched Gary Mason back to headquarters to report what we had seen and to say that, under the circumstances, I recommended the mission be aborted.

"And hurry back with the answer, Gary, before Harry and I freeze to death."

It got colder and colder. Gary should have been back by now, but there was no sign of him. We had heard some shots behind us and began to worry. Hours passed. At last Gary loomed out of the darkness.

"Where in hell have you been?"

"We can pack it in. It's off, like you suggested."

We had been lying in the frozen snow for five and a half hours. Gary explained his delay. "You're right about my having been in hell—well, almost. All of a sudden I found myself in the middle of this firefight . . . bullets flying past me right and left, from either side. I couldn't figure out who was shooting at what. Could a German patrol have come across? No way, I thought."

But that, he said, was what 6 Commando had believed when a routine Dutch Home Guard patrol passed by. Being in a new situation, each outfit didn't know much about the other, and when the Dutch *Oranje Defens* chaps challenged 6 Commando, their "Halt!" sounded so much like the German version that our side opened up and the Dutch returned their fire. It was a miracle, Gary added, that nobody had been killed or even wounded. A captain of 6 Commando had two bullet holes in his pant leg, one entering and one exiting, neither of which touched his leg.

A week later on another part of the Maas, Harry Drew participated in a patrol across—one that used the talents of 3 Troop perfectly. They set out in a rubber dinghy to cross the river and capture and bring back a prisoner. The night was dark and mild, and the patrol landed unnoticed and set off silently into enemy territory with Harry in the lead. Suddenly, they were challenged, and Harry found that they had run smack into two sentries guarding a wooden shed.

"Hasn't the Shit Signal Section informed you that there'll be a patrol out tonight?" Harry snarled at the sentries in his flawless Prussian accent. "Step forward and let me take a look at you!"

The sentries denied knowing anything and, not sure whether to trust his orders, beat a hasty retreat into the shed. Harry threatened to blow them sky-high unless they emerged. He wasn't sure how he could carry out this threat, but they came out anyway. Now Harry informed them that they were his prisoners, and he marched them quickly back to the river and into the dinghy. On the water a German machine gun opened up, and bullets began to fly alarmingly close. Our machine guns from the other bank responded, leaving a lane barely wide enough for the dinghy between the flying bullets. To make sure that the prisoners wouldn't attempt to escape by jumping overboard, Harry handed each of them a paddle.

That winter in Holland was different from the service we had seen in France, as if we were in a totally different war. The huge, flat wintry fields forced both sides to leave more space between forward positions than the distance to which they had been accustomed in the *bocage*. No-man's-land in Holland was expanded from a few hundred yards to three or four miles, allowing us to live in houses most of the time.

Some concepts changed drastically. What was considered a narrow escape in an artillery or mortar bombardment in the Netherlands would hardly have raised a comment in Normandy. What is perceived as a close shave is indeed relative.

For the first time in our experience, the Germans were better equipped than we were, at least in some ways. They had been issued pristine white snowsuits, whereas we had none. This added yet another incentive to leave a wide space between us. We were too visible. The powers that be determined that they wanted our brigade elsewhere. We were transported by truck to another part of Holland, near Maastricht and the Belgian frontier. There the Germans were holding up the Allied advance in front of the town of Roermond. Although we had a substantial foothold across the Maas there, the enemy had massive antitank defenses in place. Two deep ditches, one behind the other, cut through the flat Dutch fields, enhanced by many concrete obstacles and mines. In front of them, German infantry units were fighting stubborn delaying actions. We were to mop up these pockets of resistance and explore the possibility of circumventing the ditches.

This was thought to be a viable option, because there was a small island in the middle of the river, exactly where the antitank defenses met the riverbank on the mainland. It was called Bell Island because of its shape. If we could get a strong fighting patrol across to this place and hold it, we could then land a small reconnaissance patrol across the river farther down, behind the double ditches. This would be the preamble to a major assault, which would avoid the obstacles.

James Griffith was to participate in this operation, as was Gary Mason. The patrol went out on the night of 27–28 January 1945. The units in the area before the arrival of the Commando brigade had reported no enemy activity on the island. They thought that it might be visited only by occasional patrols, or that there was an observation post on it. They could not have been more mistaken.

We now had an ample supply of boats, so the crossing on this particularly cold night passed silently and uneventfully. No sooner had the Commandos landed and climbed the steep bank to the first dyke, which ran parallel to it on top of the slope, than six German machine guns opened up simultaneously. Because no snowsuits had been issued, the very visible landing force was hit hard, but it fought back fiercely. Our strong fighting patrol was decimated by the enemy's hail of bullets. The Royal Marine Commando major in charge was killed, along with half a dozen others, but Griffith and Mason were unscathed. Griffith was happy to be able to achieve at least some success. He found what appeared to be some important documents on

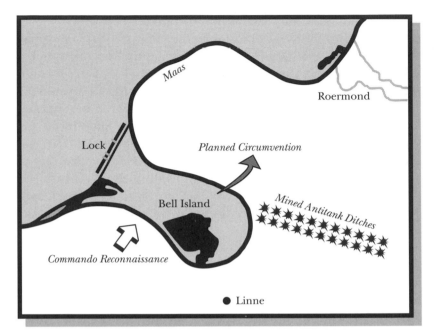

Bell Island, Holland 27–28 January 1045

a dead German officer and managed to bring them back across the river.

When the Germans opened up, Gary Mason and two of his men followed a Royal Marine Commando officer up the bank on the left flank. None was hit by the initial fusillade, but when the officer got up from where they had taken cover, he was cut down immediately. Gary and his two men managed to dive behind a pair of boats, lying high and dry upside down next to the dyke. They made it back to safety though Mason had to swim across the icy river when the swift current swept the boat with his two charges away, as they pushed off.

Eric Howarth played a prominent role in the aftermath of this operation. Surprisingly, the Germans were able to produce propaganda leaflets within a day or two, gloating over their success, even referring by name to individuals killed and captured. We responded by bringing up a loudspeaker, and from behind cover Eric requested their cooperation in letting us evacuate our dead from the island. Extraordinary negotiations followed. Eric said that he would lead a small unarmed party across to pick up the bodies. The Germans agreed.

Another boat was launched, and Eric took some men to the island on this delicate mission. After the Germans had gotten over the fact that Eric spoke perfect idiomatic German, his charisma seemed to work even on them and they became friendly, even showing him photos of their families. Suddenly, a shot rang out and whistled past Eric's ear. A die-hard Nazi had been unable to restrain himself from taking a shot at Eric. With characteristic calm and composure, Eric ignored it.

When it got dark and all the corpses had not yet been carried to the water's edge, the German sergeant-major *(hauptfeldwebel)* invited Eric to stay the night. Declining politely, Eric said he would return the next day.

By then the Germans had brought down all the bodies. They would allow only one corpse at a time to be loaded into the boat and rowed across. During the extended waiting periods, Eric finally suggested that the Germans surely realized that the war was lost and that they should therefore surrender. The *hauptfeldwebel* quickly took him aside.

"Of course we know that we have lost this damned war," he said, "but one is a soldier, after all." He appealed to Howarth, as a fellow sergeant-major, not to make his life more difficult by giving his men ideas when his job was tough enough as it was.

We learned that a few days later the entire garrison was withdrawn and severely censored for entering into negotiations with us. They and their families lost all citizen rights, and they were pilloried for their offense. In reality they had been humane and loyal, even to their lost cause. We learned this information because the old garrison was replaced by a new one of two *feldwebels* and twenty-two men who, on their first day on duty, surrendered to us by walking across a closely guarded dam connecting the island with our side of the river. They were also replaced.

After the third German garrison had settled in, Col. Peter Young, invented an ingenious punitive strike against it, reminiscent of his roller skate contraption in Normandy. From various reports he knew when the Germans were supplying the garrison. They used a sizable boat, out of sight from us around the bend downstream. Knowing the Germans' proverbial punctuality and dedication to orderly timetables, he appreciated that they would never dream of deviating from their schedule. Therefore, he collected all available explosives from nearby units and had his engineers build a raft on which to load them. The engineers timed precisely the speed of the river's current. All this accomplished, Young lit the carefully calculated fuse and pushed the raft off into midstream. It was a blustery afternoon as he watched his noble craft spin into the middle of the river and disappear around the bend. What began as a relatively quiet day was shattered by a tremendous explosion. We could not tell whether the supply boat was sunk, but the device blew out every window left in every house on our side.

Windows with shattered panes were a problem for us all along, because we appreciated living in houses, a great boon in harsh, wintry weather. Two factors aggravated the difficulty of making a war-damaged house inhabitable: the cold blowing in through the glassless windows and the usual absence of stovepipes. The enemy had removed them to heat his underground strongpoints. All houses still had iron stoves, which were useless to us because without pipes the smoke made breathing impossible.

To lick the latter situation, I went on a search mission to all nearby dwellings, occupied or not. Finding no stovepipes in any of the abandoned ones, I knocked on doors of civilian-occupied homes, behind our lines, having first researched the essential operative Dutch words for my quest. My accent notwithstanding, *kachelpijp* seemed to be understood; then I discovered that I had to qualify the word by adding *met een elleboog* (with an elbow), to steer the smoke to the outside. Kind local people behind our lines actually provided a few of the steel blue sooty implements, and the 3 Troop detachment thawed out nicely. Of course we had taken care of the window problem, by boarding them with straw-filled sacks.

After lunch one day, Eric Howarth announced that James Griffith was sending him back to the United Kingdom to be commissioned. I was surprised. "Eric! I never thought you'd agree to leave now. It'll probably mean you'll miss the Rhine crossing." "They guaranteed I'd be away only a short time," Eric said. "I'm just hopping over there, picking up my second lieutenant's pips, and coming straight back. You know that Montgomery won't allow any more commissions in the field, so this is the only way." "I'll make you a bet," I said. "For every day you're back before the Rhine crossing, I'll pay you two Dutch guilders. For every day you come back after it, you owe me two." "You got yourself a bet, Peter." It was obvious that I had the better bet. We would cross the Rhine, soon, but who could foretell how long Eric would be delayed before getting his commission and returning?

Before he left, he borrowed a set of photos from me, one of every 3 Troop detachment that had gone on D day. He had missed getting these during his prolonged stay in the hospital, and he wanted to show them to his fiancée, Audrey, and his family and also have them copied. We shook hands on our bet and he was gone.

Three troop worked together with the British 7th Armored Division, the "Desert Rats," famous from the North African campaign. The tactics we were to use were for several Commandos to ride into action clinging to the outside of their tanks. If German infantry positions were spotted, the tanks' crews would engage them with cannon and machine guns while we would dismount and eliminate troublesome antitank guns.

We didn't like this mode of operation. Those who had taken part in some early hit-and-run strikes reported that they had found the tankers sensitive to the threat of antitank weapons. When the Commandos jumped off, the tankers naturally enough wanted to keep moving so as not to present sitting targets. Theoretically, the tanks would pick us up upon completion of our task. But what usually happened was not at all convenient. By the time the last shot was fired (or at least when the Commandos had intimidated the enemy to force a lull in their firing), their rides home would turn out to be a number of specks on the horizon. Waiting for them to return was impractical and almost always futile, so the only alternative was to trek back on foot. The distances to be covered in the seemingly endless no-man's-land were a drain on everybody's good humor.

We found that loosening the Germans' hold on this part of Holland was hard work, because it took only about a dozen enemy troops to hold off our brigade for up to two days. On this occasion, they were so well dug in on the far side of a creek, overlooking the flat expanse on our side, that they could cut down anyone approaching them from the front, because we would have had to descend into the creek in their full view and then climb up toward them. Since these Germans had several handheld *panzerfaust* antitank weapons, our tank support was reluctant to come anywhere near the creek bank and confined itself to sporadic shelling and machine-gunning from a safe distance.

Finally, we planned to cross the creek a mile farther north, after we learned that the enemy did not have enough men to hold its entire length. An assault force did exactly that and then worked its way down the tree-lined far bank. Assisted by the natural cover, the men dislodged the Germans, who managed to escape through the snow toward a nearby windmill. One man succeeded in hiding there under grain sacks for another day until, driven by hunger, he decided to surrender. I can guarantee that he was well hidden, for I had ascended the windmill's steep ladderlike steps and searched each of the three levels, prodding every hemp sack en route.

The corpse of one dead German soldier presented us with the usual task of identifying his unit. The search through the pockets of this heavyset young unfortunate confirmed that he belonged to the familiar unit opposite us. Surprisingly, in his inside breast pocket he carried a large amount of money in Dutch guilders, legal tender for friend and foe alike. Our sixteen men had a standing agreement that all money found or captured would be divided equally among us. When this was done that night, Walter Hepworth declined to accept his share.

"I don't want any of your blood money," he declared. "I wouldn't touch it." We were unclear whether he meant that actually or metaphorically. Some of the paper money did have brownish red smears.

The sharing contract continued for another week when Tom Spencer, the most talented crook and scrounger of 3 Troop, announced that he was also withdrawing. "I can do better by myself than the whole lot of you together." Nobody doubted it for a moment.

By now our patrolling skills were in great demand. Our captain, James Griffith, and his orderly, the genuinely British Henderson, had been on a night patrol in the vicinity of a farm called Spielmanshof. As they approached its outbuildings, they came under withering machine-gun fire. They beat a hasty retreat, finding it hard to believe that neither of them had been hit. They were surprised that they had encountered the enemy in that place, so we had to ascertain whether this had been a chance clash with a German patrol or whether the Germans had established a solid defensive position there.

The following night a fighting patrol commanded by Major Beadle of 45 Commando set out to find the answer. The patrol consisted of fifty well-armed men plus six from 3 Troop. We left the lines of a neighboring infantry unit and headed for a farm just across from Spielmanshof, our objective. While the main body was to establish a firm base there, Griffith, Henderson, and I were to probe Spielmanshof from the left as the other three 3 Troopers did from the right, until we could determine if the enemy held that place in force.

At the very start I was disturbed at the amount of noise we were making. The patrol members were all highly trained in the art of silent movement, but if fifty-six men with weapons move into the field at the same time, the cumulative noise is bound to be audible. In the silence of a winter night, it seemed not just audible, but deafening.

I buttonholed James Griffith suggesting that the patrol go to ground and that he and I go forward until we found a good place to bring up the others. One of us would return to lead the patrol to its new position. We would repeat the process until all of us reached our objective.

"Good idea," said James, and he went off to talk to the major. My idea worked like a charm, and we reached the first farm without incident.

Then a rather surprising thing happened. "I can't get last night out of my mind," said Henderson. "The bloody machine-gun bullets practically slit my trousers. I don't think I can go out there again. This place spooks me."

There was a moment's silence.

"That's OK," James told him, "you don't need to go. Masters and I will go alone. Don't worry about it. Stay with the main body. You'll be all right tomorrow."

The farm was deserted except for an abundance of chicken and rabbits, indicating that someone had to be around to feed them, possibly the Germans in Spielmanshof.

Griffith and I, and the three others off to the right, set out toward Spielmanshof in what proved to be a bright night. To make matters worse, our searchlight beams were bouncing off the low cloud banks not far away. This device was known as "Monty's moonlight," illuminating the countryside to prevent the enemy from sneaking up unseen. Unfortunately the beams reflecting off the sky, onto the light snow on the ground and back again, made it at least as hard for us to sneak up on the enemy.

"They should have switched off the searchlights when they laid this on," whispered James. "And I know you agree with me about Henderson. He's a good lad but he wouldn't have done you or me any good out here, the state he was in. In the German Army they would have shot him for cowardice in the face of the enemy. That's why we're winning the war."

We were out so far that we could not talk or whisper anymore. We moved extremely slowly and cautiously, spread out just far enough not to be felled together by one machine-gun burst, stopping and listening every few steps. James cupped his hands over my ear to ask if I heard anything. It was unlike him to ask, I thought; but like Henderson, he had nearly been killed in this place the night before. There was another factor. I was a sergeant and he was my captain. I wasn't going to be the one to suggest, prematurely, that we get out of there. It was up to him to decide.

The scene repeated itself twice more as we crept slowly closer to what we could now make out as a barren hedgerow in front of Spielmanshof.

"How much closer do you think we can risk?" he whispered in my ear.

"How about a hundred yards?" I whispered back. "Say fifty for a start?"

He nodded.

I had actually expected that we would keep going right into the Spielmanshof farm, all things being equal.

Then I heard a noise. Metal touching wood, as when a machine-gun barrel knocks lightly against a tree trunk. The hedgerow was about 200 yards in front of us, so we were within easy range. We signaled our next move to each other swiftly, now that we were in complete accord. We got out of there a lot faster than we had moved in, but still quietly.

When we approached our base at the other farm, we had to be careful about our reentry. But we were still too near the enemy to call out. Instead we swung our compasses right and left, their luminous faces in the direction of our men. When we got very close, we started to softly whistle "Roll Out the Barrel" and "The Pennsylvania Polka," tunes of the time they would recognize.

We reported to the major that the Germans were definitely out there, an opinion confirmed by the three men from the right when they returned.

"As you know, we have not come to attack or dislodge them," the major said. "But we still need to know how strong they are or whether we just bumped into another patrol. So I want everybody to take good cover and keep well down. Only the Bren gunners and mortar men and the PIAT are to move into the most forward available cover. When that's done, I shall give the command to fire and we'll blaze away for a full two minutes. Then we'll cease fire and listen. When they respond, as I hope they will, we shall wait until their first fusillade dies down and then get the hell out of here, mission accomplished. Any questions?"

"Yes, sir," Tom Spencer said. "Can we kill some of these farm animals and take them with us? Seems a bloody shame to leave them for Jerry."

The major grinned. "All right, if you do it quickly and quietly."

"You won't know it's happening, sir."

A few minutes later the major was notified that everybody was in position.

"At your target in front. Fire."

The noise was impressive.

Two minutes later he shouted: "Cease fire. Keep well down."

There was utter silence. It seemed interminable to us 3 Troopers, who felt that to some extent our reputation was at stake. But then all hell broke loose, with at least six machine guns responding at a noise level matching ours. Of course, the Germans must have expected a major assault, unaware that such a sizable force had come that close to them. We cheered, joining in the uproar and left hurriedly after the first pause, with no one hit. Behind us we could hear enemy mortars ranging on our recently vacated positions.

There was an aftermath. We had all been ordered not to talk about where we had been. Who had undertaken what reconnaissances and where was supposed to be kept secret for overall security reasons. A few mornings later we were just putting away the mattresses and sleeping bags in our house when there was some commotion on the country road outside—horses' hoofbeats. We all rushed to the window, the only one with glass in it.

A small group of Dutch mounted partisans had ridden up to our house from the direction of no-man's-land. In the lead was a young woman of striking beauty, pale of skin, with raven black, long, straight hair framing a slim oval face. She carried a German rifle and a machine pistol and had bandoliers crossed over her shoulders.

As she reigned up her enormous dappled white horse, she displayed considerable agitation. "Spielmanshof! You haf been to de Spielmanshof!" she exclaimed.

"No way, what's a Spielmanshof?"

"But you haf been there. I know it because of this." She pointed at us, or rather just below us at the windowsill. We all looked down and saw a white rabbit skin with black spots the size of tennis balls. Tom Spencer had hung it there to dry when he had skinned what subsequently had become a delicious rabbit stew.

"I know this animal anywhere."

We changed the subject. "Anything we can do for you and your men?"

"Ja, weapons, ammunition, blankets, rations."

We gave her anything we could spare, and she and her entourage rode off.

Our search for food was never ending, so while preparing for the Rhine crossing we began to run frequent patrols across the German border. We were surprised at the number of villages and farms we encountered that looked untouched by war: undamaged buildings, abundant livestock, and well-fed people.

Upon surveying one such idyllic scene, Colonel Gray turned to me. "Would you see to it that every one of my units gets one of these by tonight?" He waved in the general direction of a gaggle of geese in the farmyard. "I think my lads deserve it; they've been fighting hard."

So I requisitioned seven well-fed geese, in fairness spreading my requests among several farms, as best I could.

One of the farmers protested vigorously. "I was in the first world war," he said, "and we would never do such a thing. It was *verboten!*"

"If that's true, times have changed," I said and asked him if he had not heard what his compatriots had done in Holland and all the other countries the Germans had occupied. "If giving up some geese is the worst thing that has happened to you in this war, you're damned lucky," I snarled at him. "You are unbombed, untortured, unmurdered."

The geese were excellent, the best meal we'd had in months. Apart from this foray, we would requisition meat and other foods, but also radios to take back to Holland as presents for our civilian hosts. The Germans had taken away or "castrated" all the Dutch radios, making it impossible to receive any broadcasts except those under their own control. While we were at it, we would order meals for ourselves.

"Fix us some ham and eggs," we would say, and one of us would accompany the lady of the house into the kitchen to make sure that all ingredients used were wholesome and nontoxic. The tommy guns we carried probably ensured prompt compliance, although no threat was ever uttered. We felt that it served them right, mild bullying, indeed, from ex-victims such as ourselves. The last shall be the first, the good book says.

24 Across the Rhine

The locale chosen for the night crossing of the Rhine seemed too obvious a place to some of us. It was the town of Wesel, a place from which roads led like sunrays to all the essential objectives of the Allied advance: Osnabrück, Münster, Essen, the industrial Ruhr area. Surely the enemy had to be sitting there, waiting for us.

To make matters worse, we received a London newspaper a few days before the actual Rhine crossing that reported its success, including the capture of Wesel. We conjectured that some war correspondent had come upon the old story of the Allies mopping up the last German resistance opposite Wesel and had become confused about which bank of the river was which. This was a dreadful mistake from our point of view. The enemy had probably seen that paper. Yet it was a fact that (other than at the Remagen bridge) no Allied soldier had set foot on the far side of the Rhine.

The bridge at Remagen is often thought of as the first Allied crossing of the Rhine on 7 March 1945, and in a manner of speaking it was. There, according to what a prisoner told me, a violent disagreement developed between an SS division that wanted to establish a defensive position on our side in front of the bridge and a German Army division that wanted to withdraw across the bridge and demolish it. My prisoner informant told me that it got so bad that each party of the dispute threatened to open fire on the other, should they attempt to interfere with their superior plan.

While the argument got more and more heated, the American First Army arrived and took both divisions prisoner. My informant said that his small remnant of the Army division was the only German presence on our bank of the Rhine, and he, a senior *feldwebel*, was ordered to fight a rear guard action to delay the Allies. He had four roads to cover, but he had only a total of thirteen men, counting himself. He put four men to watch each of three of the highways, and took up position on the most important one himself.

"I'm as good as any four *landsers,*" he said immodestly but with conviction. It was so quiet for a while that he decided he'd better take a hasty look around to check whether his men were keeping a keen lookout and to encourage them with a little morale-boosting talk: that they had been chosen to be heroes for the Fatherland, standing firm, the Watch on the Rhine—that kind of thing. All seemed fine at the first two outposts, but when he came to the third one a surprise awaited him.

"Hardly fifty yards down the road three tour busses had parked, and these Amis (GIs) were leisurely getting off, smoking and chatting and sitting down on the grass, hundreds of them. I couldn't blame my fellows for not opening fire. They were being ignored."

He rushed back to his own position where he had left his radio set, the only link to the other side of the river, and he called headquarters.

"Put me through to the General," he demanded. Of course he encountered bureaucratic resistance, but he had spent a tough campaign in Russia; he was an old soldier and he was not to be put off.

"I'm the only *feldwebel* in the *Führer's* Army on this side of the Rhine. The general will want to talk to me." They actually put him through.

"*Herr General,*" he began, "you know that secret weapon you've been telling us about? Well, the time has come to get it out of the cellar. I've been a soldier, a good one at that. But the time has come for my retirement. As for my career, I've just got to hang it up." And he hung up. Then he surrendered to us.

On the other side of the Remagen bridge, the Germans pooled all available forces to contain and seal off the bridgehead. That was the most useful aspect of that operation, as it kept many of them busy and therefore unavailable for deployment elsewhere.

Number 1 Commando Brigade prepared for an assault crossing of the Rhine in the area of Venraij in Limburg, in the south of Holland. Corporal Harris and I of 3 Troop were attached to 45 Royal Marine Commando for this operation, and other pairs of 3 Troopers were attached to 3, 6, and 46 Royal Marine Commandos.

One day the commanding officer of No. 45, Col. Nicol Gray, sent for me and said he wanted to go hunting. Could I obtain a shotgun for him from the locals? He handed me six cartons of cigarettes as a means of payment. His request illustrated two points. First, as I had discovered soon after being attached to a British Commando unit for D day, we of 3 Troop were expected to speak all languages. It simply did not occur to most commanders that just because we all spoke fluent German we did not also speak French, Dutch, and Flemish. The odd fact is that we actually did, one way or another. To speak Dutch or Flemish, we aimed halfway between English and German. If a certain word did not work, we would try one from the other language. After all, different languages originated by transpositions of vowels and consonants. It worked most of the time.

The second point was that everyone in wartime Europe considered cigarettes legal tender. In the early days, the mayor of Hauger may have been shocked by being offered cigarettes for a Manet, but as the war wore on it became standard procedure. In exchange for coffee, cigarettes, and bicycle tires, you could buy just about anything: houses, sex, or, hopefully, a shotgun.

I set out and immediately ran into a problem No civilian was allowed to have weapons of any kind, on penalty of death. It looked hopeless, but a commanding officer's demands are not to be taken lightly. Commandos are chosen and trained for being enterprising. Someone, in turning me down, said that the only guns nearby were in the hands of soldiers, the *Oranje Defens* (the Dutch Home Guard), and possibly the forester.

The forester's house was on the outskirts of town. On my way there I was challenged by British military police, for I was far from our Commando territory, conspicuous in my camouflage parachute jacket and green beret. I shook off the police easily by telling them the unvarnished truth: I was on a secret assignment for my commanding officer.

Luckily, the forester was at home and answered the doorbell. But he curtly expressed his regrets. No guns were allowed to be sold; besides, he needed his for official work.

"Well, I'm sorry to hear that. I was going to offer you cigarettes."

His eyes widened in interest. "Did you say cigarettes? How many have you got?"

"Oh, lots," I replied cheerfully. "Never mind, I'll try the *Oranje Defens*. Maybe someone there has a shotgun."

"Lots? How many shotguns do you want? I can spare three double-barreled twelve-gauge guns, with beautifully engraved locks. But they will cost you six cartons."

I did not bother to bargain, for I had two beautiful guns to spare. I gave one to Colonel Gray, who was delighted, and I took the other two to Captain Easton, whom I knew slightly. He was a Scot, presumably into hunting. More importantly, he had a jeep.

I came straight to the point by asking Easton if he would like a beautifully engraved double-barreled shotgun, and, if so, could he get another one back to England hidden somewhere in his jeep." The deal was struck. I'd give him one of the guns; he would smuggle the other for me. ("Ah, too bad about those shotguns," said the good captain when I tried to claim my prize much later. Confiscated, you know. Sorry, old man." Sometimes I have a vision of the intrepid Captain strutting through the misty Highland moors with two shotguns slung across his broad shoulders.)

Our Rhine crossing, Operation Plunder, was to lead to an Allied incursion into Germany by a night river crossing at Wesel. This was to be accomplished in exactly the reverse order of the D day landings in that the ground attack was to precede the airborne assault. The wide river was to be crossed by the Commando brigade in assault boats and Buffaloes, amphibious tracked vehicles operated by Royal Engineers. The Buffaloes sounded just like tanks but regrettably lacked comparable armor and armament. They had high sides and a trapdoor in front for the assault troops' exit.

For days we had been waiting in readiness to start the crossing. The entire bank on our side of the river was covered for several miles by a huge smoke screen that had us coughing and choking whenever the wind turned the wrong way. We even climbed trees occasionally to inhale a lung full of fresh air. The smoke, of course, was to conceal our preparations and the exact location of our landing equipment and assault force. We were even under orders to turn our

STRIKING BACK

green berets inside out, so that only the black lining showed, lest aerial reconnaissance or enemy observers or agents draw conclusions from the presence of Commandos.

Ian Harris (Hans Hajos) and I were 45 Royal Marine Commando's 3 Troop detachment. On the morning of 23 March, I was given a surprising message. An artillery unit had passed through on the nearby highway, and one of its members, Gunner Trevor, who had caught a glimpse of a green beret in spite of our precautions, asked whether one Peter Masters was nearby. Henry Trevor was none other than my cousin Hans Teweles from Vienna. I tracked him down immediately, as his battery of the 53d Welsh Division had taken up residence a mile or two down the road. We were both excited about this chance meeting. His battery invited me to lunch, which we enjoyed together reclining in a meadow. We decided to write a joint letter to my mother and his parents.

While we were scribbling it on the ground in that foreign field, the bushes barely green, his commanding officer blew a whistle, the signal to fall in so he could address the men of the battery. He had just received news that the awaited Operation Plunder was taking place that night.

"Our unit of Mountain Artillery has been given the honor of supporting 1 Commando Brigade in the biggest river crossing of the war. Prepare for your assigned tasks at once."

Great news indeed. No time to dwell upon it, though. For all I knew, 45 Commando had already broken camp in my absence and embarked in the Buffaloes to some jumping-off point. I approached the CO and explained my concern, so he continued his announcement with the remark that he had one of the Commandos with him. This was greeted with applause. He then told me he'd be only too glad to take me back in his jeep.

As it happened, my fears were unfounded, although I had not returned too soon. I was summoned to the adjutant, who introduced me to a young lieutenant of the Royal Artillery who was to be our forward observation officer. "Sergeant Masters will take good care of you," the adjutant said.

As soon as we were alone, the handsome young officer leaned toward me, looked right and left to see whether we were being observed, and said in a voice of great confidentiality: "I must ask you something, Sergeant."

"Sir?"

"You've been through this sort of fighting before, haven't you?"

"Yes, sir, more or less," I replied, wondering what was coming next.

"And do you think we will encounter the enemy?"

"Likely, sir."

"Then I must ask you a big favor, if you don't mind."

I raced through the possible options of the request to come: a quick course in survival training? A letter to his lady love? But I didn't even come close.

"When we come upon them, Sergeant," he said eagerly, "will you give me the first shot?"

Oh my, I've got me a live one this time, I thought. He thinks he's going on safari. I resolved to cock my tommy gun five minutes before the situation would demand it. But aloud I lied, "It will be my pleasure, sir."

The embarkation into the Buffaloes started at 2100. It was preceded by a massive bombardment by 77 Lancasters of No. 3 Bomber Group of RAF Bomber Command, which dropped 435 tons of bombs on the town of Wesel at 1730 hours. At 1800, six regiments of artillery began their general shelling, among them, no doubt, my cousin Henry Trevor's battery. At 2000, they started to concentrate on enemy positions at the actual landing site on Grav Island, a triangular area of swampy low ground two miles west of Wesel.

The plan called for 46 Royal Marine Commando to land first and to secure a foothold on the far bank. (They were the newest addition to 1 Commando Brigade, since 4 Commando had joined 4 Brigade for the landings at Walcheren.) Their task accomplished, 6 Commando was to lay a white tape route to the town. The entire brigade was to follow the tape in single file, to minimize the danger if minefields were encountered. Upon entering the built-up area, 45 Commando would push northeast and secure a sausage-shaped perimeter, which did not reach all the way to the bank of the Rhine. To extend the perimeter to the river was 3 Commando's task, but not until the next morning. The brilliant point was that no one was to stay in the original bridgehead.

This was an ingenious concept, which more than offset the geographically obvious choice of Wesel, about which we had had such apprehensions. The enemy had to be concerned about being misled by a diversion before he committed his mobile counterattack force, for he could not afford to hold the entire riverbank. Instead, he positioned a series of outposts to observe the river and report any attempted incursions. Only when such an attack could clearly be identified as a major one would he send in his mobile reserve.

We embarked in the vehicles, the men and equipment jampacked into the interior of the amphibious craft. My forward observer was right by my side, as was his radio operator, who had the British Army's most cumbersome radio, a 22 set, strapped to him. Normally, this piece of equipment was transported on a little trolley, but that must have been considered impracticable for Operation Plunder.

It was a clear, moonlit night as we trundled noisily toward the river. The banks turned out to be precipitous, and everybody in our craft fell forward, almost suffocating those standing in front of us by pushing them against the trapdoor at the bow. Suddenly, the craft plunged hippolike into the water, and everybody fell backward. At last we settled down and churned across the 300-yards-wide river, riding deep, the spray flying into our faces. Overhead the bombers were hitting Wesel again, 200 of them dropping more than 1,100 tons of explosives. On either side of us, Bofors guns were firing tracer, presumably to keep the Lancasters from including us in their target area. But our brigadier, Derek Mills-Roberts, must have felt that these were compromising our exact whereabouts, for I could clearly hear him shout, above the bedlam, for the Bofors to stop firing.

I don't think the gunners could hear him, for they went on firing. The noise made it impossible to determine how heavily we were being fired upon, but peering over the side I could see a Buffalo burning in midriver. Later we heard the dreadful news about that blazing Buffalo. Robbie Villiers (the lock-picking genius) and Seymour, our two-man detachment with 46 Royal Marine Commando, had been in the flaming vehicle. Both were killed.

When we touched down on the other side, our Royal Engineers drivers, wearing little yellow triangular buffalo emblems on their upper sleeves, informed us that the bank was too steep to use the trap-door, so we would have to get out by climbing over the high sidewalls of the vehicles. This presented some unforeseen problems. "How the hell are we going to get my signaler and his set out now?" gasped my artillery officer. "Don't worry," I replied, "just let everybody get out so we have some room. Then we'll lift him up horizontally and lay him on top of the Buffalo's sidewall. Then you get out and I'll climb up and lower him down to you." We did not want to have him take off his radio as it was so securely strapped on.

We managed the maneuver quite well, but soon after we had set off to join the rest of 45 Commando, my charge whispered in my ear: "Oh my God, I've lost my map."

He had put down his map case when I had lowered the radio operator down to him. I rushed back and went down on my hands and knees to search for it, but with all the comings and goings it was impossible to identify the exact place where we had been. It was a desperate situation, for all our DF and SOS tasks were marked on his map, delineating where he could lay down artillery fire in an emergency. However, we somehow found my man's opposite number who was attached to 46 Commando, and with the aid of a flashlight under a blanket, he hastily copied the information onto a spare map.

Number 6 Commando had landed in assault boats, not Buffaloes. That had not worked out well because the current was so strong that controlling the light craft proved very difficult. Worse still, some of the outboard motors malfunctioned. Several boats capsized in the five-knot current, and the men in them had to swim for it. Remarkably, one of them, Major Powell, made it ashore without losing the monocle he always wore.

Meanwhile, the tape layers did their job, paying out the broad white tape normally used to mark minefields. As in France, they carried a giant spool of it on a stick between them. Easily visible in the dark, the tape provided the comfort of knowing that one was stepping on ground where others had stepped before.

My artilleryman, regrettably, did not get his first shot, nor did he encounter the enemy on the riverbank. They were there all right,

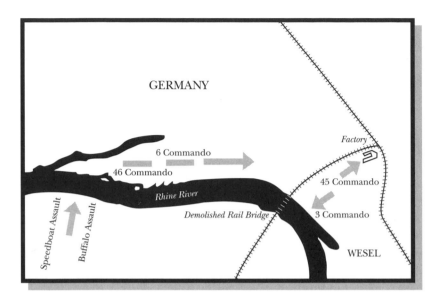

Rhine Assault 23 March 1945

but we never tangled with them as we moved inland of the German defensive posts instead of expanding along the riverbank. So we passed them unmolested as the Germans held up their counterattack until a reconnaissance could confirm that it had been a major landing. Then they sent a sizable force to the reported location, but they found nobody, as the initial bridgehead had been evacuated completely.

In the meantime, we had finished our night march on 23–24 March to the town, and 45 Commando was in the process of occupying its designated sausage-shaped area. By now I had ceased to escort my artillery officer, for 45's commanding officer, Colonel Gray, told me to accompany him and his orderly on the next phase of the operation. Abruptly, the Commando ground to a halt, and we heard the unmistakable voice of the brigadier behind us telling us to get moving. The three of us ran up the road to see what had caused the stoppage.

Suddenly, there was a terrific explosion, and all three of us were literally blown over. I saw stars, and my skin felt as if it were bursting. We had evidently been fired upon by a *panzerfaust* at close range. The German standard antitank weapon at this stage of the war, it consisted of a cone-shaped beehive head fired from a pipe containing a propelling charge. A handle like a bicycle brake activated the device, which was powerful enough to knock out a tank.

Our round had hit the ground in front of us, spattering metal fragments and gravel from the road surface and sending a considerable blast in our general direction. Amazingly, our only injury was a nasty wound in the colonel's left shoulder. A few steps farther on I saw two dead German *Volkssturm* (Home Guard) men lying facedown on a pile of debris.

Almost as a reflex, I kicked the soles of their boots. To my surprise they both got up and raised their hands. I searched them, and because I could not take them with us, I told them to walk down the road on which we had come with their hands up and surrender to the first troops they came across. They were surely the ones who had ambushed us, but they had thrown away their weapon. The colonel needed urgent medical attention, so his orderly went with him to the medics.

The reason for the delay eventually became apparent. Our lead troops had come upon three German engineers and captured them without firing a shot. Then they took them to a row of multistoried houses where Commando headquarters had been set up in the cellars: one for the colonel's command post, one next door for the signalers, and an adjacent one for our three prisoners, whom I began to question at once.

There was always a certain apprehension accompanying the capture of enemy engineers in or near the front line. What had they been sent to blow up? At times I imagined I could smell a fuse burning, so I was determined to find out as quickly as possible what their mission had been.

The standard procedure for interrogating prisoners began with the basics: search and then separate them. Ian Harris and I hastily set up our interrogation cellar, a table with a blanket thrown over it, behind which I sat as impressively as possible while Ian stood next to the prisoner.

"Unit?" I barked. These were old soldiers of unusually high rank for a German patrol.

The first POW responded routinely: "I need to give only my name, rank, and number."

And he did. I had him taken out immediately. The second one was a carbon copy of the first; but the third, ah, the third, was arrogant, luckily.

"Division?" I had demanded.

"I don't belong to a division," he said cockily.

"Battalion, then?"

"Don't belong to a battalion either." He was obviously pleased with himself at being able to tease me with his answers.

Suddenly, before my mind's eye I saw some of my training notes, stating that on page 8 or 17 of the German *soldbuch* (paybook) one may find the abbreviation ZBV. This stood for *zur Besonderen Verwendung* (for special usage) and referred to specialist nondivisional troops at the Army level, directly under Army headquarters command. I leafed through his paybook casually. There it was. I threw the book aside nonchalantly.

"Let's begin with ZBV."

He jumped as if he'd been bitten by a poisonous snake. "How do you know that? I am not saying another word."

I ordered him to be taken out and replaced by the first prisoner. "Let's start with ZBV."

He jumped as if motivated by the same reptile. "How do you know that?"

"We know everything about you. And if there were any points we didn't know precisely, they've just been filled in by your colleagues. Now we're merely checking to see whether they were telling the truth."

Soon I had the purpose of their mission, to see whether the Rhine bridge at Wesel had been sufficiently demolished. This didn't interest us, for a movable one had been constructed under the cover of the smoke screen by Royal Engineers and was waiting to be towed into position the following day.

The Germans had been captured walking along a railroad embankment. I had studied the map carefully, but I made sure that it was nowhere near me when I continued. "You came along the tracks past the factory and past the church before that." I retraced the most likely way they had come, describing all the features I had seen on the map, as if I had been there with them, or as if one of them had described it to me in detail.

And so it became the interrogator's dream: a game in which the prisoners participated as players, astonished at what I apparently knew, correcting me when I was mistaken. Harris and I worked as a team. Whenever I slowed down in my questioning, Harris would break in with a question next to the POW's ear. We kept up the momentum, bringing in one of the other prisoners when we felt we had momentarily exhausted the information from the one in the room.

Eventually, we achieved our goal with all three. They were convinced that we already knew everything about them.

Finally, I said, "And you came into that village from the north . . ." (the only village on the map in the direction from which they had come).

The prisoner interrupted: "No, we didn't come any farther."

This fact was verified by the two others, separately. It meant clearly that they had come from that village. Because they were non-divisional Army-level specialists, it was reasonable to assume that they had been stationed close to their Army command, presumably headquarters counterattack force.

I rushed to give this information to Colonel Gray, but as I left our cellar, I passed the one occupied by our signalers. They had threaded their very long, thin radio aerials through broken skylights to protrude to the sidewalk above.

"Who're you talking to?" I asked.

"Artillery on the other bank."

"What are they shooting at?"

"Nothing much. We're giving them routine targets."

"In that case I've got a good one for you. How big a one can you call for?"

"Whatever we want, including Uncle and Victory targets." In artillery parlance that meant the biggest possible concentration, the entire Army's available guns.

I gave them the precise six-figure map reference of the suspected village and heard them pass it on as I hurried up the steps to the street level and down the steps next door into the colonel's command post. I thought I had better legitimize as quickly as possible my totally unauthorized action in firing all those guns.

Colonel Gray was seated at—or rather slumped over—an improvised blanket covered table similar to the one in our cellar. A blood-stained shell dressing covered his upper arm and shoulder. As I entered, his orderly was pouring a bucket of water over the colonel's head. He had lost a lot of blood and was suffering fainting spells. Reluctant to give up his command, he had given a strict order that he was to be brought around in this manner whenever he passed out. The cold water did the job; he shook himself like a wet dog and sat up.

"May I have a word with you, sir?"

"Go right ahead, Masters."

"We have learned from prisoners where the enemy counterattack force's headquarters might be, although we're not certain, of course."

Colonel Gray brightened visibly. "Splendid!" he said. "Get the artillery on it right away."

"I have already done that, sir."

At that precise moment there was a distant rumble of loud reports, followed by the long, drawn-out, low whistle of a great many shells streaking overhead, culminating in a crescendo of explosions. The ground shook and trembled even where we were. It felt immensely satisfying. This was exactly what we 3 Troopers had been trained for.

Whether we had actually hit the enemy's headquarters I don't know, but no counterattack materialized.

I noted that Eric Howarth had missed the Rhine crossing, just as I had predicted, and I began counting the two guilders per day that our bet would earn me.

At 1030 the next morning, the sky filled with planes, and more than an airborne corps was parachuted behind German lines. The airborne operation was as delightful to watch as it must have been appalling to the enemy. I took a few of our prisoners out to watch it, to underscore the hopelessness of their situation. Until the 1st Battalion of the Cheshire Regiment reinforced us, our Commando brigade did not have enough men to guard the thousand prisoners we had taken in Wesel, so keeping their morale low was important to us. Nor was there a suitable place to put such a large number of POWs. But then someone thought of the huge bomb craters that pockmarked the ruins of Wesel, where they could easily be guarded by a couple of men with tommy guns.

The farthest point of 45 Commando's push inland was to be a wire factory directly on the railway line. That was the tip of the sausage-shaped perimeter the brigade was to take and hold. The logical approach to this objective was a green strip on our detailed map. It looked like parkland and led precisely where we wanted to go. Unfortunately, it was a series of backyards belonging to a long crescent of houses. Each yard was separated from the next by a fence or a garden wall.

The only options we had were the road in front of the houses or the back alley. We decided on the latter, despite the risk that there might be an enemy machine gun on fixed lines at the far end. All went well, and we finally reached the factory. We discovered that it was not a wire factory at all, but one that made toilet bowls. There were rows and rows of gleaming white porcelain commodes standing in military formation. The next day the enemy shelled the last shed, and the toilet bowls suffered heavy casualties, their ranks broken in many places.

One of 45 Commando's troops, under Captain Riley, had established an outpost in a house on the other side of the tracks, not far from the factory. The men reported that they had been fired upon by a German unit occupying a similar house about 300 yards from theirs, and that one man had been killed by machine-gun fire. Because this happened after the massive airborne landing, it seemed to be a surprisingly aggressive act, for the Germans must have seen, as we did, artillery pieces and vastly superior ordnance being dropped behind them, not to mention thousands of parachutists. Although the incoming planes were hard hit by flak, it was obvious that the operation had succeeded and that the enemy's position was going to become desperate in the near future. That was why I was dispatched to try to persuade them to surrender. I took along two carefully selected prisoners, both senior sergeants, one an infantryman and the other from the *Luftwaffe*.

"Do we have to do this?" asked the airman, a gnarled-looking old hand who had been around long enough to dare to ask this question.

"Of course," I explained. "According to international law, prisoners of war may be employed in lifesaving missions; by undertaking this assignment, you may save some of your comrades' lives, your lives, and our lives also." That might have been stretching it a bit, but it goes to show that in combat the man with the gun has an edge when it comes to interpreting the Geneva Convention. Unlike Arlen in Normandy, I preferred to use someone else to negotiate.

I ordered my prisoners to deliver a surrender ultimatum with a white flag (my handkerchief tied to a stick) for their protection. I introduced my two POWs to the Bren gunner who would cover them when they approached the German position.

"Meet Bill, our Brengunner," I told them. "He will shoot you if you make the slightest move other than what I'm telling you to do. You are to walk—not run—holding this white flag above your heads. You are to explain to them that their situation is hopeless, that they will be attacked by tanks very shortly, that they are grossly outnumbered, and that their only chance of survival is to surrender. They have three minutes to come out without weapons, holding their arms high above their heads. If they ask you to come over to their side, you will tell them that you are covered by a machine gun and that you cannot. Then turn about and walk slowly back here. Only if they threaten you, may you run, and if you do, you must clearly run in this direction, or you will be shot immediately. Is that understood?"

They sullenly agreed and set out apprehensively.

I watched their every step. The German soldier in the nearest slit trench listened to them and then, with a sweeping wave of his arm, beckoned them to come on in. We observed intently, particularly Bill, his finger on the trigger. But the prisoners shook their heads and pointed back in our direction. Surprisingly, the occupant of the trench climbed out of his hole and walked unhurriedly toward the house behind him. I noticed that there were some additional buildings back there. Clearly, he had gone to get instructions from a superior.

My two emissaries put their heads together as soon as he was gone, in what looked like a hasty huddle. Then they suddenly turned and ran, I should say sprinted, toward us. When they had made it to our position safely, they looked downright cheerful for the first time, delighted that they might live to see the end of the war, in spite of their forebodings. They had, indeed, been asked to come in, and they declined.

"We'll see about that," they were told by the Germans in the foremost slit trench. It sounded like enough of a threat to warrant their hasty departure. There was no response to my ultimatum whatsoever. Three minutes passed, and then three more. Captain Riley reported the situation to Major Blake, 45 Commando's second-in-command, who was now in charge, as Colonel Gray had to relinquish his post because of his injury. Major Blake ordered Riley to prepare to attack the recalcitrant enemy outpost. This filled the good captain with some dismay, because I had given him my considered estimate that what we saw in front of us was the mere tip of the iceberg. The body language of the German to whom my emissaries had spoken was that he had plenty of friends around. Riley, on the other hand, had no more than twenty-odd men, and an attack with so few seemed to me to be doomed from the outset. Yet he felt he could hardly beg off without appearing cowardly. Such are the ethics of war. He asked whether I would mind telling Major Blake the evaluation I had given him.

There was no embarrassment for me in a call that would have been impossible for him to make. I told the major the facts as I saw them, adding that with luck the position might even be carried, but that I thought few would live to tell the tale. Major Blake agreed and put the attack on hold.

A short while later Major Blake called back. He had received word that an American airborne infantry battalion with tank support from the British Guards Armored Division, which had crossed the Rhine downriver, would be coming to our aid in less than an hour. Therefore, he ordered Riley to withdraw his men back across the railroad tracks, to the factory, so as not to be in the way of the U.S. assault coming from behind him.

One more bit of excitement followed. A tank approached from where the Yanks were expected, but it was too early to be one of theirs. It was a long way off, shrouded in a cloud of dust that made identification impossible. We assumed it to be an enemy vehicle. The only antitank weapon in the outpost was one of the many *panzerfausts* that we had captured before crossing the Rhine.

Because of our shortage of antitank weapons, Ian Harris and I traveled from troop to troop in 45 Commando with a jeep load of these *panzerfausts*. With the scantiest of knowledge gleaned from the German leaflet on how to use them, we instructed the Commandos how to fire the damned things. We had captured so many that we could afford to fire not only one demonstration, but also let someone else try it.

When we stopped at Captain Riley's troop, he wanted to fire one himself. He aimed it much too low and spattered his troop with pebbles, one of which hit a Marine in the neck, leaving a nasty wound. The Marine had to be evacuated quickly, and none of Riley's troop was keen to use the weapon. The unanimous opinion was that because I was the *panzerfaust* instructor, I should do the shooting. Reluctantly, I jumped into a slit trench and reviewed the firing instructions again. They were written in such gushingly romantic and heroic German that one could not help but be skeptical about the results. If one should beware of Greeks bearing gifts, one should doubly beware of Nazis waxing romantic.

The tank was so far away that I could not identify any of its markings. The growing cloud of dust was coming right at me. Suddenly, I heard a noise behind me and saw crouched in a semicircle what seemed to be most of Captain Riley's men. None of them wanted to shoot at the tank, but neither did any of them want to miss the show.

I yelled some obscene words about them getting their heads below ground. Meanwhile, the tank was coming closer, so I could not afford to look around again to see if they really were out of sight. Like many a true war story, this one had an anticlimactic end. Just as it might have become possible to make a positive identification of the tank, the driver made a ninety-degree turn to his left and headed for the river Issel, unlamented by at least one of those watching.

We leapfrogged back across the railroad, that is, half of the troop covered the other half as it withdrew, until we reached the toilet bowl factory. We then set up a couple of Bren guns to harass the enemy position until the Americans arrived half an hour later.

We had a spectacular view of the first American attack any of us had ever seen. As it unrolled on the flat plain in front of us from left to right, tanks and infantry swarmed past, barely a hundred yards ahead. Their method seemed rather basic to us: they were using what the Royal Marines called the "bash on regardless" technique. But one tends to be overly critical when watching others perform in one's own field of expertise. There seemed to be little or no leapfrogging. They all rushed forward at the same time, intermingling with the tanks. It was hard to see how they avoided crossing each other's line of fire.

The German position continued to resist, and it inflicted considerable casualties on the advancing Americans. We awaited the outcome anxiously. I was also concerned in case my estimate of the strength of the enemy position had been wrong. After the battle was won, and a couple of German platoons surrendered and others escaped or were killed, I felt I had been justified in advising Major Blake to hold our attack.

The prisoners were handed over to us and were lined up for search and interrogation by Ian and me. Ian walked up to an *unteroffizier*, a corporal, and whacked him in the mouth. It was so unlike Ian that I was taken aback.

Ian was visibly upset and confessed that he had let his emotions run away with him. He had seen the American casualties, and it had all seemed so pointless. The Germans had lost the war but the Nazis were still killing people. "I saw that shitload of silver braid on that *unteroffizier*'s epaulettes," Ian confessed, "and just lost my temper. I forgot that he's just a lowly noncom, not the officer in charge."

This anger would occasionally surface in all of us 3 Troopers as we remembered what the Nazis had done to us Jews, to our families and friends. It didn't normally manifest itself against disarmed prisoners, but what we had just witnessed was carnage that could not have served any useful purpose. To the enemy it may have seemed a heroic last stand, but burdened as we were with our past it appeared to us to be the work of fanatics, the master race arrogantly conceding nothing. Ian never deviated from what he believed to be our sole purpose: beat the Nazis, pay them back, kill them.

Days passed and still Eric Howarth had not rejoined us. My two guilders were mounting up to quite a lot of money. I clearly was getting rich.

One day some chap from brigade headquarters drove up in a jeep. "Do you people have a sergeant-major in the Buffs?"

"No. We used to have one, but he should be an officer by now. He hasn't been replaced yet. Why?" I asked.

"Did he wear a silvered Buffs badge on his green beret?"

"Come to think of it, he did. Why?"

Eric's standard brass badge, the dragon of the East Kent Regiment, the 3d Regiment of Foot known as the Buffs, had been silvered.

The man looked solemn and awkward. "I'm afraid I have bad news for you. He was killed yesterday on the way up here."

We were in a state of shock. It couldn't be Eric. Surely he would have been commissioned before he left England and would have been wearing pips on his shoulders. We hoped it was a case of mistaken identity, but we knew it wasn't.

There was a logical explanation. Officers commissioned in one of these specially abbreviated procedures were allowed to wear their new pips only after joining their unit. So Eric, on his way back on 3 April 1945, had still been traveling as a sergeant-major. He had been riding in the cab of a truck, up front with the driver, with a load of reinforcements in the back, when a shell had hit. None of the others even had a scratch, but the driver and Eric Howarth were killed outright.

He would have owed me twenty-two Dutch guilders. Promises to the contrary notwithstanding, he would have missed the Rhine crossing on 23 March by eleven days. I would have enjoyed winning that bet and collecting, or loved to lose it.

I never saw my photos that I had lent to Eric either. I didn't have the heart to ask the family, or Audrey. Instead, I had some copies made of somebody else's set, as Eric had intended to do with mine.

25 Heroes

A few days after the Rhine crossing, James Griffith said he was going to recommend me for a commission.

"Of course you'll have to pass the War Office Selection Board first, probably in Ghent in Belgium, but that won't give you any trouble."

"James," I remonstrated (we were alone, so I didn't say "sir"), "I don't think I want to go to OCTU."

"I firmly believe that you ought to go. There's nothing to it, and you might even enjoy it."

"Now? The war is practically over and you want me to go to bullshit school squarebashing and be immersed up to my ears in pamphlets? You can't mean it. I'm a sergeant. That's the best of all worlds."

"Listen to me," James said patiently. "It'll help you with your postwar career. Take my advice. Go for it."

"If you really think I ought to be an officer, why can't they give me a commission in the field? That would save me from OCTU and keep me right here where I belong."

"You know Montgomery has ordered that field commissions are to be given only in extreme emergencies. He says it encourages fraternization with the enlisted men. You've heard that one before, right? A horrible thought."

"I bet if the brigadier wanted to give me one, he could. Why don't I talk to him?"

James stiffened a little. "It's your right to talk to the brigadier, although I wish you wouldn't."

I insisted that I did, and at 0930 the next morning Griffith took me into an upstairs room at brigade headquarters. There I met not the brigadier but Max Harper-Gow, the brigade major.

"James tells me you want to see the boss," Harper-Gow said. "I would be very grateful if you didn't. He has a lot on his mind, and we're having a hard enough time with him as it is. This might upset him and as you know it's better not to do that. Of course you're within your rights, but I entirely agree with James that you should go to OCTU. He tells me you'd make a fine officer. You can't be ordered to go, but we both honestly think it's your duty to do so."

I surrendered. Now I just wanted to get out of the stuffy building. Downstairs I could hear the unmistakable voice of Brigadier Mills-Roberts. The brigade major had been right about his mood. He was ranting and raving at a sentry, dressing down the unfortunate man for being slovenly. His back was turned to the staircase I was descending and I could not get past him. Had I tried to squeeze by, or said, "Excuse me," I would probably have been the target of the next verbal assault. But I was a seasoned old soldier by then and I knew just what to do. I got to within one step of him and snapped noisily to attention, right where I was on the stairs. He whirled around and was about to pounce on the intruder who had dared to interrupt him, when I gave him my best salute straight out of the training manual. It was perfectly executed.

A slow smile dissolved his stern features, then he beamed from ear to ear. "Good morning, Sergeant."

"Good morning, sir."

"That's more like it. Carry on, Sergeant. I want to see more smart soldiers like this one."

I felt a bit guilty, yet pleased that I had succeeded in bullshitting the old bullshitter. Out in the open I reflected on what had taken place and what was going to happen. James wished me well, I was certain. Was he really concerned about my postwar career, or was he sending me home because I had survived so far and he felt that I had done enough and wanted me out of harm's way? I shall never know.

With me back in England, Ian Harris was the sole member of 45 Commando's 3 Troop detachment, and he soon became one of Colonel Blake's most valued assistants. Blake called on him in times of stress and was never disappointed, for Ian always came through with resourceful determination and fearless action.

As a boy, Ian had attended a boarding school in the eastern province of Austria called Burgenland (literally, castle country). He became aware that all the boys in school were beating up on one little lad, the only Jewish youngster among them. Although a Jew, Ian himself had been baptized ("for the good of his future," as his parents said) and brought up as a Protestant, but he had never felt secure and constantly needed to reassure himself that he was accepted, that he belonged.

"Suddenly, I found myself participating in the bullying. I was quite shocked when the boy who was the victim looked at me in dismay: '*Auch Du?*' he said, plaintively. It sounded as bad as Caesar's '*Et tu, Brute?*' and it stayed with me all my life."

When the Nazis took over, Ian had become a target himself. Not that they knew about his origin, for the only ones aware of that were some of the teachers, and they had not given him away. But the strain of the political situation made Ian so timid that he betrayed himself by acting like a victim. When it got so serious that it even stunted his physical growth and made him run from school, his parents took him to a psychiatrist. After all, they lived in Vienna and it came naturally to seek out a disciple of Freud.

Intensive sessions proved so successful that Ian not only resumed his development but felt confident enough to return to school. He was bigger than his erstwhile tormentors now and derived great satisfaction from beating up the ones who had harassed him. His newly found self-confidence stood him in good stead when he became a soldier, the true volunteer who typified the best characteristics of the 3 Trooper.

Ian first distinguished himself on 3 April 1945 in Osnabrück when he persuaded a contingent of Hungarians in the German Army to surrender after a confrontation with their German officers. He enjoyed leading a seemingly endless column of his prisoners into captivity in a jeep. There is even a newsreel of this episode with Ian truly the leading man, looking stern and taciturn as he sat next to his driver.

But Ian's finest hour came three days later when 45 Commando was participating in the crossing of the Weser, where the enemy had made a determined stand to hold up the Allied advance. While attached to the 11th Armored Division, the Commando brigade met strong opposition from the 12th SS Training Battalion. With the Germans' fortunes of war on the wane, it was these young fanatics led by seasoned noncommissioned officers who continued to fight the hopeless fight. The fanatics were prompted by an ingrained blind loyalty to their deranged führer, and the noncommissioned officers fought "because, after all, we were soldiers," as the one on Bell Island in the Maas had explained to us earlier.

"We came under extremely heavy and accurate small-arms fire from dug-in enemy positions to the front and left flank," Colonel Blake later reported. "Owing to the flat nature of the ground, the only line of advance was along the riverbank, but every inch of ground was bitterly contested."

The colonel's headquarters suddenly found itself pinned down by young SS men in slit trenches situated only a few yards above them in the banks of the river.

"Colonel Blake looked at me and just sort of waved his chin in the direction of the trouble," Ian recalled.

As Blake wrote in Ian's citation for a Military Medal, "It was obvious that spontaneous action was necessary to save an awkward situation [a fine example of British understatement]. Corporal Harris climbed the bank and, in full view of the enemy to his left flank, fired his weapon at the enemy then at his feet, killing two and taking one prisoner."

Ian remembered dispatching the prisoner "by kicking him in the arse down the slope into the hands of our colonel and about ten members of his headquarters." Emboldened by his success, he moved forward along the top of the bank until he saw below him four Commandos with a Bren gun who were unable to see the enemy, who were rapidly approaching them.

"Since I knew what was happening on top and had used up all my tommy-gun ammunition, I told the corporal in charge to hand up the Bren gun, which he gladly did. I then plunked myself down on top of the bank and pumped the bastards full of lead."

The defenders soon spotted him, and eventually a bullet hit the magazine of his Bren gun. It split open like a steel banana peel and hit him in the left eye, destroying it completely.

The last river that had to be crossed, before the Elbe and the linkup with the Russian Army, was the Aller, a tributary of the Weser. To advance on the small town of Esse, Brig. Derek Mills-Roberts had intended to use a road bridge that had been left standing. James Griffith was assigned the task of finding out whether the bridge had been prepared for demolition, lest it be blown up as soon as the enemy became aware that the Commandos were approaching it. He and another man set out dressed in their fatigues (light canvas grayish khaki versions of the battle dress) and gym shoes; they had donned Mae Wests (life jackets) and actually floated down the river to get to the vicinity of the bridge that was their target.

Not surprisingly, the bridge had indeed been wired for demolition and, just as they got near it, it went up with a big bang. They hid on the riverbank and swam back to join the brigade, which was now en route to the other possible crossing point, a nearby railway bridge. They joined in the advance with their clothes drying on their bodies.

Bruce Beattie, who was in charge of brigade signals, thought that a brave act in itself, as it was early April in northern Germany and very cold. Once the brigade had crossed the river by the railway bridge, Mills-Roberts ordered it to form a circular defensive position.

"We dug in," Beattie recalled, "and James, who had 'captured' a German farmer, ordered him to dig his slit trench. I remember his instructions—to dig *'ein Meter—drei Meter!'*—indicating with his hands the shape he wanted.

"The following morning I was standing in my trench and was talking to James, who was standing beside it. Someone yelled at him to take cover as there were snipers about. He replied: 'Don't you know I'm bulletproof?'

"He then left me to move over to his trench. I didn't actually see him fall, but hearing shouts I—with others—rushed over to where he lay. A sniper's bullet had ricocheted and hit him in the back below the ribcage in the area of the kidney. He died instantly. That evening he was buried in the woods where he had died."

James Griffith died on 11 April, and the war in Europe ended on 8 May. It was a pitiful waste of a dashing brave man, one who had wished me well and helped me, perhaps had even saved my life when he bullied me into going to cadet school.

26 A Son to the Rescue

There's just one more story to tell: Freddy Gray's search for his parents who had been incarcerated in a concentration camp.

After the fall of Walcheren, Freddy (Manfred Gans) received a field commission. The Royal Marine Commandos were under Royal Navy jurisdiction and could therefore bypass Montgomery's orders about not granting commissions in the field. Freddy was still recuperating in South Beveland from the fighting on Walcheren when, during the last days of the war, he heard a rumor from some Dutch-Jewish sources that his parents might be alive in the Terezín (Theresienstadt) concentration camp in Czechoslovakia, which the Russians were just approaching. Immediately, on 7 May 1945, Freddy set out with a jeep and driver for Terezín, more than 450 miles away, a hundred-odd of these miles held by as yet unsurrendered Germans and another two hundred by the Soviet Army.

We all had dreamed of liberating concentration camps, and Freddy was not about to miss out on any opportunity to find his parents. Loaded to the brim with provisions, not only for the journey but also for those he hoped to find alive, he drove through the crumbling desolation of destroyed towns: Kleve, Emmerich, Bocholt, and then through his hometown of Borken. His old home was now used as regional headquarters by the Allied Military Government. It had been the Gestapo's headquarters also; they had even added a garage to the old brick building. He passed nostalgic places of past hikes, outings, and good times of childhood that were now mere piles of rubble. The fear of what might lie at the end of the long road ahead weighed on him as he and his driver pressed on. The nearest substantial city of Münster turned out to be a deserted shell with not a soul in sight except for an occasional military policeman. In Paderborn there were some refugees pushing handcarts, bicycles, and baby carriages loaded with a few miserable possessions; they were all striving to return home.

An abrupt change was evident near Kassel, where the villages looked untouched by war, the scenery as beautiful and romantic as on a prewar German travel poster. Just when Freddy had adjusted to that, he would see a village totally flattened, where pockets of resistance had held out. In Kassel the steelworks he had known were no more. Their presence in the town had caused it to be defended and therefore destroyed. Knocked-out German tanks littered the streets, rusting in the glorious sunshine. Some of the more fortunate ex-slave laborers and other prisoners had managed to steal, scrounge, or confiscate trucks on which they had hoisted national flags. They sped homeward, precariously overloaded.

At the cloverleaf where the east-west Kassel autobahn meets the one going north-south, Freddy and his English driver, Bob Bannister, were checked by American military police (MP), the only time this happened on the whole trip. Fearful of red tape turning them back, they had a few anxious moments. Although the MPs were clearly surprised to see two British soldiers so far afield, all went smoothly, and they were waved on.

Near Chemnitz the weather turned cooler. American patrols were on the road everywhere, and Freddy decided to scout around the town and ask a few questions. Did anyone know who actually held Terezín at this time—the Germans, Americans, or Russians? No one knew. Chemnitz was decked out with white flags: five or six bedsheets hung from every house. The roads were empty, and the German civilians looked at them in amazement. They started east again until they came upon a cable stretched across the road, stopping all traffic. They talked to the American and Russian sentries who stood there chatting, mostly in sign language.

"How do you Americans get along with the Russians?"

"We get along just fine," said the Yank. "They come across to loot from the Germans, which they do much more thoroughly than we do. We go over there, because out of our jurisdiction we can fraternize, meaning screw, the German girls. They're terrified of the Russians but not of us. The Russians rape; we bring them nylons."

There had been a lot of talk of Russians raping, and it is true that few, if any, restraints were put on their multinational mélange of soldiery. But much of the sexual activity, certainly that of the other Allied troops, was made possible by the moral standards set by the German women themselves in pursuit of dire material necessities, combined with a degree of sex starvation caused by the prolonged absence of most of their menfolk. To quote Bertolt Brecht, translated from the German: "First comes fodder—and then comes morality."

After being invited by a generous American colonel to spend a night resting, bathing in an opulent marble bathroom, and sharing a sumptuous meal, Freddy and his driver continued their journey the next day, 8 May. They had no idea that this was V-E Day: the German high command had surrendered to the Allies. Even if they had known, it is highly doubtful that all the elements of the enemy's armed forces were aware of that momentous decision, and that the two British Commando soldiers would not be fired upon. Communications remained in disarray for days to come.

The Americans faced insoluble problems: the masses of mobile humanity, all naturally heading for home, trying to cross the demarkation lines between the Allied zones, where they were either turned back or arrested, as well as German prisoners and returning Allied prisoners who had to be housed and fed. The American colonel was still working at 10 P.M., struggling for ways to deal with the dilemma.

"Ah, the Russians," he said. "We arrange something with them one day, and the next day they disregard every point of the agreement."

Some of his soldiers were more vehement: "Give me the real front line any day. It's easier to hold than this mess."

Freddy decided to drive to nearby Zwickau to see whether the Germans still had units fighting in the Erz Mountains, which he had to cross to get to Terezín. Nobody knew for sure. The American presence ended at Zwickau, although there were rumors of American convoys having gone almost all the way to Prague. (A good example of the prevailing confusion was that the Germans did not surrender Prague until several days after V-E Day.)

At the last American road barrier, Freddy asked where the Russians were in this area.

"Haven't seen any yet," said the guard. "There's nothing but Krauts in the Erz Mountains. If you get to your destination and back, it will sure have been as good as any Commando raid. Good luck." When they arrived in the town of Aue, which was still in German hands, there were German police in the streets and thousands of well-armed soldiers everywhere. The jeep was forced to a halt as a mass of people crowded around it—well-dressed and well-fed German men and women looking bitter and hard. Some of them asked, "Are the Russians coming? Why not the Amis? Why not you?" German soldiers, standing next to their roadblocks with perfectly good and operable antitank guns, asked if they would take them prisoner.

Freddy was glad to get out of there, but he was apprehensive about what they would encounter next. Thinking it might afford them at least a modicum of protection, Freddy picked up a wounded German soldier and his girlfriend, who wanted to return to his home.

The young German woman offered them big slices of crunchy country bread with honey. She fitted in well with the appealing landscape they were driving through, for she was beautiful in her local costume of a black skirt and embroidered white blouse. "This is gorgeous country," said Freddy in German as their passengers bade them good-bye in the village of Schwarzenberg. The young woman smiled; she looked less like an enemy and more like an angel on one of the altars of the little local churches. In her charming Erz Mountain dialect, she replied that everyone who left there always returned one day.

The country roads were empty now, the villages untouched by war. In the fields bordering the road, peasants were tilling the soil with hand tools, and woodcutters could be heard working in the forests. Occasional Czech flags showed that they had crossed into what had been that country before the Nazis usurped it. The blue triangle cutting into the white and red field, flags that must have been well hidden during the years of the German Protectorate, fluttered in the breeze of freedom over many a farm.

Suddenly, they came upon a swarm of armed Russian soldiers coming right at them. Cossacks on horseback blocked their way while two grim-looking officers galloped up alongside them.

Then, equally suddenly, they all broke into broad smiles when they recognized the British uniform. Everybody saluted, and the two Commandos drove on.

They entered a village of some 2,000 residents—and 15,000 fully armed German soldiers. The two men in the jeep were surrounded instantly.

Gray managed an innocuous question: *"Was ist los?"* (What's up?) *"Sammelstelle Infanterie Division. Nehmt Ihr uns gefangen?"* (Divisional infantry collection point. Are you taking us prisoner?)

Again they were accosted by crying women: "Save us from the Russians—they will rob and rape us."

Freddy heard himself say that the Germans had done the same in Poland, Russia, Holland, "and right here." The women answered, "there are good and bad among all people."

Many wondered why Freddy spoke such excellent German. He made it clear that he was the one who asked the questions and they were the ones to give the answers.

They drove off, slowly weaving through the crowds. They came upon masses of men in British battle dress, prisoners of war striving to get to someplace from which they could be repatriated. Some of them looked quite well, whereas others were in bad shape. Their faces lit up when they saw the Commandos, and Freddy and his driver distributed cigarettes.

"No punishment is too severe for these Nazi bastards for what they have done to us," one said to Freddy. "But wait till you see what they have done to the Jews."

Freddy's heart sank.

The prisoners were ambivalent about the Russians. Some thought them weird; others offered high praise. "They were just great. They gave us their pistols so that we could shoot the prison guards." All agreed that the Czechs wanted the prisoners to stay as insurance against Russian looting. Some had done so and had settled in with Czech women or families. They had found relative comfort, shelter, and a meal ticket, not to mention sex, after the lean years in the stalag.

Most of these men were in no hurry to go home, at least not until what they considered "proper arrangements" had been made.

Some had even managed to acquire German Army cars, but the looting insurance did not go far. The Russians, well armed but always short of transport, had swiftly relieved them of their bounty. At last, in Komotau, Freddy met the Russian Army proper. He saw long convoys of *panje* carts, each drawn by two horses. Then came tanks and field artillery, including strange-looking long-barreled antitank guns. The only truck transport was obviously British or U.S. made, lend-leased, scrounged, commandeered, or stolen, if not captured from the Germans.

Freddy stood up in the jeep all the time now, holding on with one hand, waving to and saluting every group they encountered. They all cheered and waved back. The Russian military police were women, and each carried two little signaler's flags to direct traffic. They all saluted smartly, not that there was any visible discipline. There were hopeless traffic jams everywhere, causing the officers to jump into the street and shout and gesticulate, berating one another, trying to pull rank for right-of-way. Somehow the whole circus moved forward eventually.

At an intersection a Russian military policewoman asked in English: "Are you American?"

"No, English."

Then Freddy thought perhaps she would understand German more easily, and he added *"Ich spreche auch Deutsch."*

He had guessed correctly, and she looked thrilled: *"Britisch offizier spricht Deutsch!* Like me—*ich spreche* alle *languages!"* Then she embraced him in a true Russian bear hug.

At long last they arrived at Terezín, which the Russian Army had liberated two days before. Civilians showed them the way to what they called "the Ghetto." Freddy had often been there before, in his imagination. To his amazement he felt almost calm now, when he had expected that he would die of excitement. But he had the same queer feeling in the pit of his stomach as he had during his parachute jumps.

At the camp, a blocked-off part of the town, the newly installed Russian guards at the gate jumped to attention.

"I am a British Commando officer. I understand that my parents may be here."

They summoned the guard commander, a captain. "There is one part where we have typhoid fever," he said. "If they are in that part, you must give me your word that you will not enter but return and report to me."

"I promise."

Slowly the jeep pulled through the raised barrier. Lieutenant Freddy Gray of 47 Royal Marine Commando, formerly Manfred Gans of Borken, Germany, stood on the seat next to his driver, clutching the cold rim of the windshield. He looked all about him, searching.

He saw the familiar faces of Jews—Western and Eastern European Jews of all ages—overworked and undernourished but surprisingly well dressed. Terezín had been the show camp of the Nazis for International Red Cross visits, although in reality it had always been a transit place to the gas chambers of Auschwitz.

There was a tiredness, a forlorn look to all these people, not only in their eyes but in their demeanor. He tried to smile at them but he could not. They all crowded around the jeep, some too weak to get out of its way, so the driver had to slow to a crawl. In a way it was reminiscent of the liberation of towns and villages in France, Belgium, and Holland, yet, totally different. There was no cheerful optimism, just broken human beings. All eyes were on the Commandos, but the inmates were too stunned to utter a sound. Both men, in turn, tried to appear friendly and encouraging, but they could not help looking horrified and grim. They came to a halt at the registration office, where one female inmate was still at work in spite of the late hour. Freddy asked in German if Mr. and Mrs. Gans were there.

She answered in English that they really were there, alive. She would take him to them immediately. They could hardly get through the gathered crowd now. Through some windows they could see roughly hewn double and triple bunks. Their guide finally stopped: "This is the house."

There were too many people about for Freddy's private moment, but he didn't care. He must keep calm, control himself. It was like being on parade. He entered the house, and the next moment his mother and father were in his arms, sobbing wildly. Past despair-relief-disbelief-hope-joy. Freddy looked at his father. He had been prepared for a shock, but in spite of that he had to clench his teeth not to show it. He could hardly recognize him; had he met this starved wreck of a man, his clothes hanging too large on his gaunt body, in the street, he would not have known him. His own father. The Skipper's motto helped Freddy: "Never panic." He bade his parents sit down with him. He had to lead them and gently push them to sit. They could not stop crying. Some of their friends came and tried to help calm them. Then they had to step outside on a platform rising a few feet above the huge crowd that had gathered at the marvelous news.

"*Mazeltov*," the inmates whispered, "Congratulations."

They, the miserable facsimiles of once hale and dignified humans, were cheering the good fortune of two of their own. It was heartrending. The news of this extraordinary event spread from one end of Terezín to the other. Everybody wanted to be in on it, at least with a handshake. Some young girls brought bouquets of flowers, meadow weeds really, for where would they find flowers in Terezín? Frau Gans put them into a tin can filled with water, like the good hausfrau she had always been.

Freddy then went to see the Russian commandant and gave him the Russian-language letter he had brought with him.

The commandant spoke broken German. Freddy recalls: "You found parents? Good, very good. Tomorrow I order camp sealed off—is health hazard. You not really permitted here. I close not one eye but both eyes. Your duties elsewhere. I not order you confined here. You inoculated yet?" The commandant and his three women doctors gave the impression of great efficiency. "No rush, but you leave soon, Lieutenant."

Freddy and his parents talked through the night. They told him about the horrors they had been through in the infamous Belsen concentration camp, for example, where of the 137,000 inmates only one in six survived. One day all girls under 14 were gassed. In its final days the SS had wanted to kill the entire camp population, but one commandant suggested a 24-hour postponement, why no one knew, and the Russians arrived the next day. The Jews in Terezín had consulted the psychiatrists and psychologists among them. Only these sessions and an inherent Jewish spirit of overcoming the searing scars of persecution had kept the survivors from going insane.

During that night Freddy gave an impromptu talk to the inmates about the Allied war effort. None of his listeners knew anything about D day and the heavy fighting in France, or the endless winter in Holland and Belgium, or the Walcheren landings, which were of particular interest to the Dutch Jews. They were among Freddy's parents' closest friends, as Borken was just across the border from Holland. They did not know about the starvation conditions imposed upon the Dutch population by the Nazis and the massive destruction of Germany by Allied aerial bombardment, nor about the large number of American armed forces now engaged in striving for final victory. They had not heard of the existence of a Jewish Brigade in the British Army in Italy, and they wondered about Palestine and the possibility of Jewish immigration there. It was as if they had just been through a long Rip van Winkle sleep from which they were lucky to awaken at all.

The future of the Terezín population seemed uncertain. The younger and fitter ones would survive and manage somehow, somewhere. Most of them wanted to go back to their own countries, except for the German Jews. They, and some of the others, were hoping to emigrate to Palestine but worried whether the British would let them in. Would liberated European countries admit stateless Jews, even in transit? Could there be a future for debilitated, worn-out people in Palestine, where youth and fitness were the basic requirements for a pioneering Zionist agrarian economy? The Nazis had not only tortured and killed, they had disrupted a whole society, three generations of assorted victims. The inmates of Terezín saw in Freddy a living example of one of their own kind who was fighting back. It lifted their spirits and boosted their morale in the most important manner at a most important time. Given the opportunity, they felt, they would have liked to have done something like this themselves. But they had been tricked, trapped, and demeaned, and then starved into physical and mental impotence. Maybe, just maybe, there was to be a future, after all.

Freddy's parents were forced to stay in quarantine and he had to leave. He discussed the situation with the leader of the Dutch inmate Jews, Professor Meyers, who had worked at the Peace Palace in The Hague. He was a physical wreck, but his mind was still sharp and logical. His daughter and three others had managed to leave the camp three days before the enforcement of the quarantine, to walk to Holland.

When Freddy and his driver left at ten in the morning, it was almost as if they were making a quick secret getaway. Everyone in the Terezín camp had wanted them to take letters out. Many suggested seriously that they smuggle them out, too, as stowaways in the jeep. Freddy and Bob were not sure they would be able to get out themselves.

"*Engelsk offizier,*" said Freddy with all the self-assurance he could muster when the guards at the gate, who were fully aware of the quarantine, looked doubtful. It worked. The guards not only saluted when they opened the barrier, they smiled and came over to shake hands.

On the road back to Karlsbad, Freddy took stock. He had hated to leave his parents, but he had done all he could. He had found them and brought them enough food to eat and share. His father said that the cigarettes he provided would make him a millionaire in the camp because they were better than money. Freddy knew that soon he would be able to get them to Holland, and then to Palestine.

The highway was again full of hundreds of British and American ex-POWs, scrambling west like homing pigeons. Freddy carefully selected the most feeble, an American who looked like a bundle of bones in rags that had once been his uniform. Freddy and Bob lifted him into the vehicle, although they had nothing to give him, as all food, cigarettes, and articles of clothing had been distributed in Terezín. At least he would be among loving, helping hands in a few hours.

When they reached the American lines, they handed him over. Just as Freddy entered the officers' mess, a Czech partisan led in a German general. He wished to surrender the 15,000 German troops still armed in the Erz Mountains, the ones they had passed on the way out. The U.S. colonel in charge was an enterprising soldier who boasted that he had not only attended but survived the Commando school at Achnacarry. Determined not to add to the problems of his overworked logistics staff, he referred them to the Russians, with Freddy acting as interpreter. And then he threw a banquet, where the champagne flowed even for the surrendering German general and his entourage. No sooner was that finished than the Germans were handed over to the Russian general in charge. There was a lot of saluting.

The Russian general shook hands with the Americans and Freddy and thanked them for their help. Then, with impressive efficiency and incisive clarity, this simple-looking, round-faced man issued firm orders on precisely what the Germans had to do for their surrender to take effect. There was a solid day's march to a place to be fed, for starters. The German general protested that this was too far.

"You must get used to the standards of the Soviet Army, General," replied the Russian quietly.

On the sixth day of his odyssey, Freddy reported back. He was exhausted, but he almost didn't get any sleep again, for everybody wanted to hear about his journey. He called on the Allied Military Government in Borken and was interviewed by a captain sitting in the Gans family's former living room. After declining the offer of a military government job, he made an appointment with Dutch government officials for his final self-imposed task. He arranged for transport as quickly as possible of the appropriate group of Terezín survivors, including his parents.

27 Postscript

Decades have passed. World War II is a subject for war buffs and historians to debate, and for us, who took part, to ponder. Because we were trained in the arts of war, we might occasionally sneak our reminiscences into our conversations, if our wives cannot restrain us in time.

Sometimes one hears "Forget the Holocaust. Forget the war." We Jewish soldiers cannot help but remember what to us was truly a holy war fought against a monstrous system bent on destroying us, our families and friends, and, indeed, civilized life on earth. Today, we believe in the duty and necessity to testify about what took place so that it cannot ever happen again.

The experience transformed us. Pacifists became grimly determined activists, willing to take absurd risks, not so much for the grand illusion of a better world but, more simply, to defeat the threat of evil incarnate. In retrospect, I do not wonder about what we did, but rather if we could have done even more to crush the scourge of humanity that was our enemy. I am convinced that the modest contribution of 3 Troop toward that end should not be forgotten; rather, it should serve as a boost to the morale of those who were harassed and humiliated during that dark and bespattered period of history and as a warning to the all-too-dispassionate onlookers to be more alert in safeguarding their own freedom.

We were indeed fortunate to have had the opportunity to participate in the reestablishment of human dignity. If it were possible to ask those troop members who died, they would undoubtedly affirm that they preferred their demise greatly to death in a concentration camp, a death that had been planned for each one of them by Adolf Hitler.

The motley bunch of men who had made up 3 Troop dispersed all over the globe after the war. Looking at cold statistics, of the eighty-seven troop members of the active war establishment total, nineteen were killed in action and one additional fatality resulted from an accident at cadet school. Twenty-two were wounded, seven of them so badly they had to be invalided out of the Army. Eighteen became commissioned officers, four of them in the field. The large percentage of commissions is unique in the annals of the British Army but easy to accept and understand. We were, after all, handpicked for our intelligence and initiative. Had we been British born, many of us would have begun our military careers in cadet school and reached high rank. Handicapped not only by being foreigners but also enemy aliens, we were held back further by being in a Commando troop we did not want to jeopardize by leaving when it was about to go into action. Yet it was impossible, under existing conditions, to promote us within the troop; too many chiefs, not enough Indians.

I think that the officer material of 3 Troop should have been trained and commissioned much earlier, and a cadre of special intelligence-reconnaissance detachments should have been formed, each headed by one of these officers. These detachments should then have been made available to British Commandos and other units. They should have joined the outfits with which they were going into combat much earlier and trained with them. It can be readily appreciated, however, that the formation of such officer-heavy entities, of foreigners yet, would have been far too radical for the conservative military establishment. In fact, the Armed Forces are to be congratulated for having gone as far as they did.

As Hilton-Jones wrote in his "Brief History" of the troop: "The Troop enjoyed a much greater measure of freedom and independence than that normally accorded to such small bodies, and, it must be admitted, derived no little benefit therefrom."

After victory, it came as a surprise to some of us that fit people of our ilk who had survived all previous dangers were not immortal after all, even when not exposed to enemy fire. A few eventually suffered heart attacks, several fatal. A number died of other illnesses. Many disappeared, presumably for no sinister reason. They simply did not keep in touch. Those who did cannot understand the former. How could these close friends, whose lives had been bonded by having withstood all kinds of dangers together, have forsaken their comrades? We assume, therefore, that the missing ones must no longer be alive, although occasionally one is found or simply reappears.

There is no point in listing here a detailed account of the success stories of 3 Troopers in civilian life. Instead I'll cite just a few examples. It is to be expected that carefully chosen men would continue to demonstrate the quality of initiative required for their selection and to establish successful careers. Three entered the legal profession: Brian Grant became a judge, John Wilmers became a Queen's Counsel, and Knobby Kendall became a lawyer who wrote extensively on specialized legal subjects. Kershaw rose to be international chairman of the public relations firm of Ogilvy & Mather. Kingsley was elected president of the Institution of Chemical Engineers and was appointed as an officer of the Order of the British Empire. Tennant became president of International Tyre Dealers. Dwelly rose to be a vice president of American Express. Miles worked for Cadbury, then became a vice president of the J. Walter Thompson advertising agency. Gordon took back his old name, Geiser, and held a high position at British European Airways. Ian Harris, M.M., became an international chartered accountant. Nichols, Bentley, Ross, Terry, and others became successful in the world of business, from export-import to the manufacture of knitwear. Sayers and Trevor were in fashion, design, and retailing. Gray, who took the name of Gans once again, is a chemical engineer. Bartlett returned to his birthplace, Munich, and works as an author and translator of musical subjects. James Monahan, the Irish troop officer who was not one of us refugees, but so empathetic that we would readily claim him as one of our own, was the *Manchester Guardian*'s ballet critic for forty years. After retiring as controller of European Services of the BBC, he was appointed director of the Royal Ballet School. He died suddenly in 1985, while working on a book much like this one, about 3 Troop. It would doubtless have been a more professional effort, for he was an experienced writer and a published poet. Unfortunately, he had gotten only as far as a synopsis, which I have read and consider to have been a guiding light, regrettably fragmentary. I am nevertheless greatly indebted to him, sustained by his avowed goal: "To write about these men, who they were, what they did, and what became of them."

One of the men who had an extraordinary career was Ronnie Gilbert (Hans-Julius Guttmann), who extended the covert aspect of our training after the end of the war and stayed on in Germany for many years as an intelligence chief, so effectively that he was appointed a member of the Order of the British Empire (MBE). Even the Germans wanted to give him a medal for his excellent work in tracking down war criminals. Under an ancient British law (dating back to Elizabeth I), their request was denied, but it was a triumph for one of our own lads, who had been forced to help demolish the synagogue in his hometown of Singen during *Kristallnacht*.

There were many others who were admirable for different reasons. By no means did all 3 Troopers become academicians or professionals. Some concluded that what they really wanted after their hazardous war years was the simple life, relishing peace and family above all else. Two became postmen in New York City. They did not even know of each other's whereabouts until one day Harry Drew (who took back his old name of Nomburg) bumped into Aitchison in the same post office where they both worked.

Considering that many people after the war felt that Commandos were all incipient criminals who would find it hard to settle down in civilian life, to my knowledge only two members of 3 Troop clashed with the law. One was a highly respected, ethical, and intellectual individual, whose name I choose to omit. The other was Tom Spencer. The nameless one, it was rumored, was involved in some embezzlement, possibly the victim of boredom after the excitement of living by one's wits in combat. Tom Spencer, on the other hand, had always survived by his wits and was in no way restrained by considerations of etiquette. Yet he was kind to his friends and generous to a fault. I bumped into him on a London street about a year after I had moved to America.

"Ah, you and your wife are visiting with your sister-in-law, how nice," said Tom. "But what do you eat? Meat is still in very short supply, and surely you aren't gobbling up her ration. Tell you what I'm gonna do. What meat do you like? More important: what meat does she like? Better still, come with me." He took me to a flat in Maida Vale, where a long corridor was lined with refrigerators.

"Beef, veal, lamb, pork. I'll let you have some of each, for free, of course." And he began to carve and to package. "This is my business," he said. "I'm glad to help out your sister-in-law." "Aren't you afraid of getting caught?" I asked. "Oh, I've been caught plenty of times," he continued. "I pay a five quid fine." He considered for a moment. "If I'd been caught this morning, it might have been ten quid, or more." I could not help wondering why I was the recipient of this butcher bountiful. I suppose he was genuinely glad to see me again, and perhaps still had a bit of a bad conscience for having taken my captured Walther P-38 pistol from me in that blackjack game in Holland. I do not covet weapons and own no gun. But as guns go, that Walther was a nice one.

As for myself, I had served part of my last year in the Army in the Oxfordshire and Buckinghamshire Light Infantry, my first choice of regiment when I became a commissioned officer, because I had admired them when they took Pegasus Bridge on D day. I had been dispatched to West Africa, to the Gold Coast (now Ghana) to train native troops, presumably because of my fluent German, which I spoke better than Twi or Hausa. Army logic, I presume.

It could be argued that, with my past experience, after five and a half years of service, I really belonged in Germany or Austria. But when the Army, in its wisdom, sent me to another continent, I did nothing to attempt to alter my fate, for two reasons. One was that "unexpected travel opportunities are dancing lessons from God," as Kurt Vonnegut wrote. Second, I had a certain distaste for being one of the authorities in the rubble of Nazism, where nobody had been a Nazi, and everybody claimed that they had had no inkling of what had been perpetrated right under their noses. I preferred the cleansing of the tropical rains, where the only poison to fear was from the scorpion and the black and green mamba snakes.

When my age plus length of service combined to spell my separation from His Majesty's Armed Forces, I discovered that at the ripe age of twenty-four, I would have to go to college to make myself employable. Colonel Nicol Gray, my CO in 45 Commando, invited me for a drink at the Naval and Military Club (the so-called "In-and-Out Club" in Piccadilly). He introduced me to Gen. Sir

Harry Stockton, an ancient mariner deeply enscounced in an over-stuffed club chair.

"Are you a Marine, young man?" he asked. The colonel answered for me, explaining in glowing terms the assets of my services rendered. The wizened Royal Marine general was unimpressed.

"Well, at least you had the honor and privilege to serve with Royal Marines."

"And what are your plans for the future?" Colonel Gray asked me later.

"I'm going to art school."

"Lord bless my soul, whatever for?" He looked truly puzzled. "I'm going to command the Palestine Police, if ever you need a job."

My cover still held. He obviously saw me as "British" not Jewish.

But a week later it collapsed: I was informed that I had to report to the police every month again, as an enemy alien. That seemed comical, and a little sad. But it, too, passed, and I finished college and became Britain's first Fulbright scholar to the United States. I was a graphic designer and married Alice the following spring. She had been sent to England from her Slovak village in the Tatra Mountains on a children's transport with her two sisters, the three girls being the only survivors of a large family murdered in Auschwitz. She worked for the Czech government in exile in London and in the United States for the International Monetary Fund as administrative officer for thirty-five years.

My father died in London. The old Austro-Hungarian officer had served happily as a private in the Pioneer Corps. My Aunt Ida died in London, aged ninety-four. My mother joined my wife and me in the United States. She lived with us for some years, until the arrival of our third child, when she moved to an apartment of her own. She even worked, winning two mink hats for being the best millinery salesperson at Lord & Taylor two years in a row. My sister married the scion of an Austrian half-Jewish aristocratic family and lives with her family in San Francisco.

As of this reading, our older daughter, Anne, is a graphic designer with her own design firm, and is married to an architect. We have three grandchildren. Our second daughter, Kim, is a successful author and contributing editor to *Time* and *Vanity Fair*. Her husband is a television producer. Our son, Tim, loves jazz and blues and has his own radio show, "Jazz Masters with Tim Masters." Both he and his wife work for the Discovery Channel in cable television.

The Skipper, Bryan Hilton-Jones would have been intrigued by the variety of our post-war careers. Sadly, he did not live to see the success of many of his troop. He worked in civilian foreign service, and then for a major corporation in Spain after the war. Returning from a ski excursion with his wife, his son, and two daughters, their car was hit head-on by a truck in the winter of 1969. Father and both daughters were killed instantly; the other two were almost unscathed. A terrible end for this role model of ours, this incomparable athlete to whom the physically impossible was but a minor hurdle to be vaulted with playful ease. The enemy could not kill him, although they certainly tried that night in Normandy.

Some undoubtedly achieved their successes through his inspiration, some to prove that what they deemed to be his low opinion of them was unjustified; others were simply as fiercely competitive as he was, in his quiet way. Be that as it may, he achieved the seemingly impossible goal of welding together a group of hopelessly individualistic men who were, by his own description "an argumentative bunch," into efficient weapons of war, in a war that had to be. For that we are forever grateful to him.

Who we were, what we did, and what became of us gave meaning to those of us who died and to those who are alive today.

Bibliography

Ambrose, Stephen E., *Pegasus Bridge, June 6 1944* (Simon and Schuster, 1989)

Ambrose, Stephen E., *D-Day June 6 1944: The Climactic Battle of World War II* (Simon and Schuster, 1994)

Dear, Ian, *Ten Commando 1942-1945* (Leo Cooper, 1987)

Drez, Ronald J., *Voices of D-Day, The Story of the Allied Invasion Told by Those Who Were There* (Louisiana State University Press, 1994)

Ladd, James, *Commandos and Rangers of World War II* (St. Martins Press, 1978)

Vat, Lord, *March Past: A Memoir of Lord Vat* (Weidenfeld and Nicolson, 1978)

McDougall, Murdoch C., *Swiftly They Struck, The Story of No. 4 Commando* (Odham Press Limited, 1954)

Mills, Roberts, Berek, *Clash by Night* (Kimber, 1956)

Samain, Bryan, *Commando Men* (White Lyon Publishers Limited, 1976)

Saunders, Hilary St George, *The Green Beret: The Story of the Commandos 1940–45* (Michael Joseph, 1949)

Index

United States First Army, 288
Upton, 144, 151–52

Varaville, 153, 162, 168–70, 172,
179, 193, 199, 201, 213, 229,
238, 240
V-E Day, 314
Vienna, 7–9, 21–24, 42, 51–52,
56, 130, 292
Villiers, Robbie (Egon Vogel),
34, 64, 272, 294
V-1s, 101, 272

Walcheren Island, 270–72, 293,
312, 320
Wallen, Leslie (Weikersheimer),
63–64, 98
War Office, 12, 36, 42, 56, 103,
108, 127, 307
Watson, Pat (Wasserman), 2,
18–19, 92, 270–71
Weapons, 102, 122–23, 137, 139,

148, 150–52, 164, 169, 183–84,
187, 196, 234, 247, 281–82,
294, 297, 299
Webster (Weinberger), 90–91,
149, 191
Wells, Peter (Auerhahn) 20, 91,
133, 135
Wesel, 288, 291, 193–94, 298,
301
Weser river, 309–310
Windsor, Duke of, 21–23

Wilmers, John (Wilmersdorfer),
118–20, 325
Wolkersdorfer, Sepp, 6
Wooldridge, Lieutenant, 123,
125

Young, Peter, 183, 185–86,
245–46, 248, 280

Zionists, 16, 62, 320